Proceedings in Life Sciences

VIII th Congress of the International Primatological Society,
Florence, 7–12 July, 1980

Selected Papers, Part A: Primate Evolutionary Biology
© by Springer-Verlag Berlin Heidelberg 1981

Selected Papers, Part B: Primate Behavior and Sociobiology
© by Springer-Verlag Berlin Heidelberg 1981

Main Lectures: Advanced Views in Primate Biology
© by Springer-Verlag Berlin Heidelberg 1982

Primate Behavior and Sociobiology

Selected Papers (Part B) of the VIIIth Congress
of the International Primatological Society,
Florence, 7–12 July, 1980

Edited by
A. B. Chiarelli and R. S. Corruccini

With 65 Figures

Springer-Verlag
Berlin Heidelberg New York 1981

Professor A. B. Chiarelli
Istituto di Antropologia dell'Universita
Via del Proconsolo, 12
50122 Florence/Italy

Dr. R. S. Corruccini
Istituto di Antropologia dell'Universita
Via del Proconsolo, 12
50122 Florence/Italy
and
Department of Anthropology
Southern Illinois University
Carbondale, IL 62901/USA

For explanation of the cover motive see legend to Fig. 4, p. 23.

ISBN 3-540-11024-0 Springer-Verlag Berlin Heidelberg New York
ISBN 0-387-11024-0 Springer-Verlag New York Heidelberg Berlin

Library of Congress Cataloging in Publication Data. Main entry under title: Primate behavior and sociobiology. (Proceedings in life sciences) Bibliography: p. Includes index. 1. Primates-Behavior-Congresses. 2. Social behavior in animals-Congresses. I. Chiarelli, A. B. II. Corruccini, Robert S. III. International Primatological Society. IV. Series. QL737.P9P6713. 599.8'0451. 81-14579. AACR2.

Offsetprinting and bookbinding: Brühlsche Universitätsdruckerei, Giessen

2131/3130-543210

Preface

The VIIIth International Congress of the International Primatological Society was held from 7 through 11 July 1980 in Florence, Italy, under the auspices of the host institution, the Istituto di Antropologia of the University of Florence. More than 300 papers and abstracts were presented either at the main Congress or in 14 pre-Congress symposia the week earlier (so scheduled to avoid conflicting with either the main invited lectures or the contributed paper sessions).

This volume consists of the contributed papers concerning primate behavior, with special emphasis on those social aspects that reflect on or affect primate biology. Clearly, this is one of the more important and popular subdisciplines in primatology today. We have thus restricted the subject, in agreement with the publishers, in order to ensure a successful and useful volume that is likely to be generally noticed and widely available, as these up-to-date contributions deserve.

Furthermore, we have compiled this volume in a fairly new way for congress proceedings. In view of space limitations, and the need to guarantee a high-quality and sufficiently specialized book, we subjected all manuscripts to a four-level internal review process and selected only the best 23 of the 50 submissions. We favored natural-observation work over captive studies. This rejection rate of 54% exceeds that of almost all reviewed scholarly journals. Too often primatological or anthropological proceedings have been heterogeneous, large, unselective volumes that, at least in the recent past, have repeatedly lost money (in some cases spectacular amounts). Thus we offer a reasonably compact collection of the highest-quality recent research in this book; truly the "best of" the VIIIth IPC.

The articles are arranged like the "great chain of being" with the lowest prosimians first and highest anthropoids last; while this concept may be losing ground as evolutionary theory, it is useful for organizing a volume. Those articles specifically concerning sociobiology are collected at the end.

The editors jointly share in the responsibility for this volume, thus there is no junior editor. Our names appear at the front in alphabetical order.

We thank all for participating.

October, 1981

A.B. CHIARELLI
R.S. CORRUCCINI

Contents

Contributors

You will find the addresses at the beginning of the respective contributions

Albignac, R. 25
Baldwin, P.J. 136
Bergeron, G. 142
Blanton, F.L. 100
Boehm, C. 161
Byrne, R.W. 104
Chamove, A.S. 88
Clauss, G. 30
Dienske, H. 75
Duvall, F., II 30
Everett, J. 121
Fujii, H. 52
Goosen, C. 110
Goy, R.W. 72
Heermann, P. 36
Hemmer, H. 148
Holman, S.D. 72
Hultsch, H. 30
Itoigawa, N. 64
Jensen, G.D. 100
Jonge, G. de 75
Kawamichi, M. 1
Kawamichi, T. 1

Kondo, K. 64
Koyama, T. 52
Kraberger, A. 36
Luerssen, S. 121
Luxemburg, E.A. van 75
Mathieu, M. 142
McGrew, W.C. 136
Metz J.A.J. 75
Minami, T. 64
Murdock, G. 121
Nash, V.J. 88
Quiatt, D. 121
Ribbens, L.G. 75
Richarz, K. 18
Sassenrath, E.N. 100
Schürmann, C.L. 130
Suomi, S.J. 81
Todt, D. 30, 36
Tollman, S.G. 43
Tutin, C.E.G. 136
Welker, C. 93
Wolfe, L.D. 156
Yonekawa, F. 52

Social Organization of Tree Shrews (Tupaia glis)

T. Kawamichi and M. Kawamichi [1]

Social behavior of *Tupaia* has intensively been investigated in captivity (Vandenbergh 1963, Kaufmann 1965, Sorenson and Conaway 1966, 1968, Martin 1968, Sorenson 1970, Hasler and Sorenson 1974, Richarz and Sprankel 1978, Richarz 1979). So many behavioral studies in captivity are due apparently to an interesting phylogenetic position of the Family Tupaiidae which belongs to either the Order Primates or the Order Insectivora.

Since interindividual interactions of animals in captivity are frequently observed from a short distance, the interactions can be analyzed in detail. However, social organizations are obtainable by means of field observations, because spatial organizations and social behavior may be modified in captivity qualitatively and/or quantitatively.

Our field observations on the common tree shrew *Tupaia glis* Diard were carried out in a primary forest in Singapore for 152 days between 28 September 1974 and 29 March 1975. Since the methods used for individual identification and observations on spatial organization, territory, and scent marking have been published elsewhere (Kawamichi and Kawamichi 1978, 1979), the present paper aims to provide information on aspects of family stage, family breakup, interindividual interactions, and social relationships.

Study Area and Methods

Our field study was conducted in the central part of the Bukit Timah Nature Reserve in Singapore. The reserve was uniformly covered with primary tropical rain forest, mainly of dipterocarps. A map and detailed description of the study area have been given in a previous paper (Kawamichi and Kawamichi 1979). The study area covered 22.3 hectares. The elevation ranged from 40 to 163 m.

For the capture of tree shrews, meshed cage traps baited with banana were used. Captured individuals were released after determination of sex, body weight, testis length (measured with a caliper over the scrotum), and the degree of secretion from the gular gland. All of the captured individuals were numbered by toe clippings,

1 Department of Biology, Osaka City University, Sugimoto-Cho, Sumiyoshi-Ku, Osaka, 558, Japan

and tail hair was clipped using one of 67 different patterns (Kawamichi and Kawamichi 1978).

Searching for tree shrews was made by the observers walking along forest roads.
Observations were made daily from 07.30 to 11.30 hours and from 15.00 to
18.30 hours. A network of the forest roads extended throughout the study area; all
of the forest roads were walked at least twice during the morning and twice during
the afternoon observation periods. The total amount of time spent in walking was
978 h. The behavior of tree shrews was observed from the roads with binocular tele-
scopes (9 X) until we lost sight of them in the undergrowth. Encounters with one or
more individuals occurred every 37 min on the average. The duration of observation
at each encounter was usually less than a few minutes. For the convenience of recording the positions and behavior, various names were given to individuals, capture points,
and observation sites. Capture points and moving routes were also plotted on maps.

The observations of animals were recorded as follows: Sightings; the total number
of individuals observed was recorded. Encounter; (1) solitary encounter is all observations (or sightings) of solitary animals, and (2) social encounter is all observations
of two or more individuals within 10 m of one another.

In order to analyze interindividual interactions among three participants in a social
encounter, we divided the interactions into three dyadic interactions. In the case of
four participants, it was divided into six dyadic ones. When complex interindividual
interactions involving more than one context were observed in an encounter, they
were considered separately.

The size of the home range was calculated by a weighing method. The procedure
was as follows: Step one, plot the home range on a map by connecting the most
peripheral capture points or moving routes with straight lines; Step two, cut from the
map individual home ranges. Step three, weigh each home range on a balance 0.1 mg
scale (Sartorius Co., type 2403); Step four, transform the weight of the home range
into an area size by comparing the weight of the home range with one of known
weight and size of the same paper.

A distinction between adults and juveniles was made arbitrarily by body weight.
Body weights were obtained on 117 individuals and ranged between 73 and 187 g.
Because weight data on six families indicated that the weight of the adult females was
over 147 g and that of juveniles under 144 g, 147 g and greater was taken as the
weight of adults of both sexes. Individuals who stayed in the same area for 30 days
or more were classified as residents.

Results

Home Range and Spatial Organization

Tree shrews spend most of their active time at ground level. However, they are very
agile, climbing both large vertical tree trunks and bushes. Of a total of 1905 sightings, 95.6% were on the ground or below 1.5 m and 4.4% were above 1.5 m. Climbing
was concentrated in lower heights, i.e., 1.5 to 3 m (64 times), 4 to 6 m (21 times),

7 to 10 m (2 times) and higher than 10 m (once). These observations suggest that they are principally terrestrial.

Table 1. The compositions of captured individuals and residents, and the percentages of disappearance among residents

	Adult male	Adult female	Juvenile male	Juvenile female	Total
Captured individuals	36	42	9	30	117
Residents	30	32	6	18	86
Disappeared	4	4	4	7	19
%	13.3	12.5	66.7	38.9	22.1

A total of 117 tree shrews were captured 418 times and the number of observations of individually identified animals was 1255. Of the captured individuals, 73.5% were residents. The age and sex composition of all 86 residents is given in Table 1. Each resident was captured a mean of 4.1 ± 2.2 (s.d.) times and was sighted a mean of 13.7 ± 13.6 times.

Table 2. Mean size of home ranges (m^2). Small home ranges at peripheral areas are excluded

	Male			Female			Male of pair		
	Mean	SD	N	Mean	SD	N	Mean	SD	N
Adult	10174	4606	16	8809	3706	18	8961	3050	9
Juvenile	7527	1737	4	7255	2179	9	–	–	–

Table 2 shows the mean size of home ranges. While the mean range size of adult males was 15% larger than that of adult females, the difference was not significant (Student t-test, $P > 0.05$). The mean range size of adults was 29% larger than that of juveniles and the difference was significant ($P < 0.05$).

The study area was completely covered with adult ranges of the same sex and the overlap of home ranges between residents of the different sexes was complete in the habitat (Fig. 1). There was no noted effect of inclination on the shape of home ranges. Figure 2 diagrams the home range overlap. The number of overlapping adult ranges by other adult ranges of the same sex was similar between the sexes, and the difference was not significant (t-test, $P > 0.05$). Also, the degree of overlap between adult ranges of the same sex was similar between the sexes.

By superimposing the home range maps of each sex as in Fig. 1, it was shown that adult ranges adjoined or overlapped with those of the opposite sex. Adult male ranges overlapped with about four adult female ranges, and vice versa (Kawamichi and Kawamichi 1979).

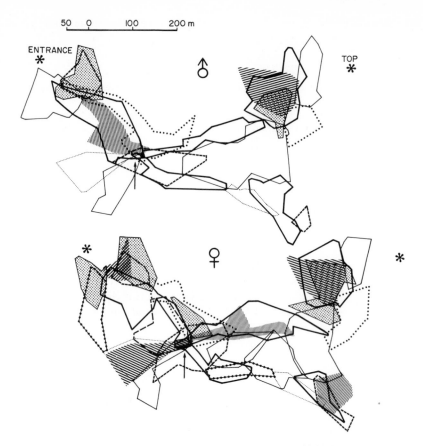

Fig. 1. Home ranges of residents between 2 October 1974 and 29 March 1975 (*top,* male; *bottom,* female). *White ranges* are those of adults and *shaded ranges* of juveniles. *Asterisks* indicate top of the reserve and the entrance. Location of a fig tree with ripe fruits is indicated by *arrows*

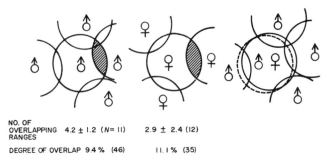

Fig. 2. Home range overlap between adults is shown schematically. Almost complete overlap of home ranges between a male and a female *(right)* indicates a pair. The number of overlapping ranges (mean ± s.d.) and the percentage of overlap *(shaded area)* were cited from Kawamichi and Kawamichi (1979)

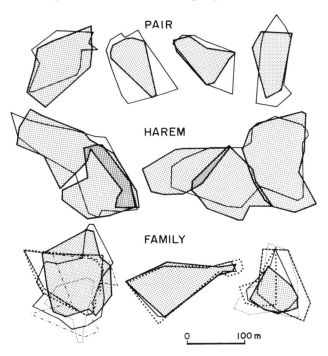

PAIR

HAREM

FAMILY

0   100 m

Fig. 3. Home range overlap of group members. *White ranges with solid line* are those of adult males, *shaded ranges* are of adult females, and *white ranges with broken line* are of juveniles. In the harem type, one adult male shared a range with two *(left)* or three *(right)* females

Among adult male ranges, there was one male range which almost completely overlapped with at least one adult female range. The size of the almost complete overlaps was highly correlated with the size of the adult female ranges (correlation coefficient, $r = 0.953, N = 12$) and the percentage of overlap varied from 53.4 to 100.0. When the home range of one particular adult male almost completely overlapped with that of only one particular adult female, they were regarded as forming a pair. The two ranges of one pair coincided very closely in shape and size (Fig. 3).

There was another type of male-female spatial relationship: One adult male range almost completely overlapped with two or three adult female ranges (Fig. 3). Such spatial association has been called a "harem" (Kawamichi 1970).

The mean range size of pairing adult males was almost the same as that of adult females (Table 2). The range sizes of harem owners L and F (16,376 m^2, 23,328 m^2), whose ranges covered two and three adult female ranges respectively, were 1.8 and 2.6 times respectively as large as the mean range size of pairing adult males. Therefore, the number of female partners per harem male was proportional to the range size of the adult males.

The mean range sizes of juveniles are given in Table 2. Juvenile ranges were patchily distributed in the study area (Fig. 1). The amount of range overlap, where the overlaps occurred, was considerable between juvenile ranges of the same sex as well as the different sexes.

The number of overlapping adult ranges by juvenile ranges of the same sex was about three in both sexes (Kawamichi and Kawamichi 1979). A considerable amount of intrasexual and intersexual range overlaps was also the case between juveniles and adults. There was one adult female range which almost completely overlapped with each juvenile range.

The size of the almost complete overlaps was correlated with the size of the juvenile ranges ($r = 0.824, N = 9$). The percentage of overlap varied from 42.5 to 100.0. Hereafter, when 43% or more of one juvenile range overlapped with only one adult female range, this adult female is regarded as the mother of this juvenile. Ten of 24 juvenile residents in the study area belonged to six mothers.

Thirty-seven adults composed of pairs and harems remained together after being marked for more than 3 months of the 6 months' study (range 95 to 167 days, mean 134 days). The ten juveniles (four males and six females) remained within the ranges of their mothers for 47 to 161 days (mean 109 days).

Social Encounters

Most of the tree shrews were solitary. Of 1591 encounters, 82.1% were the solitary encounters and 17.9% the social encounters. Of the 284 social encounters, 259 (91.2%) involved two participants, 20 (7.0%) involved three, and 5 (1.8%) involved four.

Out of the 259 cases of two participants, 194 were individually identified. Encounters between one adult male and one adult female occupied about one half of the identified cases (46.9%). In these encounters, those between partners (59 times) were 1.8 times more frequent than between nonpartners (32 times). Among the encounters between residents, intersexual encounters (118 times) were significantly higher than intrasexual ones (58 times) (Chi-square test, $P < 0.001$).

For three participants, 6 of 13 identified cases were encounters within the members of family groups. For four participants, one pair participated in 2 out of 3 identified cases. Thus, the encounters within groups as those of partners and family members attained 42.4% of a total of 210 identified cases. This high rate of encounter within groups was due to their ranging within overlapping home ranges.

Territorial Aggression

Aggressive territorial chases were recorded 34 times. Eighteen adult residents of both sexes were observed chasing another tree shrew for a total of 33 chases. Only one juvenile female resident (139 g) who did not seem to belong to any family, was observed once chasing another juvenile female. Apparently, territorial chases were directed at individuals of the same sex, irrespective of age and resident status (Kawamichi and Kawamichi 1979).

Territorial chases between adult female residents were less frequent than between adult male residents (3 vs 13). Adult females were often tolerated in invasions by neighboring adult female residents. There were four chases in which juvenile female residents were chased by neighboring adult female residents.

The exact spatial relationship between adult home ranges and territories remain unclear. Presumably intrasexual spacing among adult home ranges was the result of this intrasexual territoriality. Since the amount of intrasexual overlap was small among adult home ranges, a territory may occupy most of each adult range figured.

The coincidence of home range boundaries within a pair and the distribution of territorial chases of both sexes indicated that one and the same area was likely to be
defended independently by a pair.

Fig Tree

From early February until mid-March, one large fig tree *(Ficus dubia)* provided an
ample supply of ripe fruits (see Fig. 1). Besides a pair whose territories included the
fig tree, their three offspring, 16 residents from the surrounding area, and six vagrants
came to the tree and ate figs. The longest distance traversed by a visiting resident was
110 m. The owners of the tree chased the visitors of the same sex.

Social Systems

Pairs and harems were identified by the degree of home range overlap. In addition,
there was temporarily almost complete range overlap between an adult male and
a juvenile female. The numbers of these three types of range overlap in October–
January and in February–March are given separately in Table 3. Although mother-
offspring units broke up and membership changed among various groups, the number
of pairs (15) and harems (2) did not change during the study period, while that of
a pair containing an adult male and a juvenile female decreased from two to one.

Although juveniles move solitarily after leaving the nest, their mothers were identified also by the degree of home range overlap. Since all of their mothers were members of the pair or the harem, one or more juveniles, their mother, and her male partner
were regarded as forming a family. The ranges of the members forming a family approximately coincided with one another (Fig. 3). Table 3 shows the composition of a total
of seven family groups. Each family included one to four juveniles of both sexes. The
number of family groups decreased from six to three by the end of our field study.

Table 3. Composition of various groups. Juveniles in parentheses were those who first appeared
in March. Am = Adult male. Af = Adult female. Jm = Juvenile male. Jf = Juvenile female

		October–January			February–March		
		N	Adult	Juv.	N	Adult	Juv.
Pair	1 Pair	10	20	0	12	24	0
	1 Pair + 1 Jf	3	6	3	1	2	1
	1 Pair + 1 Jm + 1 Jf	1	2	2	–	–	–
	1 Pair + 2 Jm + 2 Jf	1	2	4	–	–	–
	1 Pair + 1 Jf + (1 or 2 young)	–	–	–	1	2	2–3
	1 Pair + (2 Jm + 1 Jf)	–	–	–	1	2	3
Harem	1 Am + 3 Af	1	4	0	1	4	0
	1 Am + 2 Af	–	–	–	1	3	0
	1 Am + 2 Af + 1 Jm	1	3	1	–	–	–
Other	1 Am + 1 Jf	2	2	2	1	1	1
Total		19	39	12	18	38	7–8

Family Breakup

Several types of groups were identified: adult pairs (with or without offspring), harems (with or without offspring), and pairs of adult males and juvenile females. Of a total of 19 groups found in October—January, 9 changed their composition by the end of our field study: One to three juveniles disappeared from four family groups and one adult pair from a family group. All members of one group disappeared from their ranges. There was a replacement of a female partner in one group. New juveniles appeared in March in two groups.

The compositions of the 19 groups observed in October—January and those of 18 groups observed in February—March are given in Table 3. During the study period, only one of the 15 pairs disappeared and one pair was newly formed. Two groups persisted as harems. An adult male-juvenile female pair was found in two groups in the first period and in another group in the second period.

Of the six family groups in the first period, five lost some or all of their juvenile members. By March, coexistence of two or three male residents had ceased in all of three groups. However, two family groups retained a juvenile female within their ranges. Also during this month, small-sized juveniles appeared in two groups. In one of these two groups, two litters coexisted. The areas used by the respective groups were stable through family breakups and membership changes.

In the last census made in March, 67 (77.9%) of all 86 residents were still within their ranges. Of the other 19 who had disappeared from their original ranges (Table 1), 8 were observed wandering. No dead animals were found. Nine of the 19 individuals were observed for the last time during 16 days between 20 January and 4 February. Seven of the nine were females. This synchronous disappearance from their original ranges occurred, despite our continuous field observations.

Table 1 shows the percentage of disappearance among residents. The highest percentage was found in juvenile males. However, the difference between juvenile males and juvenile females was not significant statistically (Chi-square test, $P > 0.20$). The overall percentage of juveniles that disappeared (45.8%) was 3.6 times as high as that of adults (12.9%). The difference was statistically significant ($P < 0.001$). However, no difference in the percentage disappearance was found between the different sexes when adults and juveniles were combined (male 22.2%, female 22.0%). Further, the sex ratio of juveniles captured in October and November was 2.0 (ten females/five males) and that of juvenile residents during the whole study period, 3.0 (Table 1). Accordingly, juvenile males seemed likely to disappear from their original family groups earlier than juvenile females.

Timing of Family Breakup

Captive behavior of *Tupaia* has been studied most intensively in *T. glis*. On the basis of the reproductive data on *T. glis* (and *T. belangeri*) in captivity (Hendrickson 1954, Sprankel 1959, Martin 1968, Shimada 1973, Richarz 1979), females experience postpartum estrus, the gestation period is 43—46 days and the litter size is usually two. The juveniles leave the nest box at 25—35 days of age and sexual maturity occurs at 90–100 days of age. We used these data to investigate the relationship between the timing of family breakups and the reproductive status of the adult females in our field study.

Disappearance of one or two juvenile males occurred in two family groups (I and VII). The final observations of juvenile males V and U in group I were 4 and 3 weeks respectively prior to the estrus of their mother. In group VII, male X left his range after 26 February; this date lay between two estrus observations of his mother. When V and U left the group, their approximate ages were 2.5 and 4 months, respectively, but the body weights were similar (128, 127 g). By the leaving time, the testes of U and X were over 10 mm in length.

The disappearance of a juvenile female occurred in three family groups (I, II, and III). Juvenile female S in group I disappeared during the middle or later stages of pregnancy of her mother. If adult female G in II became pregnant soon after her estrus on 14 December, the disappearing time of juvenile female u would similarly correspond to the later stages of pregnancy in G.

The minimum period of stay (the residence period observed + 1 month nestling period) in six juvenile females ranged from 3.5 to 6 months. In three of them, the period exceeded 5 months. Despite the fact that this exceeds the period for sexual maturity, the reproduction by these female offspring was not observed.

The gap in body weights between the four juveniles in group I ($♀$ 114, $♀$ 115 g vs $♂$ 73, $♂$ 93 g) indicated the coexistence of two litters. The coexistence was actually observed in this group by the addition of new offspring in late March. It should be noted that the coexistence was the result of the prolonged stay of the juvenile females.

Estrus and Reproductive Season

Estrus or pre-estrus behavior was observed seven times. Five of the seven cases occurred in February. The behavior was characterized by adult males intensively pursuing adult females. In five cases, adult males continually emitted a chattering sound around females as noted by Martin (1968) for *T. belangeri*. In addition to male partners, in two cases, neighboring adult males participated in following females. The male partners were apparently defeated in both cases, and a dominant male gained access to the females. The females did not actively choose their male partners among the male participants.

The onset of the mating season was indicated in December by the following facts: (1) The earliest estrus observation was made on 14 December; (2) The appearance of new juveniles occurred in two groups in early and late March. The corresponding pregnancy of these mothers would have taken place in early and late December, respectively; (3) The estrus of dd on 13 February apparently occurred after parturition, since the teats were projecting and showed twisted hairs indicating sucking. Her pregnancy had presumably begun in December.

Because small-sized juveniles were not detected by sightings and trappings from November through February, a nonreproductive phase was apparent in the first half of our study period. Among the 15 juveniles captured in October and November, the lightest body weight was found in two males (73, 93 g). The others weighed greater than 101 g. Hence, their mother's pregnancy was apparently the latest among the six family groups, and performed probably in early August. In conclusion, the 4-month period from August through November was presumably nonreproductive in *T. glis* in Singapore.

The nonreproductive season was observed under stable climatic conditions. That is, there was only a 9 min difference between the longest and shortest day of the year and a 2°C difference in the mean temperature between the warmest and coolest month of the year. Moreover, there is no real dry season in Singapore (Nieuwolt 1973). The period from December to March is the season of the northeast monsoon, which brings a large amount of rainfall to Singapore, especially during the first two months (Nieuwolt 1973). The onset of reproduction in *T. glis*, consequently, appeared to be correlated with that of the monsoon season in Singapore.

Interindividual Interactions

Various interindividual interactions were observed at social encounters. To reveal basic social relationships, we classified behavioral interactions in the following six major patterns: following, slow approach, slow leaving, chase, quick retreat, non-response, and undetermined cases.

Following: One animal slowly followed the other animal. The distance of the two individuals was usually within 1 m. A typical case was observed in males following their female partners.

Slow approach: Slow approach of one animal to the other which did not evoke the quick retreat of the latter. The approached individual either remained motionless while watching the approacher, or slowly escaped from the approacher by moving a short distance away.

Slow leaving: One individual slowly moved away from the other, while the latter did not show any particular response to the former.

Chase: Aggressive chases without bodily contact. The distance of chases varied from a few meters (lunges) to more than 10 m (pursuit). Territorial chases were observed 34 times.

Quick retreat: One individual swiftly retreated from the other, while the latter did not chase the former.

Nonresponse: Two individuals did not show a remarkable response such as approach or retreat; nevertheless, both individuals apparently perceived the existence of each other from observations of turning the head to the other individual.

Undetermined cases: These occurred when two individuals were within 10 m and did not perceive the existence of each other because of the topography or the vegetation.

Dyadic interactions in which both participants were individually identified were recorded 266 times. Most of the interactions were observed between residents. Table 4 shows the percentages of the six major interaction patterns. While following and nonresponse were frequent, slow leaving and quick retreat were only occasionally observed.

In intersexual encounters between adults, following was most frequent. Males followed females in all observations of following. Slow approach and nonresponse were

Table 4. Interindividual interactions and social relationships

			Tolerant				Antagonistic		Undetermined	Total
			Following	Slow approach	Slow leaving	Non-response	Chase	Quick retreat		
Adult – adult		Partners within pairs	18	10	1	10	2	–	5	46
		Partners within harems	10	7	–	5	1	–	–	22
		Non-partners	12	8	4	11	1	–	11	47
Intersexual encounters	Adult – juv. Family	Mother – son	–	2	1	1	–	–	5	9
		Adult male – juvenile female	–	2	–	4	–	–	1	7
		Adult female – juvenile male	–	1	–	1	–	–	3	5
		Adult male – juvenile female	5	15	1	5	5	–	3	34
	Juv. – juv. Family	Juvenile male – juvenile female	–	–	–	2	–	–	–	2
	Male – male	Adult male – adult male	5	–	–	–	16	2	5	28
		Adult male – juvenile male	–	–	–	–	2	1	2	5
	Family	Adult male – juvenile male	–	1	–	–	1	1	2	5
		Juvenile male – juvenile male	–	–	–	–	–	–	1	1
Intrasexual encounters	Female – female Family	Mother – daughter	–	–	–	6	1	1	3	11
		Adult female – juvenile female	1	–	–	3	9	3	2	18
		Adult female – adult female	2	–	–	11	5	1	4	23
		Juvenile female – juvenile female	–	–	–	–	2	–	1	3
Total			53	46	7	59	44	9	48	266
%			19.9	17.3	2.6	22.2	16.5	3.4	18.0	99.9

also frequent. Of slow approach, 76.0% were those of males to females. Of only three chases, two were made by females, when males followed the females. Interactions within a pair were not different from those within a harem. The rates of slow leaving and undetermined cases were higher in the encounters of nonpartners than in those of partners.

In intersexual encounters between adults and juveniles, slow approach and non-response were frequent. Of only five cases of following by adult males, four were observed in a pair of adult male — juvenile female. Five chases of juvenile females by adult males were lunges. In four of the five cases, the lunges were observed in tolerant contexts as following or slow approach was associated.

In intrasexual encounters, most of the encounters between males were chase and quick retreat. Chases were mainly territorial chases. Five cases of following were made by territorial residents following invaders of the same sex. The following was ceased at their territorial boundaries in four of the five cases. The residents seemed to follow the invaders, instead of chasing them, when the invaders were dominant to the residents. Similar following behavior by territorial occupants has been observed in pikas (*Ochotona princeps,* Lagomorpha; Kawamichi 1976).

In encounters between females, nonresponse and chase were frequent. Nonresponse was most frequent between females, but not observed between males. Although all observations between adult females except one were encounters between territorial residents, the interactions of following and nonresponse were observed two times as often as those of chase and quick retreat. This is because adult female residents were tolerated in invasions by neighboring adult females. Unlike encounters between mothers and daughters, chase and quick retreat were frequent in encounters between adult females and juvenile females of other family groups.

Some interaction patterns were predominantly observed in particular matches of social status. Especially, following was concentrated in encounters between adult males and adult females (75.5%). Similarly, 97.8% of slow approach and 100.0% of slow leaving were observed in intersexual encounters. In chase and quick retreat, 81.8% and 100.0% respectively were observed in intrasexual encounters. Nonresponse was not observed only in encounters between males.

Social Relationships

Four interaction patterns, following, slow approach, slow leaving, and nonresponse, indicate tolerant relationships and the other two, chase and quick retreat, indicate antagonistic relationships. In Table 4, the number of interactions indicating tolerant relationships is distributed predominantly in intersexual encounters, while that of interactions indicating antagonistic relationships predominantly in intrasexual ones.

In intersexual encounters, 97.0% of interactions between adults indicated tolerant relationships. Between adults and juveniles, tolerant interactions accounted for 88.4%. In intrasexual encounters, 79.3% of interactions between males were antagonistic, while the almost equal numbers of tolerant and antagonistic interactions were involved between females.

In interactions within family groups, those between adult partners were observed 63 times, between adults and juveniles 21 times, and between juveniles twice. In inter-sexual encounters between adults and juveniles (mother — son, adult male — juvenile female), slow approach, slow leaving, and nonresponse indicating tolerant relation-ships were observed. Intrasexual interactions (mother — daughter, adult male — juve-nile male) included chase and quick retreat in addition to slow approach and non-response. Antagonistic intrasexual relationships were suggested also within family groups, as the juveniles grew up.

In summary, basic social relationships were tolerance between the different sexes and antagonism within the sexes, together with limited intrasexual tolerance between adult female residents and within family groups.

Figure 4 schematically shows the social organization. Adult male residents were territorial to neighbors and vagrants of the same sex. On the occasions of estrus, neighboring males invaded territories and followed females in estrus. Within a family group, an adult male and a juvenile male foraged separately. Juvenile males were probably chased out of their family group by the adult male.

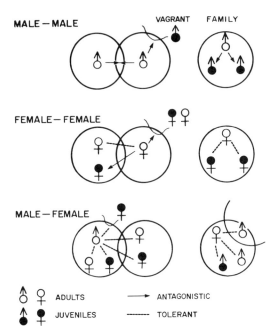

Fig. 4. Social organization is shown schematically. *Circles* indicate their home ranges

Adult female residents were also territorial to neighbors and vagrants of the same sex. Invasions by neighboring adult females were often tolerated, but the degree of home range overlap by them was partial. Neighboring juvenile females were the object of territorial chases. Within a family group, a mother and her daughter often foraged together, but two daughters foraged separately. Two litters coexisted in a family group by the prolonged residence of juvenile females.

Between the different sexes, all relationships indicate tolerance. Adult male residents were tolerant of their female partners, juvenile females, neighboring females, and female vagrants. Adult female residents were also tolerant of any males, except for the occasions of sexual approach to unreceptive females.

Discussion

Solitary Ranging Pair

Pair bonding has been suggested for *T. glis* and *T. belangeri* in captivity (Martin 1968; Richarz 1979). Our field research indicates that a new pairing pattern, that of solitary ranging pair, should be defined in *T. glis* in the wild. In spite of their solitary movements, the existence of a stable pairing situation can be identified.

Field observations of other solitary prosimians *(Perodicticus potto, Galago demidovii, Lepilemur mustelinus)* by Charles-Dominique (1974, 1977), and Charles-Dominique and Hladik (1971) revealed very similar range overlaps between the sexes. Although sample sizes were small, the formation of pairs and harems was strongly suggested in these three species. Solitary ranging-pair and harem systems have been found also in the Order Lagomorpha, *Ochotona hyperborea yesoensis* and *O. macrotis*, by one of us (Kawamichi 1970, 1971). This type of pairing is also expected to be found among other solitary mammals when more careful investigation of their spatial organization is carried out. We feel that the social category, solitary ranging pair, will occupy a position between the category of genuine solitary ranging (solitary ranging solitary species) and that of genuine pair bonding.

The coincidence of home range boundaries within pairs means that either or both recognize the range of the partner. The pair ranging solitarily on the obstructive forest floor suggests the possibility of individual recognition of scent marked odor. Von Holst and Lesk (1975) have shown that *T. belangeri* can distinguish between the sexes and even recognizes specific individuals by the odor of the sternal gland secretion. The overlapping patterns of the harem may suggest that males primarily act on the coincidence of range boundaries.

The harem may be maintained by an aggressive and dominant male who did not admit the settlement of other males for pair formation. Similar studies of *T. glis* in other localities are necessary to solve the problem whether or not the ratio of two harems to 15 pairs was stable in the species.

Our estrus observations indicated that males did not always copulate with their partners. Therefore, adult males of family groups cannot be decided as real "fathers". Here, we speculate on the functions of this pairing system: In habitats of a lower density, complete home range overlap by a pair guarantees their mating. The rate of copulation by pair partners is possibly high. In a higher density, dominance ranks among adult male residents may become apparent on the occasions of estrus. There dominant males can copulate with females other than their partners. If so, the pairing system might be more functional in low densities than in high densities.

Mechanism of Family Breakup

Although intersexual tolerance and intrasexual antagonism were suggested within family groups, actual exclusion of offspring from the family groups by adult members of the same sex was not observed. Observations in captivity by Vandenbergh (1963) and Richarz (1979) strongly suggest that juveniles are excluded from their own family groups by adult members of the same sex and that intrasexual aggressiveness is released toward juveniles after they have attained 90 days of age, at the time of sexual maturity.

Timing of the disappearance of juvenile males appeared to be correlated with the occurrence of estrus in their mothers. Because an increase in aggressiveness was apparent between adult males around females in estrus, juvenile males are conceivably excluded at this time. The timing of the disappearance of juvenile females in relation to the pregnancy of their mothers was suggested in two cases, although the possibility of accidental death could not be excluded. An increase of aggressiveness in adult females in the later stages of pregnancy was not confirmed in our field observations. The observations of tree shrews in captivity showed that "pregnancy has produced marked anti-social aggressiveness in the females" of *T. glis* (Hendrickson 1954) and that estrous females were aggressive toward other females in *T. longipes* (Sorenson and Conaway 1966) and *T. chinensis* (Hasler and Sorenson 1974).

Tolerance Between Females

A tendency for prolonged stay in female offspring was strongly suggested by the following facts: the highest percentage of disappearance in juvenile males, the lesser number of juvenile males during the nonreproductive season, and the coexistence of two litters by the prolonged stay of female offspring. In fact, three of six female offspring stayed for more than 5 months.

Mothers of *T. glis* in captivity show tolerance to their female offspring for a long period, although not to all of them (Vandenbergh 1963; Richarz 1979). Due to prolonged residence of these female offspring, the coexistence of two litters occurred in the two captive studies, as found in our field study. Juvenile females in family groups were chased by neighboring adult females when the former invaded the territories of the latter. Therefore, the juvenile females were already the object of intrasexual aggressiveness from other adult females, and were permitted to stay in their maternal ranges subject to identification as offspring by their mothers.

Because family breakups were presumably caused by intrasexual antagonism, the differential residence periods in male and female offspring were due merely to the period of tolerance toward offspring. In lemurs and lorises, female offspring remain in the maternal ranges longer than male offspring (*Lepilemur mustelinus, Perodicticus potto, Galago demidovii*. Charles-Dominique 1974; *G. crassicaudatus*, Clark 1978).

Tolerance between females was observed not only in mother-daughter relationships, but also among neighboring adult females. Adult female residents are often tolerated in territorial invasions by neighboring adult females. Also in captivity, adult females sleep together in one nest box in *T. glis* (Kaufmann 1965), *T. longipes*

(Sorenson and Conaway 1966) and *T. chinensis* (Sorenson 1970, Hasler and Sorenson 1974). On the other hand, tolerance between males has hardly been observed in captive tree shrews of various species as well as in *T. glis* in our field study. More than one adult male cannot be accommodated on one cage or even in an enclosure measuring 15 by 15 m in *T. glis* and *T. belangeri* (Hendrickson 1954, Vandenbergh 1963; Kaufmann 1965, Martin 1968).

Summary

Field observations on 117 tree shrews *Tupaia glis* were conducted over a period of 6 months in Singapore. Captures were 418, and sightings of marked animals 1255. They were terrestrial and solitarily ranging. While there was little home range overlap between adult residents of the same sex, there was complete range overlap between those of the different sexes. The latter fell within two basic patterns. Pair: One adult male range almost completely overlapped with only one adult female range. Harem: One adult male range covered two or three adult female ranges. There were 15 pairs and two harems. Each partner of the pair was territorial to the same sex, and the pair seemed to defend the same area independently.

Juveniles belong to the pair or the harem as family members. Of 19 groups (pairs, harems, or families), 9 changed their composition mainly by the disappearance of juveniles. Juvenile males tended to disappear earlier than juvenile females. The areas used by groups remained stable throughout the family breakups and membership changes. The onset of mating was observed in December and synchronous breakup of families formed during the preceding reproductive season typically occurred in late January. However, in one group two litters coexisted. Offspring were usually excluded from their family group presumably by the adult member of the same sex. Timing of family breakup appeared to be related to estrus and pregnancy in the mothers.

Basic social relationships were intrasexual antagonism and intersexual tolerance. Juveniles of both sexes, particularly females, were tolerated by the adult members of the family group. Limited tolerance was observed between neighboring adult females.

References

Charles-Dominique P (1974) Aggression and territoriality in nocturnal prosimians. In: Holloway RL (ed) Primate aggression, territoriality, and xenophobia. Academic Press, London New York, pp 31–49
Charles-Dominique P (1977) Ecology and behaviour of nocturnal primates. Gerald Duckworth, London, 277 pp
Charles-Dominique P, Hladik CM (1971) Le Lépilémur du Sud de Madagascar: écologie, alimentation et vie sociale. Terre Vie 25:3–66
Clark AB (1978) Sex ratio and local resource competition in a prosimian primate. Science 201: 163–165
Hasler JF, Sorenson MW (1974) Behavior of the tree shrew, *Tupaia chinensis,* in captivity. Am Midl Nat 91:294–314

Hendrickson JR (1954) Breeding of the tree shrew. Nature (London) 174:794—795

Holst D von, Lesk S (1975) Über den Informationsinhalt des Sternaldrüsensekretes männlicher und weiblicher *Tupaia belangeri*. J Comp Physiol 103:173—188

Kaufmann JH (1965) Studies on the behavior of captive tree shrews *(Tupaia glis)*. Folia Primatol 3:50—74

Kawamichi T (1970) Social pattern of the Japanese pika, *Ochotona hyperborea yesoensis,* preliminary report. J Fac Sci Hokkaido Univ, Ser VI Zool 17:462—473

Kawamichi T (1971) Daily activities and social pattern of two Himalayan pikas, *Ochotona macrotis* and *O. roylei,* observed at Mt. Everest. J Fac Sci Hokkaido Univ, Ser VI Zool 17:587—609,

Kawamichi T (1976) Hay territory and dominance rank of pikas *(Ochotona princeps)*. J Mammal 57:133—148

Kawamichi T, Kawamichi M (1978) Hair clipping patterns for marking tree shrew and chipmunk. Jpn J Ecol 28:65—67

Kawamichi T, Kawamichi M (1979) Spatial organization and territory of tree shrews *(Tupaia glis)*. Anim Behav 27:381—393

Martin RD (1968) Reproduction and ontogeny in tree-shrews *(Tupaia belangeri),* with reference to their general behaviour and taxonomic relationships. Z Tierpsychol 25:409—495, 505—532

Nieuwolt S (1973) Climate. In: Chuang SH (ed) Animal life and nature in Singapore. Univ Press, Singapore, pp 27—39

Richarz K (1979) Mechanismen der Gruppenbildung und -bindung bei *Tupaia glis* Diard, 1820. Anthropol Anz 37:141—176

Richarz K, Sprankel H (1978) Daten zum Territorial-, Sexual- und Sozialverhalten von *Tupaia glis* Diard, 1820. Z Säugetierkd 43:336—356

Shimada A (1973) Studies on *Tupaia glis* Diard as an experimental animal: its breeding and growth. Exp Anim 22 (Suppl):351—357

Sorenson MW (1970) Behavior of tree shrews. In: Rosenblum LA (ed) Primate behavior, vol I. Acadmic Press, London New York, pp 141—193

Sorenson MW, Conaway CH (1966) Observations on the social behavior of tree shrews in captivity. Folia Primatol 4:124—145

Sorenson MW, Conaway CH (1968) The social and reproductive behavior of *Tupaia montana* in captivity. J Mammal 49:502—512

Sprankel H (1959) Fortpflanzung von *Tupaia glis* DIARD 1820 (Tupaiidae, Prosimiae) in Gefangenschaft. Naturwissenschaften 46:338

Vandenbergh JG (1963) Feeding, activity and social behavior of the tree shrew, *Tupaia glis,* in a large outdoor enclosure. Folia Primatol 1:199—207

Social Behavior and Incest Mechanisms of Tree Shrews (Tupaia glis) Diard 1820

K. Richarz[1]

To date, only very few behavioral field studies of tree shrews exist (Chorazyna and Kurup 1975, D'Souza 1974, Kawamichi and Kawamichi 1979). It seems to be very difficult to investigate the interactions and mechanisms of bonding of these squirrel-like, very nimble, small mammals in a natural habitat. Considering these facts, it is advantageous to get a good idea of the behavioral repertoire of caged animals, first of all.

As a presupposition for comparing such data, which are gained under artificial conditions, it is necessary to know the factors which can influence behavior. Therefore, we have investigated at first the spatio-temporal structure of the behavior of solitary and paired tree shrews (Richarz and Sprankel 1978, Sprankel and Richarz 1976). Because of the limitation of space in the laboratory, investigations of group cohesion and turning out of animals are burdened with methodical difficulties. We have tried to avoid some of these difficulties by giving the animals very complex cage systems (Richarz 1979).

Methods

For the following study, the tree shrews were kept as pairs in a complex cage system. The group members were able to disperse in four cage compartments, each of which is equipped with the same inventory and is supplied with food and drinking bottles (Fig. 1; for further details see Richarz 1979). The food consisted of pellets ("Altromin Standard-Diät" for tree shrews), and was supplemented occasionally with fruit, snails, or grasshoppers. Water was provided ad lib.

All the measurable behavior elements were registered in relation to time and place of occurrence (see Richarz 1979).

1 Zentrum für Neurologie, Institut für Neuropathologie, der Justus Liebig-Universität Gießen, Arndtstraße 16, 6300 Gießen, FRG

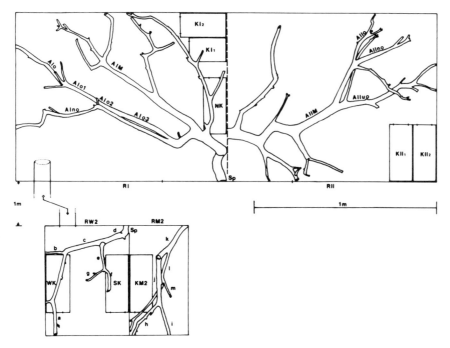

Fig. 1. View of the cage system for a family group (from above)

Results

Tree shrews are diurnal animals. The daily rhythm of activity follows a bigeminus type. The maximal activity can be observed between 8–10 a.m. and 3–6 p.m. A period of rest within narrow limits is common to all individuals around 11 a.m. A synchronization of the activity curves of sexual partners can be seen as an expression of a pair bonding (Sprankel and Richarz 1976).

Besides their temporal structure, a lot of behavior elements show a strict spatial bonding. For example, Tupaias prefer exposed sites when eating, but thereby avoid branches. In comparison with this, they prefer certain branches for defecating, the daily resting periods, and comprehensive grooming movements. In the use of such places by the individuals of a pair or a family group, relations to their rank order or the degree of bonding can be found (Richarz 1979).

From the quantitatively registered partner-orientated interactions, together with the usage of space by the animals, which were observed in long-term studies of about 5 years, the status forms of the group members and the type of social organization become recognizable.

The social organization of *Tupaia glis* is based on a permanent pair bonding. In their field research, Kawamichi and Kawamichi (1979) could verify the existence of a stable pairing situation, which they characterize as "solitary ranging pair". Our investigations have shown that the cohesion of the partners results from a permanent existence of mutual sexual attraction and from an identification with the territory (Richarz and Sprankel 1978). Among the interactions of the partners and the territorial behavior, males play a dominant role (Fig. 2). The territorial behavior is mainly expressed as scent marking by rubbing the jugulo-sternal scent-gland field (Sprankel 1961). This kind of scent marking is more important than using the abdominal glands or urine. In conditioning tests, von Holst and Lesk (1975) have shown that Tupaias can distinguish between the sexes and even recognize specific individuals by the odor of the sternal gland secretion. The function of marking the territory becomes evident by experimentally fusing the cages of sexual partners (Richarz and Sprankel 1978). Then the male follows a spatial pattern by preferring sites which were used for locomotion, respectively frequented as individual resting places in the branches, and/or which were actively or passively marked before.

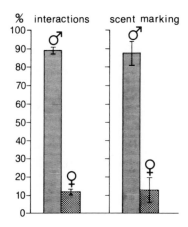

Fig. 2. Percentage of interactions and scent marking of sexual partners (findings of six pairs)

The main differences in the roles of sexual partners in all behavior parameters are a quantitative phenomenon. While males play a more dominant part, females show greater flexibility in selection of parameters. It seems that, resulting from this sex-specific unequal distribution of roles, a permanent field of tension can result, which binds the partners. In the interactions of a pair, essentially the behavior patterns from the sexual system are used (Richarz and Sprankel 1978). For example, sniffing of the genitals and courtship behavior often occur. Besides, a distinct criterium for an intensive pair bonding is lying in bodily contact. For this, the animals prefer their individual resting places together during a phase of drowsiness around noon. In this respect, as an exception, females contribute a much greater appetitive behavior.

The interactions between infants and adults are limited by the care system. For Tupaias it was called "absentee type" by Martin (1968). During the first 33 days, in which the infants grow up in a nest, only the female comes in contact with the young, visiting them only once every 48 h in the nest for suckling. During the suckling visits the young exhibit an active interaction by licking the mother's mouth.

The juveniles normally have first contacts with other group members with the leaving of the nest. Beginning with this first leaving of the nest at the age of about 33 days,

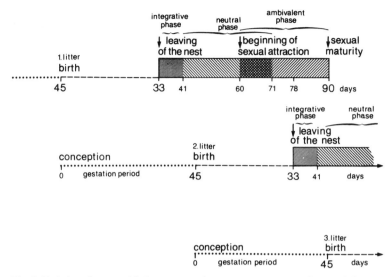

Fig. 3. Relations between birth sequences by postpartum conceptions and the temporal phases during the growing up of the young in the group

three phases can be differentiated (Fig. 3). A phase of integration of about 5 to 8 days, in which the behavior patterns between adults and juveniles are polarized on mouth licking with the adults and scent marking the juveniles, is obviously the presupposition for including the rising generation in the relational system including the space system of the adults. This phase is followed by a neutral phase, lasting about 30 days, during which the juveniles stand in connection with the adults by means of a space bonding, in which relatively few interactions occur. Through the joint use of parental resting places and through resting in close spatial neighborhood, a true retention of experience for the juveniles must be thought of (Richarz 1979).

At the age of about 60 days an ambivalent phase begins, in which the contacts between parents and offspring increase again, with an alteration and a superimposition of sexual and agonistic interactions. Besides, the sex-specific differences become recognizable: the male interacts with his daughters increasingly sexually, with the sons he is more and more aggressive; the interactions of the mother with the female off-spring are ambivalent, during which she shows, besides aggressive interactions, male behavior patterns like driving and copulatory behavior. The female scarcely has con-tact with her sons.

Lying in bodily contact has, beyond the importance for a pair bonding, significance for a group bonding. It occurs when parents and offspring use the same resting places or when the mother follows an older daughter in an ambivalent phase (Richarz 1979).

Licking the mouth, at first an element of the care system as an infantile behavior component, can be used by adults as an appeasement gesture.

Through the addition of the young a parental family arises from the pair. It seems that the type of social organization of Tupaia in connection with territoriality prevents the primitive form of a family breakup by an attractivity of the juveniles and adults, and especially by the cohesive influence of a space bonding. But a maximum of the group size is reached by two generations of brothers and sisters together with their parents. Then limiting factors set in, which seem to be based on a density stress (von Holst 1969), the possibilities of communication of the species themselves, and on incest mechanisms.

The incest avoidance begins in the ambivalent phase and seems to be reached by combined mechanisms of change of object and expulsion and/or intrafamiliar sexual suppression. The mechanisms of intrafamiliar sexual suppression are threat, psychological castration, and eventually repulsion (for explanation of the terminology see Bischof 1975).

The type of organization implies that the maturing juveniles must leave the parental territory at some time or another. This leaving occurs actively through a strong exploratory urge in certain phases of maturation. Evidence of this is a great locomotor activity of the juveniles in certain phases and the using of resting places beyond the adult nucleus in other compartments of the cage system. This happens before the juveniles have aggressive interactions with the adults (Richarz 1980).

Passively, the leaving of the parental territory occurs through a pressure from the adults on the rising generation always within the sexes. The age of about 90–100 days, in which the parents frequently have aggressive interactions with their offspring of the same sex, is regarded as the time of reaching sexual maturity (Table 1).

Table 1. Expulsion in a family group.
Age of juveniles (in days) at the beginning
of aggressive interactions with the adults

	Adults $M_2\delta$	$W_2\female$
Juveniles		
$A_1\female$	–	103
$A_2\delta$	99	–
$A_3\delta$	106	–
$B_1\female$	–	246 !
$B_2\female$	–	89
$C_B\delta$	86	–
$E_1\female$	–	96
$E_2\delta$	116	–
$E_3\delta$	117	–

It can be seen here that the females are usually more cohesive than males. Its origin might be that the territorial claim of tree shrews in the female sex is less marked and, on the contrary, the territorial independence and the separation from the ancestral group are necessary preconditions for the development of male behavioral characteristics. Through independence a dominant role is stressed more than through a territorial dependence, which accentuates a submission. A father-daughter incest is possible among Tupaias because of the ambivalent interactions between females (see Table 1, $B_1\female$) and their permanent sexual attractivity for the dominant male.

A simplified model of the tupaiid type of social organization and of its function is given in Fig. 4. As a prerequisite of this type, the maturing juveniles have the status of "jammers" and must be expelled from, or at least become neutralized for, reproduction. Expelled or exploring juveniles of a population may be able to form new territories or eventually replace a lacking sexual partner in an existing territory.

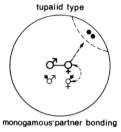

tupaiid type

monogamous partner bonding

Fig. 4. Simplified model of the tupaiid type of a monogamous pair bonding. ♂–♀,adult pair, connected by pair bonding mechanisms; ♂ ♀, mature juveniles; ● ●, infants during nest phase; - - - →, cohesive interactions; →, diffuse interactions; *circle,* territory

Summary

Long-term studies of tree shrews which were kept in complex cage systems showed that the type of social organization of *Tupaia glis* is a monogamous pair bonding. Through the addition of the young a family group can arise, the size of which is limited, among other factors, by mechanisms of incest avoidance. These mechanisms are described along with the mechanisms of pair bonding and group formation and bonding.

References

Bischof N (1975) Comparative ethology of incest avoidance. In: Fox R (ed) Biosocial anthropology. Malaby Press, pp 37–67

Chorazyna H, Kurup GU (1975) Observations on the ecology and behaviour of *Anathana ellioti* in the wild. In: Kondo S, Kawai M, Ehara A (eds) Contemporary primatology. Karger, Basel, pp 342–344

D'Souza F (1974) A preliminary field report on the lesser tree shrew *(Tupaia minor)*. In: Martin RD, Doyle GA, Walker AC (eds) Prosimian biology. Duckworth, Gloucester, pp 167–182

Holst D von (1969) Sozialer Streß bei Tupajas *(Tupaia belangeri)*. Die Aktivierung des sympathischen Nervensystems und ihre Beziehung zu hormonal ausgelösten ethologischen und physiologischen Veränderungen. Z Vgl Physiol 63:1–58

Holst D von, Lesk S (1975) Über den Informationsinhalt des Sternaldrüsensekretes männlicher und weiblicher *Tupaia belangeri*. J Comp Physiol 103:173–188

Kawamichi T, Kawamichi M (1979) Spatial organization and territory of tree shrews *(Tupaia glis)*. Anim Behav 27:381–393

Martin RD (1968) Reproduction and ontogeny in tree-shrews *(Tupaia belangeri)* with reference to their general behaviour and taxonomic relationships. Z Tierpsychol 25:409–495, 505–532

Richarz K (1979) Mechanismen der Gruppenbildung und -bindung bei *Tupaia glis* DIARD, 1820. Ergebnisse von Langzeitstudien an einer Familiengruppe. Anthropol Anz 37:141−176

Richarz K (1980) Mechanismen zur Inzestvermeidung bei *Tupaia glis* DIARD, 1820. Anthropol Anz 38:286−296

Richarz K, Sprankel H (1978) Daten zum Territorial-, Sexual- und Sozialverhalten von *Tupaia glis* DIARD, 1820. Z Säuretierkd 43:336−356

Sprankel H (1961) Histologie und biologische Bedeutung eines jugulo-sternalen Duftdrüsenfeldes bei *Tupaia glis* DIARD, 1820. Verh Dtsch Zool Ges Saarbrücken, pp 198−206

Sprankel H, Richarz K (1976) Nicht-reproduktives Verhalten von *Tupaia glis* DIARD, 1820, im raum-zeitlichen Bezug. Eine quantitative Analyse. Z Säugetierkd 41:77−101

Lemurine Social and Territorial Organization in a North-Western Malagasy Forest (Restricted Area of Ampijoroa)

R. Albignac [1]

The territory of Ampijoroa, situated in north-western Madagascar (near the city of Majunga), is characterized by a deciduous forest growing on sand, although several more humid areas surround the more or less permanent water spots.

There are numerous species of shrubs and trees. Richard (1977) identified 170 different species belonging to 35 families, a result confirmed in 1979–80. There are approximately 14,500 trees or shrubs per hectare.

Research Methods

I have mainly worked in a specially prepared study area which is transected by a grid of paths every 25 to 30 m.

In order to precisely identify the animals, I thought that it would be more useful to capture them and mark them using a double system: a permanent mark consisting of a cut on the ear, and another mark which, even if not permanent, would be easier to see. The hair on the tip of the animals tails was cut so that the identification of the individual animals would be possible.

The Lemurs were captured with the aid of blowpipe-projected syringes containing a tranquilizer (imalgene). In this way, it was possible to identify 14 sifakas, 17 avahis, and 25 sportive Lemurs within a total study area of 16 hectares.

Radio-tracking transmitters were attached to the animals' necks, in order to follow in detail the movement patterns and certain territorial and feeding behaviors. This study began in January 1979, and has been expanded since January 1980.

Results

There are several sympatric Lemur species in this area, consisting of: two diurnal species *(Propithecus verreauxi coquereli* and *Lemur fulvus fulvus),* one crepuscular, and sometimes nocturnal species *(Lemur mongoz)* and four typically nocturnal species *(Microcebus murinus, Cheirogaleus medius, Lepilemur edwardsi,* and *Avahi laniger occidentalis).*

1 Laboratoire de Zoologie, Université de Madagascar, Antananarivo, Madagascar

Most of these species are vegetarian, their diet being made up of fruits, leaves, and the bark of different trees. Only *Microcebus* eats both fruits and insects.

The territorial and social organization of the diurnal species *(Propithecus verreaux and Lemur fulvus fulvus)* differs greatly from that of the species, with a nocturnal inclination but with a relatively big body size *(Lemur mongoz)*.

Propithecus verreauxi coquereli is mainly organized into small groups, composed of from three to five individuals. Each group occupies a home range of about four to six hectares; the overlaps areas of home ranges are very important and are related to the forest food production (Fig. 1).

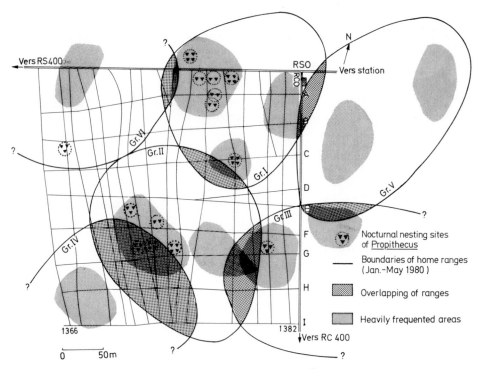

Fig. 1. Different home ranges of *Propithecus verreauxi coquereli*

The *Propithecus* diet essentially consists of leaves, sometimes of fruits, and, especially during the winter, of bark which accounts for their high population density in that part of Madagascar.

In the case of *L.f. fulvus,* we deal with Lemurs organized into real social groups, composed of at least 12 individuals. Quite differently from *Propithecus*, their home range size seems to be related to the microhabitat where they live. In the study area (that is the sandy plateau), I localized only one group, that occupying a still undetermined home range of more than 100 hectares (perhaps of 200 to 300 hectares). In contrast, in the wetter lowlands of the Ampijoroa region they are more numerous and their home range is reduced. This seems to be related to the more favorable alimentary possibilities of this fruit- and leaf-eating species.

In the case of *Lemur mongoz,* the animals live in family groups of three or four individuals. I could only localize them in the wet lowlands where they occupy large home ranges of about 100 hectares. Their habits, predominantly crepuscular and only occasionally nocturnal, are probably related to a certain competition with *L. fulvus.*

In the nocturnal species, we find more or less the same tendencies: the frugivorous and insectivorous species are more numerous in the wet lowlands, while the environmental influence seems to be unimportant for leaf-eating lemurs.

So far, we have particularly studied *Avahi laniger* and *Lepilemur edwardsi,* two abundant or very abundant leaf-eating species.

Microcebus murinus and *Cheirogalus medius* are on the contrary not so abundant, especially in the dry forest and on the plateau sands.

Avahi laniger typically lives in family groups of two or three individuals. Whatever the environment in their north-western region of Madagascar, a group home range occupies an area of about 4 hectares (Fig. 2).

Lepilemur edwardsi lives rather isolated. Nevertheless, it happens very frequently that two or three individuals (males and females) meet in the same diurnal refuge, provided that it is large enough (a wide tree hole, for example).

On the contrary, during the night they usually move separately, in a home range of about 1 hectare. The home range, especially of certain males, can be larger.

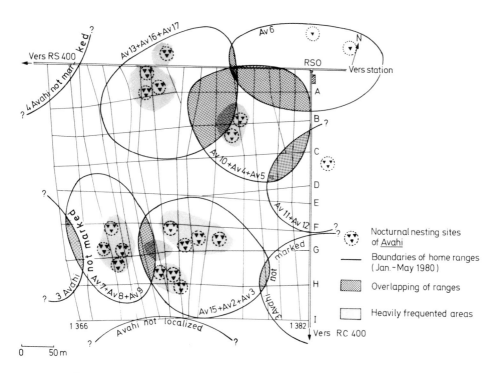

Fig. 2. Different home ranges of *Avahi laniger occidentalis*

R. Albignac

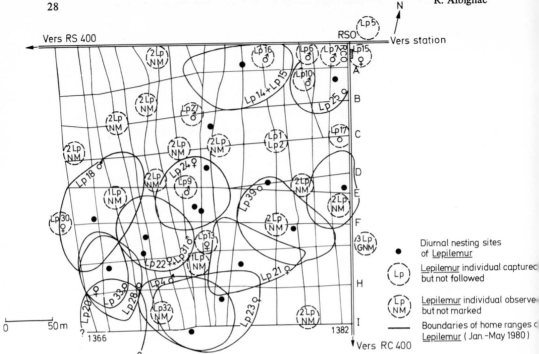

Fig. 3. Different home ranges of *Lepilemur edwardsi*

The overlaps areas of these home ranges are sometimes very extended. The animals' aggressive auditory territorial behaviors are very noticeable (howls accompanied by leaping on and shaking of branches) (Fig. 3).

The higher density of *Lepilemur edwardsi* (compared to *A. laniger*) can be largely explained by a particular alimentary behavior: these animals feed on leaves, even mature leaves, and perhaps practise coecotrophy (as observed by Dominique and Hladick 1971). The structure of alimentary canal, nutrition and digestion are presently beeing studied in order to complete these observations.

Finally, *Cheirogaleus medius* and *Microcbus murinus* always move as isolated individuals. Their number is very small in the dry forest and on sand. Within a study area of 16 hectares, two *Cheiroopaleus* and 12 *Microcebus* have been localized.

In conclusion, I would like to emphasize the intimate relationship that can exist between the diet and the social and territorial organization of West Madagascar Lemurs.

In the case of leaf-eating or bark-eating species there was no evidence of an important dietary limitation: the social and territorial organization remains unchanged throughout the year whatever the microhabitat.

On the other hand, in the case of frugivorous or insectivorous animals (that is to say the *Lemur, Cheirogalus* and *Microcebus*) the dietary factors strongly influence the size of home ranges: they are inclined to be more reduced in the wet lowlands, an environment favorable to these species.

References

Albignac R (1981) Variabilité dans l'organisation territoriale et l'écologie de *Avahi laniger* (Lému-
     rien nocturne de Madagascar). C R Acad Sci Paris 292:331–334
Charles-Dominique P, Hladick CM (1971) Le *Lepilemur* du Sud de Madagascar: Ecologie, alimenta-
     tion et vie sociale. Terre et Vie 1:3–66
Petters JJ, Albignac R, Rumpler Y (1977) Faune de Madagascar, 44 Mammifères Lémuriens
     (Primates, Prosimiens)' Orstom CNRS, Paris, 513 pp
Richard A (1977) Behavioral variation, case study of Malagasy Lemur. Univ Press, Bucknell

Factors Influencing Choice and Social Utilization of Resting Places in Captive Pottos (Perodicticus potto M.)

G. Clauss, H. Hultsch, F. Duvall II, and D. Todt [1]

The selection and utilization of sleeping and resting places by nocturnal prosimians have been studied with particular attention to its role in territoriality and in protection against potential predators. Existing reports for the potto *(Perodicticus potto)* maintain that no regular sleeping places are sought out; rather pottos sleep at any immediately suitable location taken up as daylight breaks (Charles-Dominique 1975, 1977). Also it is reported that a potto usually sleeps alone (Blackwell and Menzies 1968, Doyle 1974, Charles-Dominique 1977). As our own and other investigators' observations (Rahm 1960, Cowgill 1964, 1974, Ehrlich and Musicant 1972) made on a group of pottos kept in our laboratories contradicted the above field studies, we conducted a series of experiments pertinent to such behaviors. This was to clarify the following:
1. Which criteria are used by a potto in seeking out a sleeping place?
2. Is a sleeping place also used during the active period of the diurnal cycle? If so, then how is it utilized?
3. Do the pottos rest and sleep singly? If they do not, which individuals prefer to sleep together?

Materials and Methods

The animals under observation were four pottos (2 ♂♂, 2 ♀♀) that have been held for over 2 years in an observation chamber (2 X 3 X 4 m) in which light and temperature were automatically controlled (light/dark cycle: 12/12 h). A supplemental light source illuminated the chamber continuously with an intensity of 0.9 lux, especially during nocturnal conditions, thus allowing audio-visual filming. The food consisted of various kinds of fruits, vegetables, insects, eggs and chicken meat enriched with minerals and vitamins. They were offered with regular alternation.

Behavior of the four individually distinguishable pottos, labeled with black and white bands on the hind limbs, was analyzed per animal and age category: ad. ♂, juv. ♂, ad. ♀, juv. ♀. The adult pottos were judged as being approximately 2 years older

1 Abteilung für Verhaltensbiologie, Fachbereich Biologie, Freie Universität, Haderslebener Straße 9, 1000 Berlin 41
Offprint request to: D. Todt

than the 2 juvenile pottos according to differences in pelage structure and tooth wear patterns. For implementation of the experiments reported here the animals' chamber was restructured on several occasions. This restructuring pertained only to changes in the positioning and quality of the sleeping and resting places available to the potto.

Results

Characteristics of the Optimal Sleeping and Resting Places

In order to test which parameters are used by pottos in selection of sleeping and resting places, boxes constructed of various materials (clay, metal, paper, cardboard, plastic), and of various sizes and degrees of translucence, were placed in defined positions in the animals quarters. It was then determined which boxes were sought out and how frequently during both active and inactive phases. The results, in detail, showed that: (1) boxes of $0.2 \times 0.3 \times 0.4$ m were selected more frequently than boxes either larger or smaller than this, (2) opaque boxes were preferred to translucent boxes, and (3) given the possibility of selecting from a wall fitted with 15 adjacent sleeping/resting boxes, the pottos chose above all those boxes farthest from the floor, and then boxes immediately adjacent, or in equivalent spatial positions to one another.

After each restructuring and rearranging, all boxes were re-explored during the animals activity phases. Exploration occurred during short visits to the boxes during which the boxes were also scent marked (urine dabbing). Even during exploration the pottos showed increased frequentation of the boxes which were temporally extremely preferred to others and selected as sleeping boxes.

Once selected and established, the sleeping boxes were used exclusively. In order to determine whether the position of a box or the familiarity with a box (presumably caused by scent marking) was the deciding factor, certain boxes were exchanged (Fig. 1).

When boxes that were far apart from each other were exchanged, the animals chose the new box installed at the old position rather than the previously used box at the new position. However, prior to its selection the "new" box was often explored and scent marked during the activity period. When exchanging nearby or adjacent boxes, the animals always selected the previously used box. On the other hand, when the preferred sleeping box was changed to another position and, additionally, no box was replaced at the old position, the animals chose the old box at the new position (Fig. 1e). Some days later the former positions could be refilled with new boxes without inducing the pottos to leave the old box at the new position. From this we conclude that a familiar spatial position influences the selection of a sleeping/resting place more than did the previous use of a particular box and the thus resulting familiarity (scent) with the box.

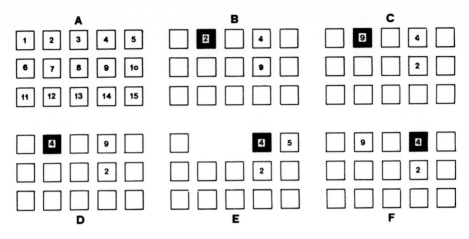

Fig. 1 A–F. Illustration of the experiments on sleeping/resting place selection; *squares,* symbols for the boxes; all boxes were numbered; entrance holes were front middle only. *Black* denotes boxes selected continuously by at least three pottos. A Starting situation – 15 boxes filled the upper third of one wall of the chamber. B The pottos selected box Nr. 2, after 7 days without boxes, box Nr. 2 was retained 5 days. C Boxes Nrs. 2 and 9 exchanged; spatial position retained – animals slept in Nr. 9. D Boxes Nrs. 4 and 9 exchanged; same position again retained. E Box Nr. 4 returned to original position equidistant from box Nrs. 3 and 9; box Nr. 4 selected again. Pottos did not select box Nr. 1 which was even nearer to the original box's position. F After 5 days in box Nr. 4 the pottos retained it even though other boxes were now placed in the originally preferred position. This demonstrates that boxes are usually selected according to their spatial position, however, familiarity with a box can also play a role

Temporal Trends in Box-Related Behavior

Attendance at boxes was observed at all times during the activity periods. But it occurred most frequently approximately 1 1/2 h before the beginning of the artificial day phase. The durations of box attendances, considered for all four individuals, showed a multimodal distribution (Fig. 2). Short "flying visits" lasted 25 ± 10 s, whereas longer visits lasted 60 ± 10 s or 120 ± 20 s. Attendances of some minutes duration were also recorded. Since pottos did not change boxes after the chamber light went on, attendances during the resting phase (light period) lasted for a full 12 h in the selected sleeping boxes.

Durations of box visitations between 20 s and 10 min occurred with an almost equal distribution for the four individuals. However, box visitations lasting longer than 15 min were predominantly performed by one particular potto (juv. ♂). All visitations observed during the nocturnal phase were basically addressed to the preferred sleeping box or the boxes adjacent to it. At present we do not know which categories of behavior were performed during the box visitations. However, there are hints that the "flying visits" consisted only in scent-marking behavior. Furthermore, visitations longer than 5 min appeared to be used as resting periods.

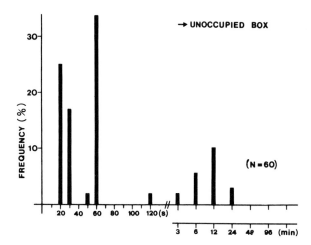

Fig. 2. Frequency distributions for durations of box visits during activity phases. Data are pooled for all four pottos. Timespan between entering and leaving a box was considered one visit. The *upper plot* is of visits to unoccupied boxes, the *lower plot* is of visits to occupied boxes (one or more animals). Durations of visits are markedly longer in the latter case

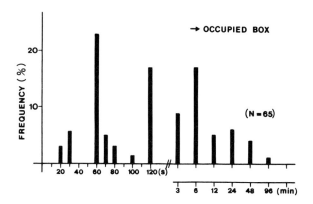

The Social Importance of Sleeping/Resting Boxes

The quantity of positions of the boxes was such that each individual could have selected its own box. However, only in singular cases did a potto remain alone to sleep. Mostly, pottos formed distinct sleeping groups (Fig. 3). When the animals did not sleep in one box, then they usually selected two adjacent boxes on the same level.

Social interactions outside the boxes consisted in: (1) contact play, (2) mutual maintenance behavior, (3) genital inspections. All social interactions were induced when one animal lingered at some preferred location outside the boxes and waited upon the approach of another individual. Detailed analysis of box visitations during the active phase showed that visitations to unoccupied boxes were significantly shorter than visits to boxes wherein another potto was detected (Fig. 2). Of all social interactions occurring within boxes 90% occurred in those boxes which were preferred sleeping boxes.The remaining 10% occurred in other preferred "alternative" boxes, these always being on the same level as the actual sleeping box.

INDIVIDUALS	♀₁	♀₂	♂₁	♂₂	♀♀₁₊₂	♂♂₁,₂	♀₁♂₁	♀₁♂₂	♀₂♂₁	♀₂♂₂	♀₁♂₁♂₂	♀₂♂₁♂₂	♀♀₁₊₂♂₁	♀♀₁₊₂♂₂	NIGHTS
♀₁	⊖	3	–	1	–	–	–	–	8	–	–	8	–	–	20
♀₂	3	⊖	1	–	–	–	8	–	–	–	8	–	–	–	20
♂₁	–	1	②	1	8	–	–	–	–	–	–	–	–	8	20
♂₂	1	–	1	⑩	–	–	–	–	–	–	–	–	8	–	20
NIGHTS	4	4	4	12	8	–	8	–	8	–	8	8	8	8	

Heading over columns: SLEEPING TOGETHER (SAME) BOX WITH

Fig. 3. Frequencies of sleeping group formation over 20 consecutive nights. Only the adult male (♂ 2) frequently slept alone

Conclusions

Our results show that a room equipped with a sufficient number of sleeping/resting places markedly influences the subsequent behavior of pottos.

Although field studies have suggested otherwise, our experiments have shown that pottos do use specific parameters in actively selecting their sleeping/resting places (Fig. 1). These factors interplay and possibly even overlap between the scent marking (social component) of the box and its position (spatial component) in the three-dimensional surroundings and are certainly used by pottos as determining factors in sleep/resting box selection. It now seems that these components are closely interconnected, but are plastic in quality, their relative importances being determined anew in each particular situation that arises.

Social interactions take place at certain spatially determined locations, both inside and outside the boxes used for sleeping/resting purposes. We suppose that under natural conditions places scent marked by more than one potto could be locations suitable for such interactions. That pottos form sleeping groups contradicts previous findings from field studies. It remains unclear whether group sleeping behavior is due or not to laboratory conditions that limit the pottos ranging behavior. Further experimentation is planned to clarify this matter.

Acknowledgments. We thank our technical staff M. Böhnisch, M. Schmiske, and J. Strassert for continued and effective assistance.

References

Blackwell KF, Menzies GJ (1968) Observations on the biology of the potto *(Perodicticus potto M)*. Mammalia 32:447–451

Charles-Dominique P (1975) Vie sociale de *Perodicticus potto* (Primates, Lorisidées) étude de terrain en forêt équatorial de L'Ouest Africain au Gaban. Mammalia 38:355–379

Charles-Dominique P (1977) Ecology and behaviour of nocturnal primates prosimians of equatorial West Africa (transl Martin RD). Columbia Univ Press, New York

Cowgill UM (9164) Visiting in *Perodicticus*. Science 146:1183–1184

Cowgill UM (1974) Cooperative behaviour in *Perodicticus potto*. In: Martin RD, Doyle GA, Walker AC (eds) Prosimian biology. Duckworth, London

Doyle GA (1974) Behaviour of prosimians. In: Schrier AM, Stollnitz F (eds) Behaviour of non-human primates, vol V. Academic Press, London New York, pp 1–142

Ehrlich A, Musicant A (1972) Social and individual behaviors in captive slow lorises. Behaviour LX:196–220

Rahm U (1960) Quelques notes sur le Potto de Bisman. Bull IFAN 22, 1:331–342

The Lateral Balancing of Handedness Tested in Slowly and Rapidly Moving Lorisidae

D. Todt, A. Kraberger, and P. Heermann [1]

The handedness of primates may follow either from learning mechanisms, especially operant conditioning, or from a functional asymmetry of hemispheres. However, in contrast to handedness in man, the lateral preference of hand application in non-human primates may show significant temporal fluctuations. This has been evidenced by long-term studies in Cercopithecidae (Cole 1957, Warren et al. 1967, Ettlinger and Moffet 1964, Beck and Barton 1972, Lehman 1978, Flowers 1975, Todt and Götz 1980) and Callithricidae (Rothe 1973). In accordance with the common finding that these fluctuations occur particularly prominently (1) in young individuals, and (2) during test situations easy to settle and familiar to the animals, we suggest a hypothesis providing both an explanation of lateral fluctuations and a basis for further experiments. There is a central component that promotes a lateral balancing of handedness: After successful conditioning of a particular hand (skill 1), this component generates lateral variation of handedness, specifically without the precondition of a previous unsuccessful application (= frustration of the conditioned hand). Consequently, the component guarantees that not only one, but both hands can be trained correspondingly on the long run (skill 2; Fig. 1).

We guess that this component could be advantageous especially for aboreal species which (e.g., concerning patterns as "targeting", "reaching", "grasping") cannot afford an extreme specialization of only one hand. This seems to be more plausible in rapidly

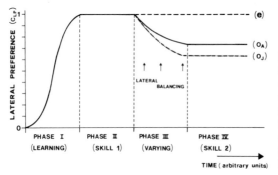

Fig. 1. The hypothesis of lateral balancing of hand application (see text). e, expected hand preference when positive reinforcing of a preferred hand continues, and no lateral balancing occurs. O_A (respectively O_J) observed preference in adults (respectively juveniles) after lateral balancing during phase III

1 Abteilung für Verhaltensbiologie, Fachbereich Biologie, Freie Universität, Haderslebener Straße 9, 1000 Berlin 41

than in slowly moving species. Therefore, we have examined the hypothesis of "lateral balancing of handedness" by comparing hand application in pottos *(Perodicticus potto)* and galagos *(Galago senegalensis)*. Our questions:

1. Would prosimian species turn out to be handed? If so, would hand preferences remain consistent during different tests (tasks)?
2. Would there occur individual differences? If so, could they depend on the age of subjects?
3. Would there occur temporal fluctuations in the handedness of particular individuals? If so, would this support or reject the mentioned hypothesis?

Methods

The tests were carried out on four pottos *(Perodicticus potto;* 1 ad. ♂, 1 juv. ♂, 1 ad. ♀, 1 juv. ♀) and four Senegal galagos *(Galago senegalensis;* 1 ad. ♂, 1 ad. ♀, 2 juv. ♀) which had lived in captivity for more than 2 years. Each species was kept in a separate room, and both species were examined under corresponding conditions. Test situations (Fig. 2):

(A) Free reaching of food pieces. The food (pieces of fruits, eggs, insects) was offered in open bowls on a board.
(B) Reaching foods through an open window in a transparent plastic box installed over the bowls.
(C) Reaching foods through two open windows in an equivalent box.
(D) Reaching foods through a window in an equivalent box after pushing down a plastic door.

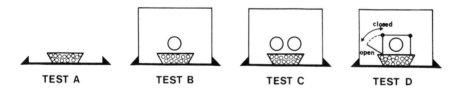

Fig. 2. Test situations. During test *B* and *C* open windows of a transparent plastic box allow "reaching through" and taking food pieces out of bowls. During test *D* a subject can reach through the window after having pulled down a transparent plastic door (bimanual test)

Each test situation was offered during several successive nights (tests A, B, C: 5 nights; test D: 10 nights). The behavior of the animals was recorded on video tape using the low-light camera NATIONAL WV-268. During dark phases (12 h) the rooms were illuminated continuously via a low-intensity light of 0.9 lux to allow recording. For evaluation of the temporal ordering of the behavior the video records were labeled electronically by a timer (FOR.A.VTG 33) down to frames of 20 ms.

The preference strength of handedness was estimated via $C_{LP} = \sqrt{(R - L)^2}/(R + L)$; C_{LP} = coefficient of lateral hand preference; R = frequency of right-handed. L = frequency of left-handed action patterns (here: frequency of "reaching"). Additionally $C_{SA} = (S - U)/(S + U)$; C_{SA} = coefficient of successful application; S = frequency of successful hand application; U = frequency of unsuccessful application. For analysis of intratest and, additionally, intertest consistency of lateral preferences we computed $C_{CC} = \chi^2/(\chi^2 + N)$; C_{CC} = corrected coefficient of contingency; N = number of tests.

Preparing for an interspecific comparison of handedness we checked an array of diverse motor patterns hand-performed by pottos and galagos (Kraberger 1980; Heermann 1980). We looked for pattern types of short and consistent duration, and, additionally, of clear-cut start and termination. Based on these criteria, we selected the pattern type "reaching" which was measured from the start of a goal-directed hand movement until touching the object. In contrast to "reaching", patterns like "grasping", "holding", "manipulating" showed multimodal distributions of duration. Furthermore, they seemed unsatisfactory for an interspecific comparison because of morphological/anatomical hand differences between pottos and galagos.

Results

Test-Dependency of Hand Preference

A single "reaching" lasted significantly longer in pottos than in galagos (Table 1). Nevertheless, individuals of both species performed this pattern type with lateral preference either for the right or the left hand. The distinctness of the preference depended significantly on the test situations. It was lower for "free reaching", higher for "reaching through", and highest for "reaching through" during test D which required bimanual action patterns (Fig. 2; Table 1).

Individual Differences in Handedness

As given in Table 1, individuals of both species could differ in a preference for either the right or the left hand. Additionally, they could differ in the strength of that preference. In both species, the latter differences turned out to vary with the animals' age. During test situations A, B, and C the juvenile individuals were significantly less handed than the adult ones. Only during test situation D were individual differences rather small (Table 1).

Temporal Fluctuations and Consistency of Handedness

In both species the strength of lateral preference could vary temporally. These fluctuations depended on the test situation and, additionally, on the animals' age. However, the fluctuations could show species-specific differences: the medium C_{LP}-values

Table 1. Handedness of "reaching" tested in four pottos:(*Perodicticus potto*) and four galagos (*Galago senegalensis*) during four tests (A, B, C, D; see Fig. 2). C_{LP}, coefficient of lateral preference; C_{CC}, corrected coefficient of contingency. Both C_{LP} and C_{CC} were computed for the five sessions of the 4th night only (see Fig. 4). α, significance based on χ^2-test; f A, frequency of "reaching" acts

Subjects		Preferred hand	Duration of reach (s)	Test A				Test B				Test C				Test D			
				C_{LP}	C_{CC}	α(%)	f A	C_{LP}	C_{CC}	α(%)	f A	C_{LP}	C_{CC}	α(%)	f A	C_{LP}	C_{CC}	α(%)	f A
Potto	ad. ♂	L	0.99±0.13	0.70	0.7	0.1	208	0.81	0.8	0.1	113	0.88	0.8	0.5	96	–	–	–	12
	ad. ♀	L	0.87±0.22	0.76	0.7	0.01	343	0.88	0.8	0.01	349	0.92	0.8	0.1	318	–	–	–	10
	juv. ♂	R	0.91±0.19	0.50	0.5	0.01	418	0.75	0.6	0.01	425	0.82	0.7	0.01	460	0.99	0.99	0.01	436
	juv. ♀	L	0.85±0.18	0.43	0.4	0.1	297	0.52	0.5	0.1	277	0.76	0.7	0.1	251	–	–	–	35
Galago	ad. ♂	R	0.62±0.17	0.72	0.6	0.1	214	0.79	0.6	0.1	424	0.79	0.7	0.1	463	0.94	0.8	0.1	347
	ad. ♀	R	0.56±0.16	0.66	0.6	0.1	226	0.82	0.8	0.1	511	0.86	0.8	0.1	536	0.95	0.8	0.1	369
	juv. ♀1	L	0.45±0.16	0.48	0.5	0.01	253	0.67	0.7	0.01	523	0.77	0.8	0.1	498	0.92	0.8	0.01	513
	juv. ♀2	R	0.49±0.19	0.42	0.5	0.1	219	0.65	0.6	0.1	534	0.74	0.7	0.1	402	0.91	0.6	0.1	377

observed for galagos during sessions of tests A, B, and C resulted rather from a rapid alternation of right and left hand than from a lateral change of hand application. In contrast to this, pottos did not perform rapid and frequent alternations of right and left hand (Fig. 3).

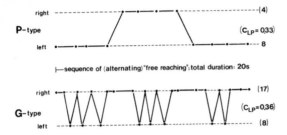

Fig. 3. The different types of performing frequencies of "free reaching" towards an object. Lateral changings *(on top)* are typical for pottos; whereas lateral alternations *(on bottom)* are typical for galagos. C_{LP}, Coefficient of *L*ateral *P*reference (see text)

The C_{LP}-values computed for the test situations A, B, and C were plotted against time (succession of sessions of nights). The resulting curves showed a shaping similar to that one predicted by our hypothesis (Figs. 1 and 4). The decrease of preference strength, which during tests B and C occurred on both species, could *not* have been generated by any frustration of the conditioned hand. This follows from the C_{SA}-values (coefficient of successful application) computed for that hand (Fig. 4). Especially this outcome supported our hypothesis. In parallel, the C_{LP}-values calculated for test A did not contradict the hypothesis. This follows from the conclusion that the individuals of both species were familiar with test A, thus being already in the state of skill 2 when being examined here. At present it remains unanswered whether the C_{LP}-values of tests B and C would have declined, thereby approaching toward the C_{LP}-values of test A, if the test presentation would have been continued further.

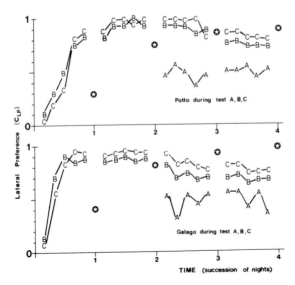

Fig. 4. Temporal variation of handedness during tests *A, B, C* observed in 20 sessions during 4 successive nights in a potto *(on top)* and in a galago *(on bottom)*. *Stars* show the strength of successful application of the preferred hand measured via C_{SA} (see text)

During test D, which required bimanual hand application, only one of the animals (Senegal galago juv. ♀) showed a low decrease in its lateral preference starting in the eighth night. Evaluation of test D showed that galagos were significantly more capable of learning how to manage the presented task than were pottos. However, present data do not allow to compare and distinguish long-term characteristics of handedness studied under test D (Fig. 5).

Conclusions

Although the relatively small number of tested individuals does not allow final statements concerning the complete spectrum of lateral hand preferences in galagos and pottos, it is evident that both species may develop and show distinct handedness. As known for other nonhuman primates (Warren et al. 1967, Ettlinger and Moffett 1974, Lehman 1978, Rothe 1973, etc.) some individuals preferred right- and others left-hand application. Also the finding that the preference strength of handedness depended on the animals' age and, additionally, on the tasks which had to be manipulated, is in accordance with results of other investigators.

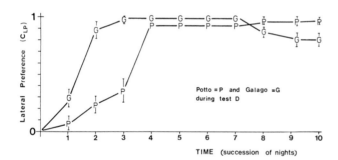

Potto = P and Galago = G during test D

Fig. 5. Lateral preference observed in a potto *(P)* and a galago *(G)* during the bimanual test *D* represented during 10 successive nights (see text)

Species-specific differences in long-term fluctuations of handedness were not found to be significant between the tested pottos and galagos. Furthermore, these fluctuations supported our hypothesis for both species. The support resulted from the decline of hand preference, which occurred although the success of the preferred hand did not decrease parallely. However, compared with the results of corresponding tests carried out in Cercopithecidae (Todt and Götz 1980), this decrease was less prominent in monkeys. Further studies may help to understand this difference. Such studies should include tests that examine the lateral hand preference of Lorisidae in other functional contexts of behavior, particularly locomotion and play.

Acknowledgments. We thank our technical staff M. Böhnisch, M. Schmiske, and J. Strassert for continued and effective assistance.

References

Beck CH, Barton RL (1973) Deviation and laterality of hand preference in monkeys. Cortex 8: 339–363

Cole J (1957) Laterality in the use of the hand, foot, and eye in monkeys. J Comp Physiol Psychol 50:296–299

Ettlinger G, Moffet A (1964) Lateral preferences in monkey. Nature (London) 204:606

Flowers K (1975) Handedness and controlled movement. J Psychol 66:39–52

Heermann P (1980) Handeinsatz beim Senegal-Galago. Diplom-Thesis, FU Berlin

Kraberger A (1980) Wahlstrategien des Verhaltens von *Percodicticus potto* am Beispiel des Handeinsatzes. Diplom-Thesis, FU Berlin

Lehman RAW (1978) The handedness of rhesus monkeys. Neuropsychology 16:33–47

Rothe H (1973) Handedness in the common marmoset *(Callithrix jacchus)*. Am J Phys Anthropol 38:561–565

Todt D, Götz M (1980) Laterale Präferenzprofile beim Handeinsatz von Meerkatzen (Cercopitheciden). Verh Dtsch Zool Ges Berlin 1980, p 370

Warren JM, Abplanalp JM, Warren HB (1967) The development of handedness in cats and rhesus monkeys. In: Stephenson HW, Hess EH, Rheingold HL (eds) Early behaviour. John Wiley, New York, pp 73–101

Adaptive Strategies Adopted by a Free-Ranging Troop of Vervets When Placed in a Specially Designed Enclosed Environment

S.G. Tollman [1]

> *". . . we are far from understanding the complexities of behavioural adaptation to any given environment."*
>
> Dolhinow (1972, p. 16)

Cercopithecus aethiops has successfully adapted to all the different types of African environments which range between high rainfall forest and arid grassland where food shortages occur. Their adaptability has been accounted for in terms of anatomical generalization, relative lack of sexual dimorphism, and behavioral flexibility (e.g., Gartlan and Brain 1968, Chance and Jolly 1970, Rosen 1974). But — what are the seemingly successful strategies employed by these monkeys as they cope with, and then adjust to, a novel situation? In this research project a free-ranging troop of vervets was caged in the open, in the range of an unknown wild troop, and the process whereby this social unit dealt with this strange situation instantly, and then adapted to it in the long term, was examined.

The Subjects

Before capture, the free-ranging troop had lived relatively undisturbed at Beachwood Golf Course, a lush, well-tended 45.6 hectare tract of subtropical land. Even man-made changes ceased in 1961, when the clubhouse was completed. The troop was relatively large (about 40 individuals), well fed, and so well protected that overpopulation may distort the ecological balance in that area (Campbell, pers. comm.).

Procedure

After a 16-week field study, eleven of the forty free-ranging Beachwood individuals were trapped within 24 h of each other, and caged in a 6.5-meter radius "luxury" geodesic dome. For a description of the cage, the capture and establishment of the troop, see Tollman and Lucas (1976). The following table illustrates the change in troop composition upon caging.

Ten weeks of intensive monitoring of behavior was conducted, from the moment of the troop's capture and caging, until the troop had apparently adapted to their new

1 Department of Psychology, University of Natal, Durban, 4001, South Africa

Table 1. Changes in troop composition upon caging

Category	Free range troop	Caged troop
Adult male	2	1
Adult female	9	5
Immature vervets	25	3
Infants	4	2
Total	40	11

environment. A total of 346 h were recorded. The techniques employed consisted in random troop scans, focal sampling, and automatic bursts of 8 mm movie every 15 min for 30 s. Continuous monitoring of the first 2 weeks was followed by randomly assigned half-hour observation periods, six times per week for 8 weeks, and concluding with a resumption of continuous daily observations for 5 days during the 19th week. Details of collection of data and analysis can be found in the unpublished M. Sci. thesis by Tollman (1977).

Ethograms for each monkey and the troop as a whole were developed. The ethograms record both the frequency and the duration of each behavior pattern, and also permit comparison between animals. Interaction matrices were constructed, and charts were designed which enabled plotting the troop's position in space, as well as individual movement.

Results and Discussion

In the field, the troop's activities, like their surroundings, were predictable, well ordered, and the social roles clearly defined. Upon caging, this social group had to cope with an environment which was unfamiliar, and therefore initially constituted a threat to their survival. The most drastic alteration that these vervets had to cope with was probably the unfamiliarity of the cage territory, coupled with the fact that it was part of the range of another troop. In addition, troop movements were impossible in the cage and, despite careful planning to provide for all the facilities seen in the wild, space and resources were restricted. Furthermore, even though the caged vervets were taken from the same troop, and thus possessed established familial and social bonds, the troop had been reduced, the composition changed, and some close ties must have been broken.

Immediately after caging, the 11 Beachwood vervets seemed to explore their surroundings tentatively. Within an hour the local troop arrived and vigorous intertroop encounters ensued initiated by both the local dominant male and the caged male, and their respective troop members immediately supported them. The caged troop, however, had to deal with unforeseen contingencies. The cage wire prevented physical contact between the troops. Movement was restricted to a confined space and height domination was impossible. By nightfall of the first evening, troop behavior as seen

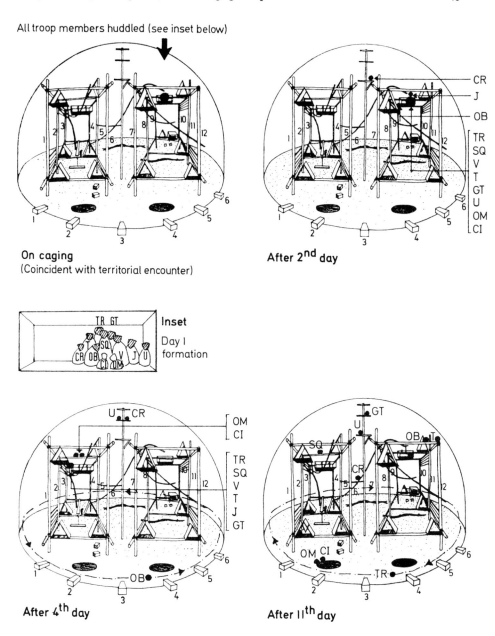

Fig. 1. Diagrammatic representation of daytime changes in troop. Spatial distribution during adaptation. Mature: *TR* Adult male; *OB* adult female; *SQ* adult female; *V* adult female; *I* adult female; *J* adult female. Immature: *GT* subadult male; *U* juvenile; *CR* juvenile; *OM* infant; *CI* infant

in their familiar Beachwood environment had disappeared, and they all huddled together, as illustrated in Fig. 1, high up in the only shelter protected on four sides.

Adaptation to the cage seemed to be effected in three phases. In phase 1, the troop's apparently confident relationship with its environment collapsed. It followed caging and unsuccessful territorial fighting and so the vervets' responses during this phase were to a strange and threatening situation. Phase 2 consisted in a gradual adjustment to this novel environment, while during phase 3 the vervets appeared to have adapted to the cage environment.

The crisis – that is, transfer to an unfamiliar and confined area, and territorial subservience – promoted social cohesion within the troop and decreased activities disrupting bonding. The behavior mechanisms elicited upon caging were significant increases in proximity by reduction of interpersonal distances, in activities concerned with physical contact, and in social facilitation, as well as a significant decrease in intratroop agonism (see Figs. 2–6). The troop seemed initially to function as one organism.

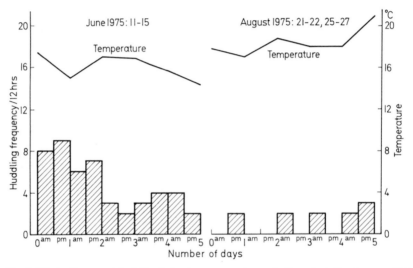

Fig. 2. Illustrating vervet huddling behavior upon caging and after adaptation to cage. Note: (i) Significant difference in huddling: p < 0.002 *(sign test)*. (ii) No apparent relationship between huddling and temperature

The increase in physical contact was exhibited at first by huddling behavior as distinct from sitting together. The monkeys seemed to bunch together as closely as possible, thereby increasing surface contact, and sometimes put their arms around each other. At night, the vervet troop retained this huddle conformation and they all slept together in one bunch. In this study, these behaviors were independent of climatic temperature as suggested by Struhsaker (1969) and Gartlan and Brain (1968). Thus, it seems that troop proximity is an important factor in an unpredictable situation.

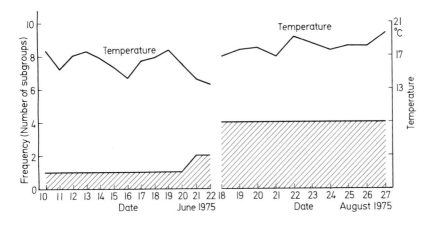

Fig. 3. Illustrating the relationship between sleeping subgroup formation, time and temperature. Note: (i) Significant increase in subgroup formation between commencement and completion of study p <0.008 *(sign test)*. (ii) No relationship between temperature and subgroup formation

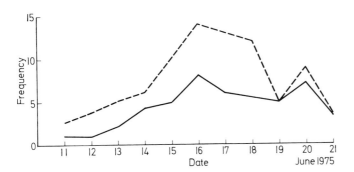

Fig. 4. Indicating significant correlation between grooming and territorial fighting. Rs: 0.95. Significant correlation: p <0.01. —— Mean No. of grooming individuals/time sampling round (11 x 5 minutes). – – – – Total No. of territorial fights/day

During this huddling phase, movement was minimal — faeces were liquid and smelly, and the vervets went to sleep far later than in the field. It seemed that the vervets were clustered together in a state of heightened vigilance, and physical preparedness.

The female-infant unit appeared to stabilize and integrate the caged troop. During phase 1 increased suckling occurred, thus providing some behavioral continuity between field and cage. Gartlan and Brain (1968) found an intensification of the mother-infant bond in the ecologically impoverished area of Chobi. The female-infant unit appeared to form the nucleus of the huddle toward which the other vervets were

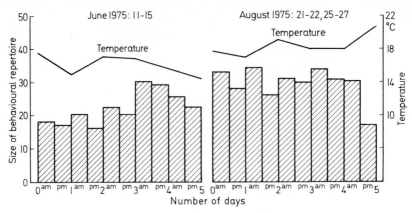

Fig. 5. Comparison of the range of vervet behavioral repertoires on caging and after adaptation. Note: (i) Significant increase: p $<$ 0.02 *(sign test)*. (ii) No apparent relationship with temperature variation

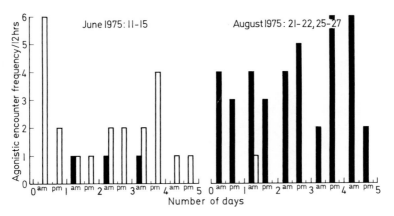

Fig. 6. Changes in inter- and intratroop agonism upon caging and after adaptation. Note: (i) intra-troop agonism increased significantly: p $<$ 0.002 *(sign test)*. (ii) Intertroop agonism decreased significantly: p $<$ 0.02 *(sign test)*. ▭ Intertroop. ▆ Intratroop

attracted. The initial troop huddling formation was relatively invariant. The troop congregated in the only shelter closed on five sides. The adult male was barely visible as he crouched behind, while the female-infant units were in the center of the front line, and therefore the most prominent troop members to any observer. Since different responses would be evoked by the sight of a leader adult male and the sight of a female-infant unit, it is postulated that this troop formation may have been a sub-missive display to inhibit the attacking behavior of possible territorial adversaries. This hypothesis could be tested by noting whether the response of a dominant male to strange female-infant pairs, and strange dominant males, is different. The role of the female-infant unit in this study is in agreement with the statement by Lancaster

(1975) that "both field and captive colonies suggest that it is the matrifocal core which provides a primate group with stability and continuity through time" (p. 26). Further support for this hypothesis came from the fact that it was the feeding female who initiated grooming activity in the cage.

After the initial immobile period, increased physical contact was also apparent in an increase in grooming activity and mating. Grooming appears to have many functions. In this study increases in grooming correlated significantly with the renewal of intertroop fighting (Fig. 4) – throughout the study, grooming appeared to function as a tension-reducing activity. This corresponds with Sade's observations (1965) that a relaxing effect on grooming participants is common. Regarding an apparent increase in sexual activity, Wilson's sweeping negation of Zuckerman's hypothesis (1932) that mating provides the motivational bond uniting primates into social groups seems an overstatement. While mating may not serve as major role in promoting social cohesion, it seems incorrect to discount it completely.

During phase 2, the inactive, huddling troop emerged from the protected shelter for progressively longer periods, and their range of behavioral activities expanded. Social facilitation during the initial phase of emergence was amplified – all the troop members did the same things at the same time. Increased coordination of the activities of other troop members must have been heightened. Synchronization of troop activity diversified during adaptation, and there was a significant increase in the behavioral repertoire of the troop after adaptation (Fig. 5). This synchronization of activity appears to approximate Stumpfer's (1970) findings with humans that there is a positive interrelationship between fear and affiliative tendencies. The social group seems to exert a force drawing the individual toward it, and the strength of the force seems related to the hospitality of the environmental circumstances.

Tinbergen (1965) pointed out that social organization is an integration of both positive and negative forces. Unity within the troop in order to meet any contingency seemed maximized, and disruptive factors were decreased. As shown in Fig. 6, intratroop agonism was minimal during the initial phases of caging, and only after most intertroop agonism was eliminated, was a significant increase in intratroop agonism exhibited.

Resolution of the territorial conflict coincided with the Beachwood troop's apparent adaptation to their new environment. During phase 1 the caged troop appeared to collapse, during phase 2 the caged adult females recovered and initiated active intertroop fighting, while during phase 3 the caged adult male's "leader" role was restarted and the local male retreated, and has not been seen sitting on the cage since, although he is often in the vicinity.

The submission of the Beachwood troop to their local counterparts seemed to be led by the adult male, whose behavior disintegrated after an unsuccessful confrontation with the local troop due to environmental constraints inhibiting movement and space domination. The troop response to this cue was to form a submissive but vigilant huddle around the adult male. Thus the cue for the troop's initial response seemed to be the male – but it was the behavior of the adult females during this intertroop confrontation that appeared to contribute toward its resolution and, consequently, toward the adaptation of the troop to the caged environment. It was the adult females who surrounded the adult male in the enclosed shelter, appearing to "protect" him, and flanked him when he moved. It was the adult females, too, who initiated the

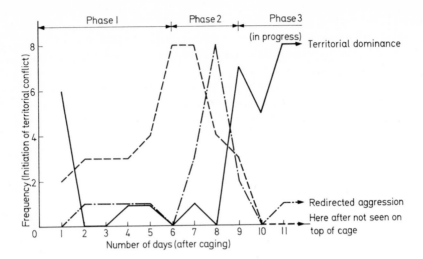

Fig. 7. The leader vervet in territorial encounters. Note: Phase 1. Collapse of caged troop. Phase 2. Recovery of caged adult females (initialing active fighting). Phase 3. Recovery of caged adult male – retreat of local male. ——— Caged adult male. – · – · Caged adult female. – – – Local dominant male

resumption of territorial fighting after the caged adult male collapsed. The territorial activity of the females in this study appears to support Lancaster's suggestion (1975) that in species like the vervet, where dimorphism is "minor", there may be very little difference in the aggressive potential of males and females. The behavior of the females in this study contradicts Wilson's statement (1975), cited from Gartlan and Brain (1968), that the adult male vervet chased territorial intruders 0.7 of the time, subadult males 0.3 of the time, and other age/sex categories did not show this behavior at all (see Fig. 7). It is suggested that this discrepancy may be due to the limited time during which Gartlan carried out his study, that unpredictable intertroop fighting may not have occurred, and that the monkeys may not have been identifiable. The activity exhibited by the adult females during my study may indicate a capacity for behavioral flexibility which is not present in the males. Conversely, though, the troop consisted of five adult females, and only one adult male, he may not have therefore been expandable in terms of troop survival and reproduction. Furthermore, after the females initiated the resumption of territorial conflict, the dominant adult male became increasingly involved in the territorial encounters. His increasing involvement was paralleled by a progressive involvement of the subadult male for whom he seemed to form a focus, and a growing acceptance of one of the local males as peripheral to the caged troop. The climax fight, which finally caused the local dominant male's retreat was initiated by the adult male and occurred when the peripheral male joined the caged troop against the locals.

Conclusion

Living in social groups, according to Kummer (1971), is the strong point of primate adaptation, as it enables members to meet the demands of the environment.

This investigation suggests that the success of the vervet may, in part, be due to the versatility of the troop's social organization, where the social structure varies with environmental characteristics — adverse conditions promoting cohesiveness, and favorable circumstances producing diversity of behavioral activities. The capacity and flexibility of the adult female to fulfill such a wide spectrum of roles ensured the retention of all behaviors necessary for the everyday functioning of the troop. Does this behavior, then, free the adult male to act as the "sensor" of environmental conditions and, by being a focus for the troop, to direct the unit's responses in relation to the prevailing environmental conditions? The transition of the male from outgoing leader to withdrawn submissiveness served as a signal for all troop members to huddle together, to enhance their attention toward one another, and to increase their level of awareness, so that the troop became consolidated as a single, united entity to deal with an unpredictable situation.

Acknowledgments. I thank Mr. J.W. Lucas, Senior Lecturer at the University of Natal, who inspired this study, and all the members of the Psychology Department, University of Natal, who supported, advised, and helped so enthusiastically throughout the execution of the study. The assistance of the Human Sciences Research Council and the Natal University Research Fund is gratefully recorded. The opinions expressed and conclusions drawn are those of the author, and are not to be regarded as a reflection of the opinions and conclusions of these institutions.

References

Chance M, Jolly C (1970) Social groups of monkeys, apes and men. Jonathan Cape, London

Dolhinow P (ed) (1972) Primate patterns. Holt, Rinehart & Winston Inc, New York, pp 352–393

Gartlan JS, Brain CK (1968) Ecology and social variability in *Cercopithecus aethiops* and *Cercopithecus mitis*. In: Jay PC (ed) Primates: Studies in adaptation and variability. Holt, Rinehart & Winston Inc, New York, pp 253–292

Kummer H (1971) Societies: Group techniques of ecological adaptation. Aldine Atherton Inc, New York

Lancaster JB (1975) Primate behaviour and the emergence of culture. Holt, Rinehart & Winston, New York

Rosen SI (1974) Introduction to the primates: Living and fossil. Prentice Hall Inc, New York

Sade DSS (1965) Some aspects of parent-offspring and sibling relations in a group of rhesus monkeys with a discussion of grooming. Am J Phys Anthropol 23:1–18

Struhsaker TT (1969) Correlates of ecology and social organisation among African cercopithecines. Folia Primatol 11:80–118

Stumpfer DJW (1970) Fear and affiliation during a disaster. J Soc Psychol 82:263–268

Tinbergen N (1965) Social behaviour in animals with special reference to vertebrates, 2nd edn. Methuen, London

Tollman SG (1977) The behavioural adaptation of a troop of vervet monkeys to a caged environment. Unpublished M Sci Thesis, University of Natal, Durban

Tollman SG, Lucas JW (1976) The design and maintenance of a primate troop enclosure. Proc 28th Annu Congr S Afr Psychol Assoc. University of the Witwatersrand, WUSPO

Wilson EO (1975) Sociobiology: The new synthesis. Bel Knop Press of Harvard University Press, Cambridge Mass London

Comparative Studies of Gregariousness and Social Structure Among Seven Feral Macaca fuscata Groups

T. Koyama [1], H. Fujii [2], and F. Yonekawa [3]

Group differences in gregariousness and social structure among various feral groups of Japanese monkeys have been reported in field studies of provisioned monkeys, which began in the 1950s (Kawamura 1966, Kawai 1969, Yamada 1966, 1971). These reports, however, have been mostly based on intuitive and subjective impressions, such as "more vs less cohesive group", or "group strictly vs loosely controlled by the leader". The reported group differences were attributed to differences between leaders' characters or to the differentiation of the social roles of group members in relation to their age and sex. The first purpose of this study is to demonstrate group differences in gregariousness by applying uniformly controlled experimental methods. The second purpose is to discuss the social structure of Japanese monkeys with respect to group differences in their gregariousness.

Methods and Procedure

The distribution and the habitat of Japanese monkeys extend to all the Japanese archipelago except the nothernmost island (Hokkaido), from 31° to 41° latitude north, but climatically and ecologically there may not be very extreme differences among the habitats. Seven baited free-ranging groups which inhabited the western part of Japan were used for the present study (Fig. 1). The investigation was carried out for about 10 days in the birth season of each group, at which time group members are believed to be most cohesively integrated. Three groups, Miyajima, Katsuyama, and Arashiyama, were investigated in 1974, and the other three groups, Choshi-A, Gagyusan, and Tsubaki, in 1975. Awaji was investigated in 1978 (Table 1).

Three kinds of experiments were done for each group: (1) measuring the degree of gregariousness, (2) measuring the level of tension, and (3) recording the monkey's responses to man. Simple methods were used because of the restriction of time and incomplete identification of group members.

1 Present address: Faculty of Home Economics, Ochanomizu University, 2-1-1, Ohtsuka, Bunkyo-ku, Tokyo, 112 Japan
2 Faculty of Human Sciences, Osaka University, 286-1 Yamada-Ogawa, Suita, Osaka, 565 Japan
3 The Short-term Treatment Center for Emotionally Disturbed Children, 7-1, Shintsutsumi, Komatsujima, Sendai, 983 Japan

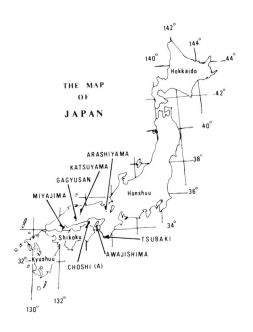

Fig. 1. Map of Japan and location of observed seven Japanese monkey groups

Table 1. The selected seven groups

	Miyajima	Katsuyama	Arashi-yama	Choshi-(A)	Gagyusan	Tsubaki	Awaji
The total number [a] of population	60	174	161	431	143	150	130
Year when baiting began	1961 [b]	1958	1954	1956	1955	1955	1967
Fission of the group	–	1 (1973)	1 (1966)	1 (1968)	6 [c]	–	–
Period of investigation (birth season)	Jun '74	Jun '74	Jun, Jul '74	May '75	May '75	Jun '75	May '78

a   Number of infants less than one year old excluded
b   This group was originally baited at Shodoshima in 1961, and transplanted here in 1962
c   See Furuya (1969)

The degree of gregariousness of a group was measured by the number of monkeys who were in a circle of 8 m diameter within which a fixed amount of wheat and beans were homogeneously scattered. The circle was drawn at the center of each group's feeding area. The monkeys were observed for 30 min in each trial, the average number of trials being ordinarily eight for the seven groups. During the observations the location of animals was recorded every minute by two observers with 35 mm cameras. The result of each trial was represented by the maximum number of animals counted in 30 min of each trial. Frequencies of agonistic vocalizations given by the monkeys in the circle were counted as indices of the level of tension among the group members. Vocalizations were recorded throughout each trial by a cassette tape recorder connected to a parabolic microphone, and total amounts of syllables were counted later. The level of tension was measured in three situations in addition to the experimental situation: resting, normal feeding, and traveling situation. The monkey's responses to an approaching experimenter, such as flight distances and displays, including facial expressions, were recorded by a portable video tape recorder.

Results

Gregariousness

In Fig. 2, the thick column shows the mean number of animals in the circle and the thin line shows the largest number of them in the circle during the trials. In Choshi-A, for example, 129 monkeys were the largest number counted in the circle, while 94 was the average number. In Katsuyama and Gagyusan, only an average of 22 and 18 monkeys respectively were in the circle, and 30 and 26 at most. Miyajima is a more gregarious group than Katsuyama or Gagyusan, 50 being the largest number in the circle and 36 the average.

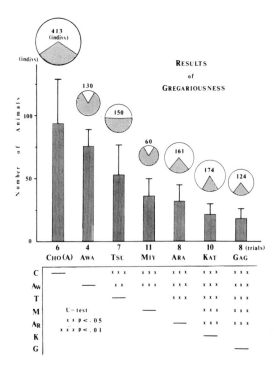

Fig. 2. Maximum and mean number of animals in an 8 m diameter circle *(columns)* and their percentage in relation to total group members *(shaded area of the circles)*, and results of U-test

The percentage of group members in the circle is represented by the shaded area of the fan. In Katsuyama and Gagyusan, only about 30% of the members were in the circle. In Awaji and Miyajima, on the other hand, more than 80% of the total group members were in the circle. In Choshi-A, only about 30% of the members were in the circle, although the group is a gregarious one.

An overall test suggested that the results for each group did not come from the same populations (Kruskal-Wallis test: χ^2 (H) = 42.8, p < 0.01). Then the results for each group were compared in pairs by the Mann-Whitney U-test. In terms of both the mean number and the largest number, Choshi-A and Awaji were the most gregarious groups, and Tsubaki, Miyajima, and Arashiyama came next. Of the seven groups, Katsuyama and Gagyusan were the least gregarious groups.

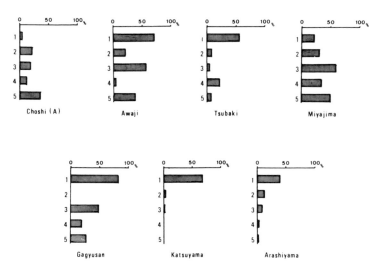

Fig. 3. Duration of the five highest ranking central males' stay in the circle expressed in a percentage of the total observation time

Figure 3 shows how long the five highest ranking central males in each group stayed in the circle expressed as a percentage of observation time. The alpha males of Miyajima and Choshi-A were not the longest stayers. For these two groups, there was no consistent relationship between the duration of the central males' stay in the circle and their dominance hierarchies. In contrast, the alpha male in Katsuyama, Gagyusan, and Awaji stayed longer than any other central males, namely for a period of more than 60% of the total observation time. In Tsubaki and Arashiyama, the alpha males were the longest stayers and the duration distributions for both groups of central males were similar to those of Katsuyama. In general, the duration of central males' stay decreased in the order of their dominance hierarchies. The fourth- and fifth-ranking males were still young (5 to 7 years old) in Awaji, Gagyusan, and Tsubaki. They were estimated to be the sons of dominant females, as they stayed in the circle for a comparatively long period.

Table 2. The ratio of the duration of the alpha male's stay in the circle accompanied by the other central males to the total duration of his stay

Central males' ranking	2nd	3rd	4th	5th
Miyajima	0.49	0.63	0.12	0.45
Katsuyama	0.12	0.04	0.00	0.00
Arashiyama	0.40	0.00	0.00	0.00
Choshi-(A) [a]	0.00	0.00	0.00	0.00
Gagyusan	0.00	0.59	0.19	0.00
Tsubaki	0.00	0.04	0.08	0.00
Awaji	0.00	0.61	0.06	0.22

a In Choshi (A), the lower- than the second-ranking central males
   showed as high a ratio of duration of the stay together with each
   other as the alpha male of Miyajima showed in the table above
   (for example, pairs of the third- and the fourth-ranking males,
   and the third- and the fifth-ranking males, showed 0.44 and 0.76
   respectively)

The ratio of the duration of the alpha male's stay in the circle, accompanied by the other central males, to the total duration of his stay (Table 2) reveals that the Arashiyama, Gagyusan, and Awaji's alpha males were each tolerant of a particular central male in the circle. On the other hand, Katsuyama and Tsubaki's alpha males occupied the circle exclusively. The alpha male of Miyajima was tolerant of other central males. In Choshi-A the very old alpha male often stayed alone except when

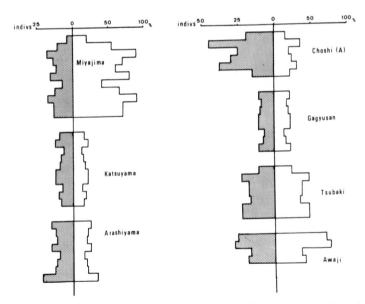

Fig. 4. Number of adult females in the circle when the maximum number of animals was recorded in each trial *(left shaded sides)*, and the ratio of the number of females in the circle to the total number of females in the group *(right sides)*

accompanied by the sixth-ranking young male (the ratio: 0.33), but the other central males tolerated each other in the circle, as in Miyajima.

The bars on the left side of Fig. 4 indicate the number of adult females in the circle when the maximum number of animals was recorded in each trial. The bars on the right side indicate the ratio of the number of females in the circle to the total number of females in the group. In Choshi-A, Tsubaki, and Awaji many adult females were in the circle, but in other groups small numbers of females were in the circle. As for the percentage of females who were in the circle, Miyajima and Awaji showed very high scores. In Tsubaki, about half of the adult females were in the circle. In Katsuyama and Gagyusan, at most 20% of the females were in the circle.

The Level of Tension

Group differences in levels of tension measured by vocal aggression are illustrated in Fig. 5. The thick column shows the mean frequencies of vocal aggression in all trials for each group, and the thin line shows their highest frequencies. The column of Choshi-A was higher than that for any other group, as indicated by the results of gregariousness. Gagyusan and Katsuyama showed low levels of frequencies here again. In terms of the frequency of vocal aggression, the rank order of Awaji was very different from that for gregariousness. Awaji showed as low a level of tension, as did Gagyusan and Katsuyama. Miyajima was not statistically different from Gagyusan

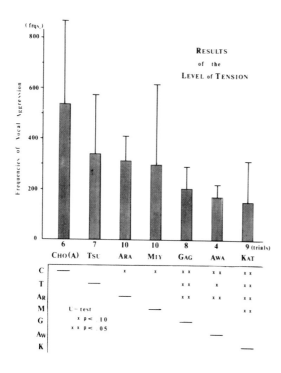

Fig. 5. Maximum and mean frequencies of vocal aggression (columns), and results of U-test

and Awaji because of its wide fluctuation in the frequencies of vocal aggression and because of the small amount of data in Awaji. The highest overall and mean frequencies recorded there seem to distinguish Miyajima from Gagyusan and Awaji. Tsubaki, Arashiyama, and Miyajima had medium level tension. Although an overall test testified to group differences in levels of tension (χ^2 (H) = 21.5, p < 0.01), they were not so clear here as in gregariousness, because the frequency of vocal aggression varied more than the number of animals in the circle. The differences in tension, however, are efficiently shown by considering both the mean frequencies and the highest frequencies.

The occurrence of vocal aggression during a single trial is illustrated in the lightly shaded histogram (Fig. 6). The solid line shows the change in the number of animals in the circle, and the horizontal arrows show the duration of the highest ranking or other central males' stay in the circle. The vocal aggression, which occurred within the first few minutes, was caused by the confusion resulting from many animals entering the circle. After that, it was often given in response to the central males' entrance to the circle or their withdrawal. When any one of the central males entered the circle, there seemed to be the following two sequential patterns: (1) A central male followed by adult females and juveniles entered the circle, and they got into disputes with females who had been occupying the circle; (2) a central male entered the circle alone, and as soon as he entered, the adult females and juveniles who had been staying homogeneously in the circle without forming subgroups attached themselves to the entering male, and formed subgroups. The members of one subgroup tried to exclude other subgroup members, and they were involved in disputes.

As for the solid line in this figure, there are three patterns shown by the change in the number of animals in the circle. In the most gregarious group, Choshi-A, the number of animals reached the highest point soon after the experiment started, and it decreased in a steep gradient, giving a concave curve. In the other groups except Tsubaki, the number of animals decreased with a less steep gradient, giving a convex curve. Tsubaki has a particular pattern of maintaining a high level of gregariousness throughout the 30-min period.

Correlation Between Gregariousness and the Level of Tension

The seven groups were charted on the dimensions of gregariousness and level of tension (Fig. 7). There is very high correlation (r_s = 0.886, p < 0.05) between gregariousness and level of tension in the rank order of the six groups, excluding Awaji. Level of tension also positively correlates with gregariousness among the six groups (r = 0.960). This would indicate that the more gregarious groups had higher levels of tension. As it will be discussed later, the results of Fig. 7a should be examined from another viewpoint first. In Fig. 7b, the abscissa is the percent ratio of the maximum number of animals in the circle to the total group members of each group, and the size of the circle indicates the maximum number of animals in the circle of the experiment. That means the group with a larger circle is more gregarious than one with a smaller circle. Katsuyama, Gagyusan, Arashiyama, and Tsubaki show a lineal relationship among them. This suggests that they might be typical groups of Japanese monkeys. Choshi-A, which had a large population size, is plotted at the top left in

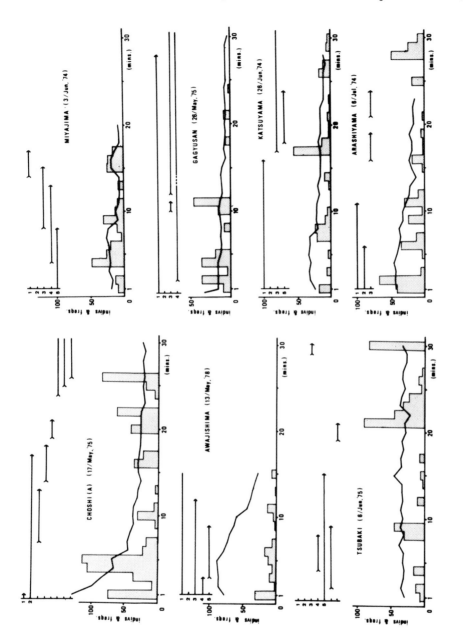

Fig. 6. The occurrence of vocal aggression during a single trial *(histogram)* and the change in the number of animals in the circle *(solid line)*. The *horizontal arrows* show the duration of the highest ranking central males' stay in the circle (males without number were not identified)

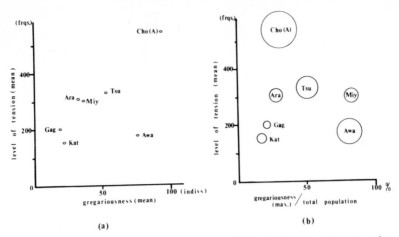

Fig. 7. a Correlation between gregariousness and the level of tension. **b** Position of seven groups according to the level of the tension and the percent ratio of maximum gregariousness to the total group members. *Size of circles* represents maximum number of animals in the circle

this figure, while Miyajima with a small population size is plotted at the middle right. Both of them are outside of the line which can be drawn from Katsuyama to Tsubaki. Awaji is located outside of the line, too. Thus, the latter three groups seem to be aberrant, but these deviations may have adaptive significance for the groups for the following reason. There are no groups plotted in the area where more than 50% of the group members could enter the circle with as high level of tension as in Choshi-A. The fact that Awaji is plotted at this point, the bottom right in the figure, may indicate that Awaji optimally adapted to a densely crowded situation, for about 80% of the group members were able to enter the circle at as low a tension as in Katsuyama and Gagyusan.

Discussion

Gregariousness and the Relationships Among Central Males

The results clearly showed differences in gregariousness among the groups. These differences approximately correspond to those which previous field workers reported intuitively in terms such as cohesive or not-cohesive, and strictly or loosely controlled groups.

The relationships among the central males of the groups were presented with respect to the duration of their stays in the circle. If the duration of the alpha male's stay reflects his ability to control, as a leader, the other males, Miyajima and Choshi-A's alpha males would have weak control over the other central males in their groups. In contrast, the alpha males in Katsuyama, Gagyusan, and Awaji would have strong control, because they stayed in the circle for more than 60% of the total observation time. Awaji, however, is one of the most gregarious groups, while Gagyu-san is the least gregarious group. The same contrast is seen between Katsuyama and Tsubaki, that is, the duration distribution is similar despite the difference in gregari-ousness. In addition, Katsuyama shows a different duration distribution from that of Gagyusan, though the former is as gregarious as the latter.

The relationships among the central males were also analyzed with respect to the ratio of the duration of the alpha male staying with each of other central males to the total duration of his stay in the circle. The results in Fig. 3 and Table 2 suggest that neither the ability for control nor the character of the leader may necessarily determine the gregariousness of the group.

The number of adult females who were able to enter the circle was presented in Fig. 4. Generally, the number of females in each group who were able to be in the circle increased with group gregariousness. Since the adult females are usually accom-panied by their offspring, the number of adult females in the figure may well reflect the gregariousness of the group. There might be two alternative situations in the circle: in the circle of highly gregarious groups there might be one or two central males accompanied by many females and juveniles, or there might be more than one or two central males in the circle (see also Fig. 6) accompanied by a relatively small number of females and juveniles. Miyajima and Choshi-A were in the latter situation. while Tsubaki and Awaji were in the former one. The results also showed a general tendency for a small number of the females to enter the circle, while almost all females in Miyajima and Awaji were able to stay in the circle.

Discussion of the Correlation Between Gregariousness and the Level of Tension

Why did the more gregarious group have higher levels of tension? Group members would normally keep proper interindividual distances, as a reflection of the intrinsic regulatory function for maintaining the unity of each group (Hediger 1964, Eibl-Eibesfeldt 1970, Hinde 1974). Our experimental situation was designed to reduce markedly the intrinsic interindividual distance between the group members. If their distance regulating function operated effectively, the group members could have avoided the excessive disputes seen in Choshi-A. Presumably, the regulatory function operated more effectively in Katsuyama and Gagyusan than in any other groups, because their group members kept proper distance from each other and avoided disputes. On the other hand, it operated less effectively in Choshi-A, because most of the group members were involved in disputes resulting from their excessive gregarious-ness. Yet the data from Awaji need another principle to explain their uniqueness. A large difference in dominance relationships among group members was found between Awaji and Katsuyama by our other experimental studies (paper in prepara-tion). In Awaji, submissive group members tend to approach dominant ones without receiving any aggression. Such peculiar dominance relationships may contribute to Awaji's being one of the most gregarious groups with a low level of tension.

Social Structure of Japanese Monkeys

The analysis in Fig. 6 suggests that a group of Japanese monkeys may include in it several subgroups in which adult females and juveniles are arranged around one of the central males, who is called a core male, and also suggests that the social structure of Japanese monkeys may consist in dynamic interaction among the subgroups. The members in a subgroup are called followers of the core male (Maeda 1967, Fujii 1975). As was seen in Fig. 4 and in Fig. 6, the gregariousness and the tension in our experiments might relate on the one hand to the size of subgroups, and on the other to cohesiveness of a subgroup resulting from the intensity of psychological bond between followers and a core male as a leader. Consequently, the group with large subgroups would be liable to become gregarious. And in the group which has cohesive subgroups supported by strong psychological bond between leaders and followers, the entrance of core males into the circle would bring many disputes, because the females and juveniles who usually follow the core males would differentiate themselves from other subgroup members in the circle when their core male entered. In this sense, the behavior of females and juveniles who follow the dominant core male might be more important for the gregariousness or the cohesion of group than the behavior of dominant males. This conclusion is different from that of Kurokawa (1975), who concluded the dominant males determined the group cohesion.

Group differences in gregariousness and level of tension may derive not simply from differences in superficial social structure such as group size, or age/sex composition, but from the difference in dynamics among group members such as the spatial regulatory function among the group members or the psychological relationship between leaders and followers in subgroups.

Acknowledgments. The authors are indebted to Associate Professor N. Itoigawa, Faculty of Human Sciences, Osaka University, for his invaluable advice and encouragement. The authors wish to express their gratitude to Dr. R.A. Hinde, MRC Unit, Cambridge, for his active interest and criticism. Thanks are also due to Dr. L.M. Fedigan, Dept. of Anthropology, University of Alberta, for correcting this manuscript.

This study was supported by the fund to Dr. H. Fujii, F. Yonekawa, and T. Koyama for Cooperative Studies of Kyoto University Primate Research Institute in 1974, 1975, and 1977, and by Japanese Government Grant to Dr. H. Fujii (No. 171027) in 1976.

References

Eibl-Eibesfeldt I (1970) Ethology: The biology of behavior. Klinghammer E (transl). Holt Rinehart and Winston, New York

Fujii H (1975) A psychological study of the social structure of a free-ranging group of Japanese monkeys in Katsuyama. Contemp Primatol 5th Int Congr Primatol Nagoya 1974. Karger, Basel, pp 428–436

Furuya Y (1969) On the fission of troops of Japanese monkeys. II. General view of troop fission of Japanese monkeys. Primates 10:47–69

Hediger H (1964) Wild animals in captivity. Sircom G (transl). Dover Publications Inc, New York

Hinde RA (1974) Biological bases of human social behaviour. McGraw-Hill Inc, New York

Kawai M (1969) Ecology and society of Japanese monkeys (in Japanese). Kawade-Shobo, Tokyo

Kawamura S (1966) Culture of non-human primates: from the observation of feral Japanese monkeys (in Japanese). Shizen 11 (11):28–34

Kurokawa T (1975) An experimental field study of cohesion in Katsuyama group of Japanese monkeys. Contemp Primatol 5th Int Congr Primatol Nagoya 1974. Karger, Basel, pp 437–444

Maeda Y (ed) (1967) Studies on behavior of Japanese monkeys in Katsuyama troop (in Japanese). Univ Press, Osaka

Yamada M (1966) Five natural troops of Japanese monkeys in Shodoshima Island. I. Distribution and social organization. Primates 7 (3):315–362

Yamada M (1971) Five natural troops of Japanese monkeys in Shodoshima Island. II. A comparison of social structure. Primates 12 (2):125–150

Behavioral Differences Between Feral Group-Reared and Mother-Reared Young Japanese Monkeys

K. Kondo, T. Minami, and N. Itoigawa [1]

We have studied effects of isolation on behaviors of Japanese monkeys such as distortions of social behaviors, restrictions in contact with physical environment, and development of stereotyped behaviors (Itoigawa 1967), and have found that these effects depend on the development of monkeys (Minami 1974). The stereotyped behaviors, especially locomotive stereotyped behaviors, increase in encountering situations where some degree of "tension" appears to be present (Yamaguchi 1977). We consider that the stereotyped behaviors reflect emotional disturbance in monkeys.

In recent years, a large amount of developmental studies in nonhuman primates have been concerned with effects of early social isolation on behaviors, and most of these studies have described effects of isolation on infants aged less than one year. A few studies, however, have been made to clarify effects of rearing conditions before isolation on later behavioral development of infants.

The purpose of this study is to compare effects of the following two pre-isolation conditions on social and stereotyped behaviors in young Japanese monkeys who were isolated at an age between 2 and 3 years. One of the two pre-isolation conditions was rearing monkeys in a feral group, and the other was rearing them only with their mothers. Effects of the two pre-isolation conditions on social and stereotyped behaviors were tested by the following two experiments: one, the group formation by monkeys who had been reared by either one of the two pre-isolation conditions (Experiment 1), and the other, the introduction of adults to each group (Experiment 2).

Experiment 1: Group Formation

Subjects

There were two groups, each consisting of two males and one female. One group was the feral-reared group and the other was the mother-reared group. The subjects of the feral-reared group were born in a free-ranging group at Katsuyama in Okayama prefecture. They were captured at about 2 years of age and sent to the Osaka University Laboratory. The subjects of the mother-reared group were born in the Laboratory

1   Department of Psychology, Faculty of Human Sciences, Osaka University, 286-1 Yamada-Ogawa, Suita, Osaka, Japan

and reared only with their mothers until 2 years of age. Their mothers were born in the Katsuyama group and captured as adults, except for a female subject's mother who was captured at 2 years of age.

The subjects of each group were caged in isolation at an age between 2 and 3 years. The isolation cage (50 × 70 × 180 cm) denied visual and tactual access to other monkeys. After the isolation period, the grouping was made for the subjects of each group.

Procedure

The group formation consisted of four phases (Table 1). In phase 1, the subjects were put together for 30 min once a day for 8 successive days. In phase 2, feeding was done during the period of grouping. The procedure of phase 3 was the same as in phase 1. In phase 4, the grouping was made all day and they were no longer separated. The grouping of each phase began when the front and side doors of the isolation cages were opened, allowing the subjects' interactions in the isolation and social cages (200 × 200 × 200 cm; Fig. 1).

Table 1. Schedule of group formation

Phase	Days	Group formation	Observation	Feeding during observation
1	1			
	2			
	3			
	4	30 min daily	30 min daily	–
	5			
	6			
	7			
	8			
2	9	30 min daily	30 min daily	+
	10			
3	11	30 min daily	30 min daily	–
	12			
4	13	all day	30 min daily	–
	14			

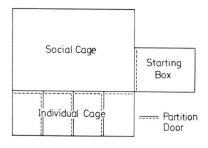

Fig. 1. Experiment cage

Social behavior and stereotyped behaviors were observed according to predefined behavioral categories with 15 sec intervals for 30 min by three observers, each of whom participated in observing one of the three subjects throughout the experiments.

Results

Figure 2 shows dominance relations among the subjects which were determined by the occurrences of approach and withdrawal in each phase of the group formation. Throughout the group formation, the feral-reared subjects showed more social interactions than did the mother-reared ones. In the feral-reared group the dominance relations (mR7 > mC7 > fL7) were established early in phase 1. Although reversal of the dominance relations occurred between mR7 and mC7 in phase, 2, the dominance relations remained stable for the remaining phases. In the mother-reared group, the dominance relations were not stable. The male subjects tended to withdraw from each other, and mLP3 and fLN3 did not interact with each other at all. Play-initiating behaviors occurred in the feral-reared group, but they did not occur in the mother-reared group. Inter-group comparison of the stereotyped behaviors shows that apparently more frequent and more variable patterns of the stereotyped behaviors occurred in the mother-reared group than in the feral-reared group (Table 2).

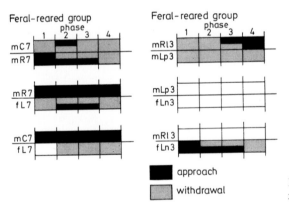

Fig. 2. Occurrence of dominance relations in group formation

Experiment 2: Introduction of Adult Monkeys

Subjects

The subjects of the feral-reared group and the mother-reared one were the same for experiment 2 as for experiment 1. The introduced adults were born in the Katsuyama group and captured there as adults. They have experienced many social encounters with other monkeys in the Laboratory.

Table 2. Occurrences of stereotyped behaviors in group formation

Subjects	Behaviors	Phase			
		1	2	3	4
Feral-reared group					
mC7	Fur-pulling				+
mR7	Hanging-swing	+		+	++
	Bipedal-sway	+		+	+
fL7	Jumping	++			
Mother-reared group					
mRl3	Hanging-swing	++		+	
	Bipedal-sway	+			
	Pacing	+			
mLP3	Eye-poke	+	+	+	+
	Fur-pulling				+
	Pacing	++	++	++	
	Twirling	++	+	+	+
	Somersault	++	+	+	+
fLN3	Pacing		++	++	++
	Twirling		++	++	++
	Rolling	++	++	++	
	Circling		+	++	

$+ < 10\%$ $++ \geqslant 10\%$

Procedure

The following two tests were conducted to investigate the subjects' responses to the adults who were introduced into each group. Test 1 was the 30 min daily introduction of each of six adults to each group in the order female (day 1), male (day 2), male (day 3), female (day 4), female (day 5), and male (day 6). The test was started by opening the partition door between the social cage and the starting box (100 X 60 X 70 cm; Fig. 1). After the 30 min daily test the adults were confined to the starting box, which denied visual contacts between the group's subjects and the adults. The subjects' behavior were observed for 30 min respectively before and during the introduction of the adults.

Test 2 was the introduction of a pair of adult male and female for 30 min daily for 4 days. After the 30 min daily test the adults were confined to the starting box, which allowed visual and tactual contacts between the group's subjects and the adults all day.

Results

Figure 3 shows the percent occurrences of social behaviors such as approach, withdrawal, and lip-smack in test 1. The frequency of social behaviors did not differ
greatly, but the feral-reared subjects showed markedly more frequent lip-smacks than
did the mother-reared ones. The mother-reared subjects recklessly approached the
adults many times. The results of the social behaviors during test 2 (Fig. 4) show
similar tendencies to those of test 1. Figure 5 shows the number of occurrences of
aggressive behaviors, such as chase, attack, bite, and other agonistic behaviors from
the adults to the group's subjects. The mother-reared subjects received more aggressive
behaviors from the adults than did the feral-reared ones. Especially the female subject
(fLN3) of the mother-reared group received violent attacks and was severely injured.

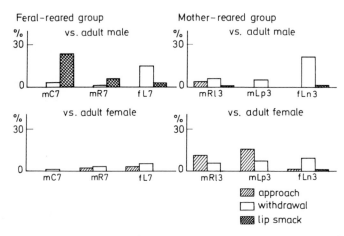

Fig. 3. Percent occurrence of social behaviors to adults in introduction of adults (Test 1)

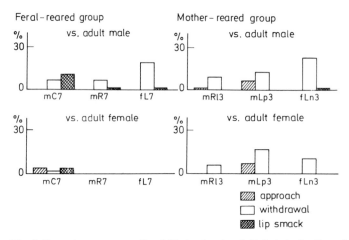

Fig. 4. Percent occurrences of social behaviors to adults in introduction of adults (Test 2)

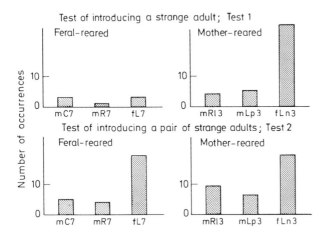

Fig. 5. Total number of aggressive behaviors from adults

The female subject (fL7) of the feral-reared group received aggressive behaviors as often as did fLN3, but she warded off aggressive behaviors from the adults and was not injured. Most of the aggressive behaviors occurred when the mother-reared subjects recklessly approached the adults and did not show any distinct facial expressions to these. Namely, aggressive behaviors from the adults occurred mostly through the subjects' inappropriate reactions to the adults' social responses.

Table 3. Occurrences of stereotyped behaviors in introduction of adults (Test 1)

Subjects	Behaviors	Before introduction	During introduction
Feral-reared group			
mC7	–		
mR7	Sway	+	+
	Jumping	+	+
fL7	Rock	+	
	Fur-pulling	+	+
Mother-reared group			
mRL3	Auto-grasp	++	
	Fur-pulling	+	
mLP3	Fur-pulling	+	
	Eye-poke	+	+
	Auto-bite	+	
	Jumping	+	+
	Pacing	++	++
	Twirling	+	++
fLN3	Pacing		+
	Twirling		+

$+ < 10\%$ $++ \geqslant 10\%$

Table 4. Occurrences of stereotyped behaviors in introduction of adults (Test 2)

Subjects	Behaviors	Before introduction	During introduction
Feral-reared group			
mC7	Pacing		+
mR7	Pacing		+
fL7	Pacing		+
Mother-reared group			
mRL3	Auto-grasp	++	
	Fur-pulling	++	
	Auto-bite	+	
	Pacing		+
mLP3	Fur-pulling	++	
	Pacing	+	++
	Twirling	+	++
fLN3	Auto-grasp	+	
	Pacing		++
	Twirling		++

+ <10%   ++ ≥10%

The mother-reared subjects showed more frequent and more various patterns of the stereotyped behaviors during the introduction of the adults than did the feral-reared subjects in test 1 (Table 3). The frequency and patterns of their stereotyped behaviors during the introduction of the adults showed prominent differences from those before the introduction of the adults. In test 2, similar tendencies were seen to those in test 1. The feral-reared subjects showed only pacing during the introduction, while the mother-reared ones showed greater variabilities of the stereotyped behaviors by the introduction of the adults (Table 4).

Discussion

The results of the experiments indicate that most behaviors of the mother-reared subjects contrast markedly with those of the feral-reared ones. In the group formation, the mother-reared subjects showed less frequent interactions with each other, and stable dominance relations were not established. During the introduction of the adults, they recklessly approached the adults and received aggressive behaviors mainly because they reacted in inappropriate manners to the adults. The mother-reared subjects showed less adequate social behaviors, more frequent and more various patterns of the stereotyped behaviors, and probably more emotional disturbances by social encounters than did the feral-reared subjects. On the other hand, the feral-reared subjects established the dominance relations in the early stage of the group formation and showed play behaviors frequently during the group formation. They showed lip-smacks to the adults and warded off the adults aggressive behaviors.

The rearing with mother is certainly one of the requisites for proper development of infants' social behaviors (Mason 1960, Minami 1974), but it would not be sufficient. Peer interactions as well as maternal interactions are important for proper social development of infants. Suomi and Harlow (1975) described that reinforcement from peer interactions refine and perfect the appropriate social behaviors. In a free-ranging group, group members of both sexes of varying ages contribute to social development of infants and to facilitation of "normal" maternal behaviors of mothers. Effects of these group members on social development of infants should be examined to investigate determinants of infant development.

References

Itoigawa N (1967) A review on behavioral studies of development in nonhuman primates (in Japanese). Machikaneyama Ronso, vol I. The Literary Society, Osaka Univ, pp 15–35

Mason WA (1960) The effects of social restriction on the behavior of rhesus monkeys. I. Free social behavior. J Comp Physiol Psychol 53:582–589

Minami T (1974) Early mother-infant relations in Japanese monkeys. Contemp Primatol 5th Int Congr Primatol Nagoya, pp 334–340

Suomi SJ, Harlow HF (1975) The role and reason of peer relationships in rhesus monkeys. In: Lewes M, Rosenblum LA (eds) The origins of behaviors. ETS Symposium on friendship and peer relations. Wiley, New York, pp 153–183

Yamaguchi K (1977) Effects of group formation on the stereotyped behaviors in separate reared Japanese monkeys *(Macaca fuscata fuscata)* (in Japanese). Annu Anim Psychol 39:33–41

Effects of Prior Experience with Infants on Behavior Shown to Unfamiliar Infants by Nulliparous Rhesus Monkeys

S.D. Holman and R.W. Goy[1]

Group-living nulliparous primates are strongly attracted to, and, when opportunities arise, will touch, groom, hold, cradle, and carry neonates in their group (rhesus monkeys – Hinde et al. 1964; langurs – Jay 1962). Whether these interactions provide practice with infants for young females so that eventually they will display adequate care to their own babies is conjectural. In the present study we have attempted to evaluate the influence of prior experience with neonates and infants by comparing the behavioral responses displayed by two groups of differently socially-reared nulliparous rhesus monkeys *(Macaca mulatta)* to young infants.

The two groups were composed of 20 singly housed, young nulliparous females. Eleven animals (median age, 4.5 years) had been reared in the laboratory (LR) with mothers and/or age-mates only, and nine animals (median age, 3.7 years) had been reared in two large, breeding troops (TR) and therefore had lived with all the various age classes including infants for approximately 3 years prior to their permanent removal. For six females from one troop, interactions with newly born infants during the previous birth season had been observed and recorded.

The experimental procedure (Series I) consisted in five daily half-hour exposures to a 1–12-day old unfamiliar rhesus infant in a large (0.75 X 3.2 X 0.75 m high) cage. Approximately 6 months subsequent to the last test for each female, the whole series of testing (Series II) was repeated for all females in the TR group and seven animals of the LR group. Behavior of the female and infant was recorded on a check sheet list divided into 15 sec intervals. Occurrence of a behavior was recorded only once during each interval in which it was observed. The total sum of 15 sec intervals over the five tests was then analyzed.

Under similar experimental procedures we have found that 90% of multiparous females, which have not lived with infants for over 1 year, will immediately pick up, hold the neonates ventro-ventrally, and show strong attachment to them (Holman and Goy 1979). In the present study of nulliparous females ventro-ventral carrying was seen only in one (11%) of the TR and two (18%) of the LR females in Series I. In Series II, a statistically significant increase was seen in the TR group (67%), but not in the LR group (17%). Although the number of 15 sec intervals of testing during which the infant was held or carried ventro-ventrally was still small for TR females (median, 2.0), it was statistically significantly greater than the same measure for LR females (Table 1).

1 Wisconsin Regional Primate Research Center, University of Wisconsin, 1223 Capitol Court, Madison, WI 53706, USA

Table 1. Behavior displayed by troop (TR) or laboratory reared (LR) nulliparous females during two series of five 30 min tests with 1–12-day old unfamiliar infants

Behavior [a]	TR		LR	
	Series I	Series II	Series I	Series II
Ventro-ventral	0	2 [c]	0	0
Cuddling	0	11 [c]	0	1
Approaching	100	123 [c]	57	38
Prox-within 60 cm	270 [b]	212 [c]	174	91
Touch	30 [b]	50 [c]	4	1
Insp. infant's genitals	3	2 [c]	0	0
Groom	25 [b]	15	1	0
Lipsmack	15 [b]	6 [c]	31	17
Present	0 [b]	1	3	4
Threaten/mouth	1 [b]	0.5	0	0

a   Median frequency of the total sum of 15 s intervals for each individual
b,c Significantly different from LR Series 1 (b) or LR Series II (c). (All Mann-Whitney U tests, p ⩽ 0.05)

Unlike multiparous females (Holman and Goy 1979), in nulliparous females the duration of ventro-ventral holding was for short periods only, and the nulliparous females did not often initiate this interaction. Rather it was usually the infant that oriented itself toward the female and maintained ventro-ventral holding through its grip. At the end of these short episodes, the female always broke the infant's tenacious grip and usually leapt out of the infant's grasp and away from close proximity. Similarly, a greater number of the TR females were seen cuddling (non ventro-ventral holding) infants, but a significant difference between these groups was not observed until Series II ($\chi^2_1 \equiv G = 7.7, p < 0.02$).

Comparisons of touching and grooming during Series I and II, and approaching and inspection of the infant's genital area in Series II, revealed that medians of the number of 15 sec intervals during which these responses were displayed by the TR females were consistently greater than those of the LR females (Mann-Whitney $U \geqslant 77, p < 0.05$, Series I; $U \geqslant 51, p < 0.05$ Series II, Table 1). Generally, the LR females seemed indifferent to or apprehensive of the infants, in that in both series they spent significantly more time at a greater distance from the infant, showed a greater frequency of 15 sec intervals of purse-lipped lipsmacking to it, and, in Series II, displayed a greater frequency of presenting to the infant than did the TR females (Table 1). These last two behavior patterns are often displayed in some social contexts by anxious and subordinate animals. Conversely, the TR females occasionally threatened or punished a too clinging infant by gently mouthing it. The number of 15 sec intervals in which threatening or mouthing was seen while never high, was significantly greater for the TR females than for the LR females ($U = 76, p = 0.05$, Series I only).

Although the TR females had been housed singly for approximately 10 weeks before behavioral testing commenced, it is thought that the stress experienced on removal from their troop depressed their behavior in the Series I tests to some extent.

As the TR females became habituated to laboratory housing, behavioral activity in the Series II tests improved. No significant change in behavior was seen in the LR females between Series I and II.

The longest and what appeared to be the most intense interaction recorded during observations made of TR females while living in their troop was "holding". TR females often held infants ventro-ventrally and frequently carried an infant from place to place. For each of six nulliparous females of the TR group we calculated their rates of holding infants (number of holds per 1000 min of observation) while they were still living with their natal troop. The rate of holding was significantly positively correlated (Spearman's coefficient $\geqslant 0.89$, $p < 0.05$) with touching and proximity to the infants in both series of tests given to them after they were separated from their troop and individually housed (Table 2). There was an association, but, because of small numbers ($N = 6$), no significant correlation between holding and cuddling, inspection of the infant's genital area or grooming.

Table 2. Relationships between prior holding and/or carrying of familiar infants and responses shown toward unfamiliar infants

An identification in troop	Median holds/ 1000 min	Behavior during test			
		Series I		Series II	
		Touch	Prox. within 60 cm	Touch	Prox. within 60 cm
78039	7.92	82	349	78	283
AE25	5.75	68	364	56	273
Z48	4.17	30	270	32	196
Z35	2.92	30	251	50	212
78047	1.25	22	185	28	103
AA85	0.58	20	101	16	122

We conclude that the type of prior rearing can affect later interactions with infants. Furthermore, it does seem that prior experience with familiar infants influences later responses to unfamiliar infants. The nature of this influence is such that responses associated with timidity or fearfulness of the strange infant are less likely to be displayed, and responses indicative of tolerance of the strange infant are more likely to occur. In no way, however, did prior experience with familiar infants, even when that experience indicated strong affiliation, increase the tendency of nulliparous females to display behaviors characteristic of adopting females or normal mothers (Holman and Goy 1979).

Acknowledgments. Supported by NIH grant RR 00167 to WRPRC and NIMH grant MH 21312. Publication no. 21-009 of the Wisconsin Regional Primate Research Center.

References

Hinde RA, Rowell TE, Spencer-Booth Y (1964) Anim Behav 12:219–220
Holman SD, Goy RW (1979) Abstr. Eastern Conf Reprod Behav, New Orleans
Jay P (1962) Ann NY Acad Sci 102:468–476

Studying Effects of Maternal Care in Rhesus Monkeys at Different Levels of Resolution

H. Dienske, E.-A. van Luxemburg, G. de Jonge, J.A.J. Metz, and L.G. Ribbens [1]

The ultimate aim of our study in rhesus monkeys is to detect possible effects of the type of mother-infant relationship on the developing infant. We chose to study play with peers as the most important characteristic to be influenced, as play is the most common interaction with group members in early life, and because play is probably an exercise for the development of social skills.

This paper discusses our choice of experimental methods and the results of an attempt to find "natural" parameters for the quantification of mother-infant interactions in rhesus monkeys. Moreover, a few results are described.

Methods

Various difficulties are inherent in studies on the effect of the style of maternal care on the developing infant.

1. The degree of genetic relationship between a mother and her infant is so great that any correspondence between mothering style and the infant's characteristics may be ascribed in part to inheritance. To eliminate this systematic effect, we exchanged infants during the infants' first week of life.

2. Many individuals exert influences on the mother-infant diad in a monkey group. Social play is influenced by the mother's place in the dominance hierarchy (Tartabini and Dienske 1979). As our study is basically analytical, we lessened social complexity by placing only two mother-infant pairs together. Signs of dominance appeared to be exceptional.

3. Even singly caged pairs are quite diverse in their types of relationships. This is a disadvantage if one compares different classes of mothers living under different experimental situations, as large samples are required. We exploited interindividual differences by sampling mothers in such a way that a rather continuous range from overprotective to quite rejective mothering could be expected.

To avoid sampling biases, each diad was its own control in experiments. Three experimental situations were provided each week. (1) Pairs were singly caged during 3 days. (2) On 2 days, two pairs remained together; these tetrads consisted of the

1 Primate Center TNO, 151 Lange Kleiweg, 2288 GJ, Rijwijk, The Netherlands

same monkeys each week. (3) To study the "boldness" of infants, during the remaining 2 days of each week we offered a situation in which at least one infant had to leave its mother in order to play with its peer (see de Jonge et al. 1981). In each of these three situations, the behavior of all four individuals of a tetrad was recorded in order to determine the influence of each individual on the infants' development.

4. In a pilot study (Dienske and Metz 1977), it was found that the alternations of on- and off-mother were inhomogeneously spread over the observation time. During the day, sleeping and waking were alternated with a cycle duration of about one hour. To study nonstationarity, we chose long, continuous observation periods (viz., 10,000 s; i.e., 2 h 47 min).

5. Most studies on mother-infant interactions in monkeys have used a one-zero sampling on check sheets with a time base of 15 or 30 s (see, e.g., Simpson and Simpson 1977). When using a computer-connected event recorder in our pilot study, we found that many body contact bouts were of even shorter duration than a few seconds. For an accurate account of the contributions of mother and infant to body contact, it was necessary to measure bout lengths accurately (Dienske and Metz 1977). Difficulties may arise if the time unit is long in comparison to the mean bout length (see Goosen and Metz 1980). We used a time unit of 0.1 s.

6. The main behavioral changes are known to take place during the first 2 months of life; thereafter such changes are slow. Therefore, we made observations more frequently at ages of less than 2 months.

Results

Levels of Resolution

In the literature, rhesus mother-infant interactions have been described at a variety of arbitrarily chosen levels of analysis. We felt that the degree of arbitrariness could be reduced. During a formal analysis of the alternations between on- and off-mother in rhesus monkeys, we found a few levels of resolution that emerged in a natural way from an unprejudiced analysis of the data. Units of a higher level of resolution exerted strong constraints on those of the next, lower level. In other words, if one neglects divisions at a higher level, the results of any analysis at a lower level become unnecessarily complicated.

The Nap-Wake Cycle. During the light period of the day, mother-infant interactions appear to be dominated by alternations between napping of the infant and its being awake. The uninterrupted body contact bouts during napping lasted about 100 times longer than those during waking, which has a tremendous influence on data representations of body contact (see Dienske and Metz 1977). This seems obvious, but it was usually neglected (see Simpson 1979).

Markovian States in the Alternations Between On- and Off-Mother. Analysis of the bout lengths of body contact and off-mother revealed that the alternations between these two acts could be appropriately described as a continuous time Markov chain with three behavioral states: on, nipple, and off (Dienske et al. 1980). In a continuous time Markov chain, the transitions between its states do not depend on previous history. If less than these three states were distinguished or if no distinction at the higher level of resolution (the nap-wake cycle) was made, the simple Markovity was replaced by an inconveniently complicated situation (Dienske and Metz 1977, Dienske et al. 1980). This demonstrates how a parsimonious approach may reduce arbitrariness in the choice of behavior categories.

During a number of awake phases (mostly near the end), the infant became less active and more contact prone ("drowsy") or sometimes showed temper tantrums if its mother refused contact. When tests for Markovian properties (see Dienske et al. 1980) were applied to such inhomogeneous awake phases, significant deviations were common. Splitting these awake phases into fully awake and drowsy subphases often resulted in clear improvements.

Markovian Microstates. When the infant is on- or off-mother, it is able to perform a variety of acts. It appeared that the transitions between these acts could also be described as a continuous time Markov chain. In Fig. 1 transition rates are represented for the brief acts within off-mother (microstates) as if one were examining the off-state through a quadrangular magnifying glass. These transition rates are usually at least one order of magnitude greater than those among the macrostates (i.e., on, nipple, and off). The transitions within the on and the nipple states are also Markovian, but have quite different rates; Markovity at the level of the microstates would be lost if one did not make distinctions at the level of the macrostates.

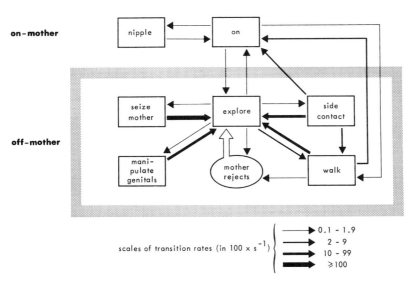

Fig. 1. Example of transition rates among behavioral microstates that occur during off-mother. Transitions among the macrostates nipple, on, and off are also given

"Point" Events. Terminations of Markovian states have no durations. In reality, terminations proceed very rapidly. Therefore, they are regarded to be "point" events of
which the durations are neglected. In spite of their brief durations, state terminations
may be short chains of acts, such as mother breaks on-nipple → infant vocalizes. The
type of point event is used to account for the separate contributions of mothers and
infants to the duration of body contact (see Dienske et al. 1980).

Summary. The results of our analysis are summarized in Fig. 2. It illustrates how each
lower level is embedded in the next higher one.

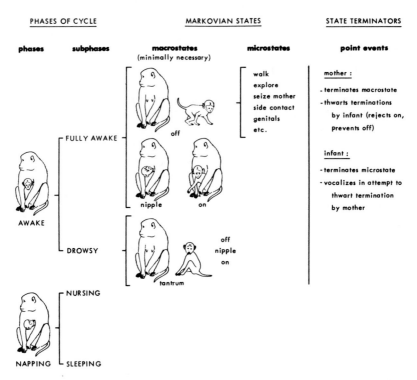

Fig. 2. Summary of the various levels of resolution that resulted from our analysis of mother-
infant interactions in rhesus monkeys

Effects of the Experimental Situations

Effects on the Nap-Wake Cycle. The durations of the nap-wake cycle and its phases or
subphases are not as a rule influenced by the three experimental situations described
earlier, viz., single pairs, tetrads, and leaving maternal protection for play (van Luxemburg et al., in prep.). However, when pairs were not separated from each other, the
two infants synchronized their awake phases. Activity synchronization increased the
time available for playing with each other (de Jonge et al. 1981).

Effects on the Body Contact States. From a number of tests it followed that Markovity applied to body contact in each of the three experimental situations. In the situations that permitted social play, the infants spent more time off-mother, which increased play opportunity, as most play occurs when one or both infants are off their mothers (de Jonge et al. 1981).

Effects on the Microstates. The most important effect on the microstates is the emergence of social play. How far a Markovian approach applies to play remains to be studied.

Effects of Different Styles of Maternal Care on Infant Behavior

Diversity in relationships most clearly follows from making or breaking of body contact by one pair member and the partner's reaction. Only a few mothers prevented or terminated off-mother after ages above 1 month. Maternal prevention or breaking of body contact is the greatest source of individual variation.

On the level of the nap-wake cycle, maternal refusal of napping (which always takes place in body contact) often leads to long bouts of vocalizations (napping conflicts). Results obtained by van Luxemburg et al. (in prep.) demonstrate that these napping conflicts do not reduce the portion of time spent in napping, but conflicts speed up the nap-wake cycle (i.e., shorter phase durations). De Jonge et al. (1981) found that napping conflicts reduced the time available for social play.

During fully awake, however, vocal protests against breaking or prevention of body contact are scarce and rarely persistent; vocalizations did not affect the durations of the macrostates within subphases. Connections between discord over contact and social play remain to be studied.

Conclusions

The hierarchial organization that resulted from our analysis accounts for time scales in behavior. The levels of resolution we found are based on the principle that distinctions at one level must be made if this leads to increased simplicity at a lower level. Simplicity was searched for by testing whether bout length distributions were of a simple kind, such as exponential or normal distributions. As test results demonstrated a reasonable fit, the given levels of resolution are not arbitrarily chosen, but follow from the time structure in the behavior shown by our mother-infant pairs. This approach also proved to be useful in other contexts of behavior (Metz 1974, Goosen and Metz 1980, de Jonge and Ketel, in press).

Most of our "simple", directly measured parameters correspond to those of Hinde and White (1974), and Simpson and Howe (1980). However, most of our "derived" parameters (i.e., calculated from simple; see Hinde and Herrmann 1977) are different. They directly followed from the mathematical properties of continuous time Markov chains, which established and limited the number of "derived" parameters (Dienske and Metz 1977, Dienske et al. 1980).

Our parameters are purposely designed for a separate characterization of mothers and infants with respect to the time they allot to mutual interactions. Educational effects are being studied in our experiments at all of the levels of resolution described in this paper.

Acknowledgments. This project was supported in part by the Foundation for Fundamental Biological Research (BION), which is subsidized by the Netherlands Organization for the Advancement of Pure Research (ZWO).

References

Dienske H, Metz JAJ (1977) Mother-infant body contact in macaques: a time interval analysis. Biol Behav 2:3−37

Dienske H, Metz JAJ, Luxemburg E van, Jonge G de (1980) Mother-infant body contact in macaques. II. Further steps towards a representation as a continuous time Markov chain. Biol Behav 5:61−94

Goosen C, Metz JAJ (1980) Dissecting behaviour: relations between autoaggression, grooming and walking in a macaque. Behaviour 75:97−132

Hinde RA, Herrmann J (1977) Frequencies, durations, derived measures and their correlations in studying diadic and triadic relationships. In: Schaffer HR (ed) Studies in mother-infant interactions. Academic Press, London New York

Hinde RA, White LA (1974) Dynamics of a relationship: rhesus mother-infant ventro-ventral contact. J Comp Physiol Psychol 86:8−23

Jonge G de, Ketel NAJ (1981) An analysis of copulation behaviour of *Microtus agrestis* and *M. arvalis* with regard to reproductive isolation. Behaviour, in press

Jonge G de, Dienske H, Luxemburg E van, Ribbens L (1981) How rhesus monkey infants budget their time between mothers and peers. Anim Behav 29:598−609

Metz JAJ (1974) Stochastic models for the temporal fine structure of behaviour sequences. In: McFarland DJ (ed) Motivational control systems analysis. Academic Press, London New York

Simpson MJA (1979) Daytime rest and activity in socially living rhesus monkeys. Anim Behav 27:602−612

Simpson MJA, Howe S (1980) The interpretation of individual differences in rhesus monkey infants. Behaviour 72:127−155

Simpson MJA, Simpson AE (1977) One-zero and scan methods for sampling behaviour. Anim Behav 25:726−731

Tartabini A, Dienske H (1979) Social play and rank order in rhesus monkeys *(Macaca mulatta).* Behav Process 4:375−383

Genetic, Maternal, and Environmental Influences on Social Development in Rhesus Monkeys

S.J. Suomi[1]

Interest in the development of social behavior by young primates has generated considerable research effort over the past two decades. Social ontogeny has been studied in many primate species, both in the laboratory and in feral settings, and among the different primates perhaps the most thorough ontogenic data base exists for macaques, especially rhesus monkeys *(M. mulatta)*. As a result, we presently know a great deal about how these monkeys develop socially in a variety of different rearing environments.

It is now well established that rhesus monkey infants growing up in feral environments normally spend most of their first month on or in close proximity to their biological mothers. In succeeding weeks and months these infants leave their mothers with increasing frequency in order to interact with others in their troop, especially peers. By the end of their first year most infants have established complex social relationships with their peers and with older siblings, while interactions with their mothers have declined substantially from previous levels. Over the next 3 years of life such developmental trends largely continue, although they differ somewhat for male and female subjects. Virtually the same general pattern of social ontogeny has also been reported for laboratory-born rhesus monkeys reared in assembled social groups containing (at least) mothers and peers.

Despite the overall consistency of this basic ontogenic sequence, there are substantial *individual differences* in how rapidly and thoroughly these infants expand their behavioral repertoires and develop social relationships with others as they grow up. Such individual differences in social ontogeny are potentially of considerable interest from *ethological* and *sociobiological* perspectives, to the extent that they predict and/or underlie differential reproductive success when the infants grow to sexual maturity. Such individual differences are also of great potential interest from a *psychological* perspective, to the extent that they parallel and/or influence differences in "personality" traits or characteristics of the subjects. Finally, such individual differences are potentially important from a *clinical* perspective, to the extent that they permit identification of individuals at high risk for subsequent display of psychopathology.

1 Department of Psychology and Primate Laboratory, University of Wisconsin, Madison, Wisconsin, 53706, USA

Given these considerations, it is not surprising that recent research on macaque social ontogeny has focused on identification of factors contributing to such individual differences. Among the most thoroughly investigated of these factors have been those involving the maternal care an infant receives and the nature of the relationship it develops with its mother. Several studies have revealed that infants who develop "insecure" or "anxious" attachments with their mothers, in the terms of Bowlby (1969), are less likely to leave their mother's immediate presence and to interact with others in their social unit throughout at least the first 2 years of life than are infants whose relationships with their mothers are more "secure" or better "meshed" (Hinde and Simpson 1975). Other studies have shown that mothers who display unusually high levels of rejecting behavior toward their offspring tend to rear infants who maintain higher-than-normal levels of mother-directed activity and correspondingly display lower-than-normal levels of exploration and peer interaction throughout early development. Additional social deficits (hyperaggression and excessive disturbance behavior) often emerge in these infants later in life (cf. Suomi 1979a). Thus, differences in maternal treatment can clearly influence the nature and magnitude of differences between individuals in their social development.

Another obvious source of intersubject variability in macaque social ontogeny involves the nature of the infant's social rearing environment beyond its biological mother. Several authors have reported that the number and/or sex of available peers during ontogeny can influence the schedule and manner in which the infant disengages itself from its mother (White and Hinde 1975, Suomi 1976, Goldfoot 1978). Other studies have shown that the number, age, and sex of available siblings can also significantly affect an infant's social development (e.g., Suomi 1977a; Berman 1978), as can the presence or absence of adult males (e.g., Suomi 1977b). Thus, the nature of an infant monkey's entire social network helps determine the pace and direction of its social development in addition to and/or in interaction with any maternal influences (cf. Suomi 1979b).

A third potentially important factor contributing to intersubject ontogenic variability derives from possible constitutionally based *temperament* differences between infants, especially with respect to intrinsic *fearfulness* or *anxiety* (cf. Thomas et al. 1968). A frightened or anxious infant is less likely to leave its mother and interact with others in its social network than is an infant who, in Bowlby's (1969) terms, is "secure". Thus, a frequently fearful or chronically anxious infant may actually experience functional social deprivation even if it is reared in a "normal" social environment. Of course, if it also has a punitive mother and/or is reared in a highly stressful social setting, its functional deprivation should be even greater, and its social development should suffer accordingly.

For these reasons, recent research at Wisconsin has focused on assessing individual differences in fearfulness or anxiety in rhesus monkey infants. In addition to behavioral measures of fearfulness we have sought to obtain indices of autonomic reactivity in these subjects. Our rationale for examining autonomic variables has been based on the long-standing belief that fearfulness and/or anxiety has autonomic components (cf. James 1890, Spence 1964). Thus, in an initial study by Baysinger et al. (1978), measures of heart-rate change in an aversive conditioning paradigm were obtained from rhesus monkey infants and then correlated with behavioral measures for fearfulness/anxiety displayed by the infants as they grew up.

In this first study, ten infants were separated from their mothers at birth and reared, with inanimate surrogates, in the laboratory nursery. Beginning at 28 days of age, each infant was exposed to eight conditioning trials on each of 10 days, for a total of 80 trials. On each trial a 70 db 1 kHz pure tone served as a CS for a 105 db white noise US occurring 10 s after the CS onset. The subject's mean heart-rate change (in beats per minute) during that 10-s period was calculated for each trial. After the last day of conditioning each subject was moved out of the nursery and placed, with its surrogate, in a single cage in a colony housing room. Subjects remained in their cages throughout the rest of their first year of life. During this time their home-cage behaviors were scored for 5-min periods four times each week by trained observers watching over closed-circuit television. In each observational period the durations of behaviors encompassed by each of ten predefined categories were recorded.

Measures of heart-rate change and subsequent behaviors were compared in the following manner. First, each subject's heart-rate change scores were averaged over all 80 trials, yielding a single *mean heart-rate change* score for each infant. These scores ranged from -13.2 bpm to $+2.24$ bpm; with eight of the ten subjects displaying mean heart-rate *deceleration* during conditioning trials, consistent with findings from the human literature (cf. Graham 1980). Second, behavioral category scores for each subject were averaged over four time periods: 1–3 months, 4–6 months, 7–9 months, and 10–12 months of age. Four of the ten categories *(self-directed, surrogate contact, passive,* and *locomotion)* accounted for over 90% of the subjects' behaviors during these periods. Finally, each subject's mean heart-rate change score was successively paired with its mean duration score for each category in each of the above four time periods, and Pearson correlations were then calculated for the ten subjects. These correlations are presented in Table 1.

As indicated in the Table, infant heart-rate change scores obtained at 1 month of age were highly predictive of differences between subjects in *self-directed* behavior throughout their first year of life. Indeed, the heart-rate change scores accounted for

Table 1. Correlations between mean heart-rate change scores and 3-month mean levels for four behaviors

Behavior categories	Months of age				
	1–3	4–6	7–9	10–12	Overall
Self-directed	0.82 [b]	0.92 [c]	0.88 [b]	0.90 [b]	0.93 [b]
Surrogate	0.94 [b]	0.60	0.48	0.50	0.73 [a]
Passive	0.05	0.14	0.08	0.65 [a]	0.12
Locomotion	-0.38	-0.39	-0.50	-0.30	-0.63

a $p < 0.05$, b $p < 0.01$, c $p < 0.001$

Operational definitions of behavioral categories:
Self-directed: grasping any part of the body with the hands or feet and/or huddled posture with head below the shoulders in fetal-like position and/or repetitive rocking while sitting or huddled;
Surrogate contact: any contact of the infant with the surrogate's terrycloth cover;
Locomotion: movement in any direction of at least one body length;
Passive: absence of locomotion and failure to change body orientation or posture for at least 15 s after which scoring begins

a remarkable 86% of the total intersubject variance for that category over the whole year. Correlations between 1-month heart-rate change and levels of other behaviors during each 3-month period were considerably more modest, except for *surrogate contact* during months 1–3. This pattern of predictiveness for the heart-rate change scores is significant, in that during the first 3 months of life surrogate-reared infants display fear and anxiety by increasing their levels of surrogate contact and self-directed behavior (cf. Harlow and Zimmermann 1959, Suomi and Harlow 1976). In succeeding months surrogate contact drops and self-directed responses become more prominent in displays of anxiety (cf. Harlow and Harlow 1969). Thus, in the present study those behaviors most characteristic of fearfulness/anxiety in each time period had the highest correlations with the 1-month heart-rate change scores. Behaviors *not* characteristic of fearfulness/anxiety failed to correlate significantly with heart-rate change scores during any time period (except for *passive* during months 10–12). These findings suggest a strong continuity between early autonomic responsivity (as indexed by heart-rate change) and expressions of anxiety by monkey infants reared with surrogates but otherwise isolated socially.

The relationship between early heart-rate change and expressions of fearfulness/anxiety later in life was further explored in a second study. Here, as before, rhesus monkey infants were each run through a total of 80 conditioning trials during their first month of life and their heart-rate during these trials monitored. Of the 12 subjects 11 displayed average heart-rate deceleration during the CS-US intervals, essentially replicating the performance of the previous subjects. Unlike the previous subjects, however, these infants were reared in peer groups after their conditioning trials; thus, they received considerably more social stimulation than had their surrogate-reared counterparts. In addition, the present infants were briefly separated from their peer groups at 41 days of age and were again separated at 91 days of age for a 7-day period, unlike the previous subjects who had remained undisturbed in their home cages during the same chronological period. As before, observational behavioral data were collected on these infants during 5-min sessions several times each week of the study, and category scores obtained during various time periods over the subjects' first 9 months of life were correlated with the earlier heart-rate change data. The obtained values of these Pearson correlations are presented in Table 2.

As indicated in the Table, highly significant positive correlations were found between 1-month heart-rate change scores and levels of *self-directed* behavior during all time periods except the two base-line periods. Additionally, significant negative correlations between heart-rate change and *play* behavior during the time periods immediately following the 7-day separation were disclosed. The only other behavioral category that correlated significantly in any time period with heart-rate change was *passive,* in the final base-line period only. The pattern of significant correlations shown in Table 2 is consistent with the hypothesis that heart-rate change is predictive of behavioral displays of fearfulness/anxiety, in that the highest correlations were obtained for behaviors characteristic of anxiety but only during or shortly after exposure to environmental "stressors" (group formation and social separation). For example, play behavior is usually suppressed when an infant is stressed (cf. Suomi 1979a) – in the present study, play showed a significant negative correlation with heart-rate change only following the 7-day peer separation. The only other significant

Table 2. Correlations between mean heart-rate change scores and behavioral category levels during subjects' first 9 months of life

Behavioral categories	Days of age						
	30–40 (group formation)	41 (brief separation)	60–90 (presepara-tion base-line)	91–98 (7-day separation)	99–106 (7-day reunion)	107–135 (28-day postsepara-tion)	242–270 (final base-line)
Self-directed	0.91 [c]	0.80 [c]	0.40	0.69 [a]	0.71 [b]	0.73 [b]	0.41
Social contact	0.12	–	– 0.27	–	0.18	0.24	– 0.05
Play	0.35	–	– 0.41	–	– 0.58 [a]	– 0.63 [a]	– 0.15
Passive	0.19	– 0.15	0.44	0.34	0.25	0.19	0.81 [b]
Locomotion	0.01	– 0.43	– 0.01	0.20	0.12	0.23	0.09
Exploration	– 0.17	– 0.27	0.31	– 0.53	0.04	0.06	– 0.20

a $p < 0.05$, b $p < 0.01$, c $p < 0.001$

Operational definitions of behavioral categories:
Social contact: tactile and/or oral contact with another monkey;
Play: any type of socially directed play activity (including rough-and-tumble, approach-withdraw, and noncontact type play);
Exploration: tactile and/or oral manipulation of inanimate objects on or in cage;
Self-directed, Passive, and *Locomotion:* same definitions as in Table 1

correlation – *passive* during the final base-line period – followed the pattern shown in the previous study.

The results of these two experiments thus suggest that individual differences in early heart-rate change parallel individual differences in subsequent displays of fearful-ness/anxiety. The facts that infants in the two studies had different rearing histories, were subjected to different stressors at different points in development, and yet still showed the same general pattern of behavioral correlation with early heart-rate change, suggests that this relationship may be quite robust for young rhesus monkeys, at least when all members of a comparison group share the same form of rearing environment.

Now, all subjects in both experiments came from our laboratory breeding colony, and post hoc examination of breeding records revealed that several sets of these sub-jects were half-siblings to one another. More precisely, one pair and two trios of subjects in the first experiment and one pair and one trio of subjects in the second experiment had been sired by the same breeding colony males. Additionally, two breeding colony males each sired one of the subjects in both experiments, while two breeding colony females also had offspring in both studies. Thus, it was possible to compare differences in heart-rate change scores between half-sibs with those between unrelated individuals, both within the subject sample for each experiment and across the two samples. *F* tests of relative variance among scores of half-sibs compared to relative variance among scores of unrelated individuals indicated that for all such comparisons half-sib variance was significantly less than that between unrelated sub-jects (all p's < 0.05).

In view of the facts that all subjects in both experiments were separated from their mothers at birth, were reared in the same nursery according to the same general procedures, and were exposed to the same schedule of conditioning trials, it is difficult to account for the intersubject variability in heart-rate change scores in terms of maternal and/or environmental factors. Instead, genetically based explanations appear more plausible, particularly given the half-sibling comparisons. The present data are insufficient to differentiate between alternative genetic models, but they clearly are highly suggestive that differences between subjects in heart-rate change have some genetic basis. Given the obtained relationship between heart-rate change and subsequent behavioral indices of fearfulness/anxiety, one can additionally infer that temperament differences between subjects with respect to relative anxiety are also likely to reflect genetic factors.

It remains to be demonstrated explicitly in what manner and to what degree such temperament factors actually interact with maternal care and social network variables in influencing the course of social ontogeny in rhesus monkey infants. The findings of the second experiment did reveal that temperament differences could account for behavioral differences between infants but only in relatively stressful environmental settings, thus reflecting one type of temperament-environmental interaction. However, to date none of the subjects assessed for heart-rate change have subsequently been reared by their biological mothers, and so consideration of temperament-maternal care interactions presently represents pure speculation.

Nevertheless. the present two studies do provide a basis for empirical development and testing of ontogenic models which reflect genetic, maternal, and social environmental sources of influence. The ability to assess temperament factors in a context independent of maternal and/or environmental influences and in a manner not exclusively dependent on behavioral indices represents a most useful research tool in this regard. Furthermore, the capability to breed subjects who can be expected to possess high vs low anxious temperaments (we have already identified specific members of our laboratory breeding colony who consistently have produced high vs low anxious progeny, based on a post hoc survey of breeding records) permits the preassignment of such infants to different maternal and/or social environment rearing conditions, thus satisfying a major requirement for direct experimental testing of various ontogenic models. Our laboratory is currently in the process of carrying out such experimentation, and I hope to be able to present the results of these tests at the next Congress of the *International Primatological Society*.

Acknowledgments. Research described in this paper was supported in part by funds from the National Institute of Mental Health (USPHS Grants MH-11894 and MH-28485), from the National Science Foundation (BNS77-06802), and from the University of Wisconsin Graduate School. The contributions of C.M. Baysinger, C. Cronin, R.D. DeLizio, L.E. Ohman, and J.P. Taylor in helping to collect and analyze the data are gratefully acknowledged.

References

Baysinger CM, Suomi SJ, Cronin C, Ohman LE (1978) Infant rhesus monkey heartrate changes predict behavioral levels later in life. Abstr Meet Am Soc Primatol 2:2–3

Berman CM (1978) The analysis of mother-infant interaction in groups: possible influence of yearling siblings. In: Chivers D, Herbert J (eds) Recent advances in primatology, vol I. Behaviour. Academic Press, London New York

Bowlby J (1969) Separation and loss, vol I. Attachment. Basic Books, New York

Goldfoot DA (1978) Development of gender role behaviors in heterosexual and isosexual groups of infant rhesus monkeys. In: Chivers D, Herbert J (eds) Recent advances in primatology, vol I. Behaviour. Academic Press, London New York

Graham FK (1980) Distinguishing among orienting, defense, and startle reflexes. In: Kimmel H, van Olst E, Orlebeke J (eds) The orienting reflex in humans. Erlbaum, Hillsdale, NJ

Harlow HF, Harlow MK (1969) Effect of various mother-infant relationships on rhesus monkey behaviors. In: Foss B (ed) Determinants of infant behaviour, vol IV. Methuen, London

Harlow HF, Zimmermann RR (1959) Affectional responses in the infant monkey. Science 130: 421–432

Hinde RA, Simpson MJA (1975) Qualities of mother-infant relationships in monkeys. In: The parent-infant relationship, Ciba Foundation Symposium 33 (new series). Elsevier, Amsterdam

James W (1890) The principles of psychology, vol II. Holt, New York

Spence KW (1964) Anxiety (drive) level and performance in eyelid conditioning. Psychol Bull 61:129–139

Suomi SJ (1976) Mechanisms underlying social development: A reexamination of mother-infant interactions in monkeys. In: Pick A (ed) Minnesota Symposium on child psychology, vol X. University of Minnesota Press, Minneapolis

Suomi SJ (1977a) Development of attachment and other social behaviors in rhesus monkeys. In: Alloway T, Pliner P, Krames L (eds) Attachment behavior. Plenum Press, New York

Suomi SJ (1977b) Adult male-infant interactions among monkeys living in nuclear families. Child Dev 48:1255–1270

Suomi SJ (1979a) Peers, play, and primary prevention in primates. In: Kent M, Rolf J (eds) Primary prevention of psychopathology, vol III. Social competence in children. University Press of New England, Hanover New Hampshire

Suomi SJ (1979b) Differential development of various social relationships by rhesus monkey infants. In: Lewis M, Rosenblum L (eds) The child and its family. Plenum Press, New York

Suomi SJ, Harlow HF (1976) The facts and functions of fear. In: Zuckerman M, Spielberger C (eds) Emotion and anxiety. Erlbaum, Hillsdale, NJ

Thomas A, Chess S, Birch H (1968) Temperament and behavior disorders in children. Univ Press, New York

White LE, Hinde RA (1975) Some factors affecting mother-infant relations in rhesus monkeys. Anim Behav 23:527–542

Personality and Dominance Behaviour in Stumptailed Macaques

V.J. Nash and A.S. Chamove [1]

Primatologists working in both laboratory and field settings have acknowledged the role of dominance and its influence on primate social behaviour. They have however largely ignored the role of personality in an individual's behaviour. This paper presents briefly some findings from experimental research which attempts to do both, to determine the effect of being in a particular dominance position on behaviour and to discover if there are patterns of behaviour characteristic of individual monkeys regardless of dominance position.

Initially we performed a factor analysis on the behaviour of a group of 13 laboratory-born stump tailed macaques over a variety of situations, which yielded a strong first factor of "dominance", emphasising the pervasiveness of this phenomenon. In brief, dominant animals (as determined by standard measures such as priority of access to preferred items, etc.) exhibited the following characteristics: Dominants (1) showed more positive social behaviour, (2) did less visual monitoring, (3) were more disturbed when removed from the rest of the group, and (4) exhibited more self-aggressive behaviour. The question arose as to whether these characteristics were a function of their dominance position or their personality.

The early work on personality in animals in the 1930s involved selective breeding which resulted in the identification of strains of rats which were characteristically different: Hall's "hi/lo" emotional rats (Hall 1934), Tryon's "maze-bright/maze-dull" rats (Tryon 1930), and Hall and Klein's "aggressive/non-aggressive" rats (Hall and Klein 1942). More recent studies on primates have used factor analyses of social behaviour in an attempt to parallel the work on human personality. Van Hooff's (1970) component factor analysis on the behaviour of a semi-captive group of chimpanzees yielded four factors: (1) a "socially positive" factor, (2) a "play" factor, (3) an "aggression" factor, and (4) a "submission" factor. Similarly, Chamove et al. (1972) in their factor analysis on laboratory-born rhesus social behaviour identified (1) a "sociable" factor, (2) a "hostile" factor, and (3) a "fear" factor, which they state "are not dissimilar to those which gave rise to the three major factors in research on human personality — extraversion/introversion, psychoticism and neuroticism" (p. 502). A principle components analysis on ratings of laboratory rhesus monkeys by Stevenson-Hinde and Zunz (1978) produced three main components: (1) Confident — Fearful, (2) Active — Slow, (3) Sociable — Solitary. In summary, all of these

---

1   Department of Psychology, University of Stirling, Stirling, FK9 4 LA Scotland

investigations identify a sociable dimension in primate personality, a fearful dimension, and two report finding an aggression dimension.

Richards (1974) notes that animals react differently to isolation according to dominance position and suggests that dominance is related to a basic property of the complete personality of the individual, rather than being a social property manifested only when several individuals are together. Using their Emotions Profile Index, Buirski, Plutchik, and Kellerman (1978) obtained ratings on wild chimpanzees, characterising dominant animals as aggressive and distrustful, subordinates as timid, trustful, and impulsive. Since dominance is such an important phenomenon and has such a pervasive and restrictive influence on behaviour, it is only through experimental or statistical control that one can separate dominance from personality. This study uses experimental manipulation. It attempts to sort out which characteristics of a given animal are due to its dominance position and which to personality.

Table 1. Dominance positions in regroups

Animal number	15	17	5	11	10	8	13	2	4	3	25	27	6
Dominance in group of 13	1	2	3	4	5	6	7	8	9	10	11	12	13
Regroup number 1	1	2	3	4	5								
2		1	2	3	4	5							
3			1	2	3	4	5						
4				1	2	3	4	5					
5					1	2	3	4	5				
6						1	2	3	4	5			
7							1	2	3	4	5		
8								1	2	3	4	5	
9									1	2	3	4	5

The current study, almost completed, involves a manipulation of the same group of 13 animals, testing subgroups of 5 animals for 4-week periods to assess the effects of changes in dominance on behaviour. The format of regroups is shown in Table 1 and consists of nine regroups of 5 animals adjacent in dominance position in the group of 13.

Figure 1 shows percentage positive social behaviour for four animals (numbers 11, 10, 13 and 2) over differing dominance positions, and can be said to be only indirectly related to dominance. The apparent inverted U-shape curve can be explained by the nature of the regroups. As Boelkins (1967) reports, animals interact mostly with those animals occupying adjacent dominance positions. In the case of the dominant (position 1) animals of the subgroups, the animal or friend usually above them is absent and that is likely to affect their level of social behaviour. Similarly, when subordinate (position 5), the animal usually below them is absent. However, when in intermediate positions (2, 3, and 4), they have both adjacent friends with which to interact.

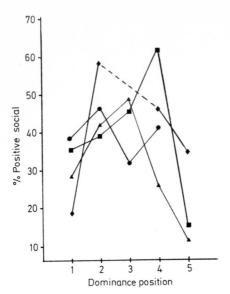

Fig. 1. Percentage positive social behaviour for four animals over differing dominance positions

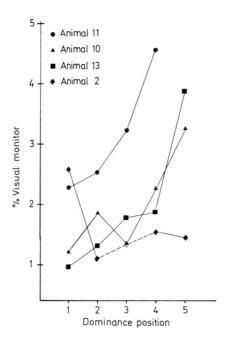

Fig. 2. Percentage visual monitoring for four animals over differing dominance positions

The data for visual monitoring (Fig. 2) over differing dominance positions are more directly linked to dominance and support our previous finding and that of Chance (1976) that subordinate animals do more. The individual patterns in the data may reflect an individual adaptation to the differing dominance positions — how relaxed an animal is. Animal number 2, when dominant, seemed ill at ease for much of the time.

The data for self-aggression shown in Fig. 3 again show individual patterns and contrary to initial findings do not appear to be a purely dominance linked characteristic. They may reflect how disturbed an animal is in a particular dominance position. Certainly, animals exhibit more self-aggressive behaviour when subjected to frustration or stress (Nash 1980), and here it may be linked to how well an animal adapts to a position of dominance or subordinance.

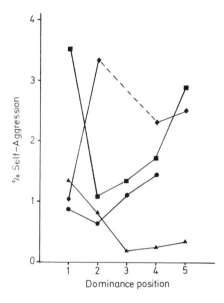

Fig. 3. Percentage self-aggression for four animals over differing dominance positions

It is clear from the results that some of the behaviours which initially seemed to be correlated with dominance are a function of the personality of the individual in that dominance position and not of dominance per se. If this were the case, the one would ideally expect a linear relationship between dominance position and behaviour. This is not the case; there are apparent individual reactions to changes in dominance. The problem remains of how to separate adequately dominance effects from personality effects. Manipulating dominance may give us some ideas as to the characteristics associated with it, but one is also changing the environment in which an animal can display his personality (e.g., by manipulating the number of friends with which he is used to interacting). There is also an element of interaction between dominance and personality, with some animals adapting better than others to positions of dominance/ subordinance. While dominance position is an important influence on an individual's behaviour there are other factors involved, although the study of social behaviour without dominance may be a difficult task.

Acknowledgments. This research was undertaken whilst the first author was in receipt of a post-graduate studentship from the Science Research Council. Thanks to R.N. Campbell for advice and support.

References

Boelkins RC (1967) Determination of dominance hierarchies in monkeys. Psychonom Sci 7: 317–318

Buirski P, Plutchik R, Kellerman H (1978) Sex differences, dominance and personality in the chimpanzee. Anim Behav 26:123–129

Chamove AS, Eysenck HJ, Harlow HF (1972) Personality in monkeys: factor analyses of rhesus social behaviour. QJ Exp Psychol 24:496–504

Chance MRA (ed) (1976) The social structure of attention. Wiley, London

Hall CS (1934) Emotional behaviour in the rat. 1. Defecation and urination as measures of individual differences in emotionality. J Comp Psychol 18:385–403

Hall CS, Klein SJ (1942) Individual differences in aggressiveness in rats. J Comp Physiol Psychol 33:371–383

Hooff JARAM van (1970) A component analysis of the structure of the social behaviour of a semi-captive chimpanzee group. Experientia 26:549–550

Nash VJ (1980) Personality and dominance behaviour. Ph D Dissertation, in preparation

Richards SM (1974) The concept of dominance and methods of assessment. Anim Behav 22: 914–930

Stevenson-Hinde J, Zunz M (1978) Subjective assessment of individual rhesus monkeys. Primates 19:473–482

Tryon RC (1930) Studies in individual differences in maze ability. J Comp Psychol 11:145–170

Natural and Dependent Rank of Female Crab-Eating Monkeys (Macaca fascicularis) in Captivity

C. Welker [1]

When establishing our breeding group of *Macaca fascicularis* in 1975 by successive introduction of females into a group of one male and two females, we observed some strategies of females to get a higher social position (Welker et al. 1980). We got the impression that interactions within the first minutes after the introduction were the most important ones for their later rank. It seemed that there were a priori different types of females, low-ranking and high-ranking ones.

During the following years there occured only few alterations in the hierarchy. The once achieved rank position was generally stable. Infants, born in the group, received the same social position as their mothers in a male and female hierarchy.

Before starting further research about an innate disposition for high ranking or low ranking, we started some experiments to answer the question to what extent the observed ranks were natural or dependent; that is, dependent mainly on special connections to the highest-ranking individuals of the group.

After each experimental step (cf. Fig. 1), which continued usually 12 days, we made a food competition test. Thereby each animal was locked together with each other individual of the group successively and a piece of egg or a nut was placed on the floor of the cage. Since eggs and nuts were a very attractive food for all our animals and the tests were made before feeding, we could be sure that all the animals were interested in the food. Record was kept of which animal took the food and what interactions occurred. The experiment was always made three times in succession. For each food competition test all possible combinations were tested. As a result of the observations we were able to establish various rank orders. Example 1: A and B are sitting on a board. A takes the food, goes back to the board and eats. B remains seated. That is, A has a higher rank than B. Example 2: A and B are sitting on a board. A takes the food, flees or remains seated on the floor. B threatens or pursues A. That is, B has higher rank than A.

The animals were observed for 3 h daily by two of six observers with whom the animals were familiar, and a record was kept of the interactions of the whole group (one observer 2.5 h), of single individuals (one observer 2 h), and in addition video-tapes were made of the whole group (one observer 0.5 h), and of single individuals (one observer 0.5 h). The quantitative data of the undirected positive social behavior,

1 Institut für Zoologie und vergleichende Anatomie, Heinrich-Plett-Straße 40, Universität Kassel, 3500 Kassel, FRG

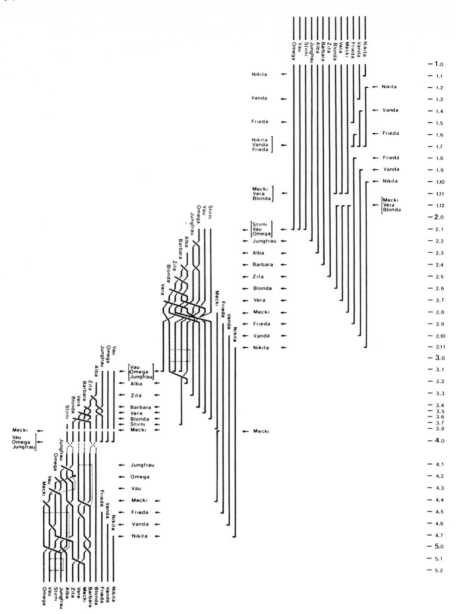

Fig. 1. Results of the food competition tests; rank of individuals and sequence of experimental steps

such as contact sitting, of the active social interactions as for example grooming, and of the agonistic interactions observed in the whole group, are demonstrated for three individuals in Figs. 2, 3, and 4. Each point of the curve represents the mean of one experimental step which continued usually 12 days long (with the exception of 3.4–3.8, which continued only for 6 days).

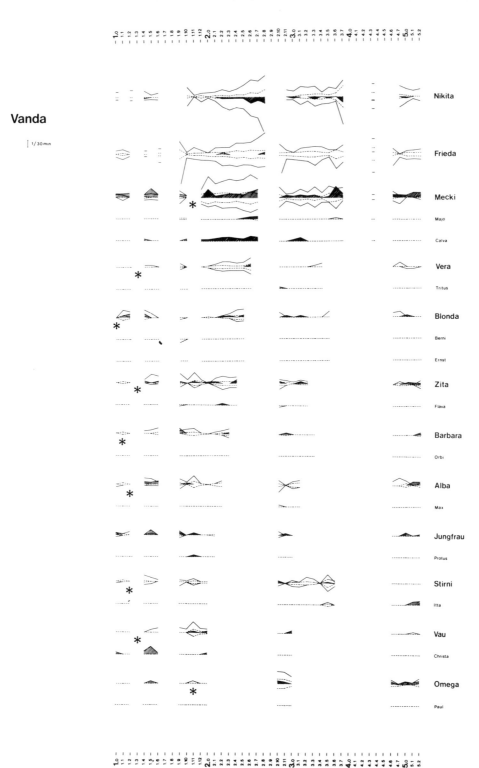

Fig. 2. Interactions between the high-ranking female "Vanda" and each of the other individuals of the group. *Above,* interactions which started from Vanda; *below,* interactions which started from the other individual. *Solid line,* active social interactions; *broken line,* undirected positive social behavior; *shaded,* agonistic interactions. The *asteriks* indicate that the female is carrying a newborn

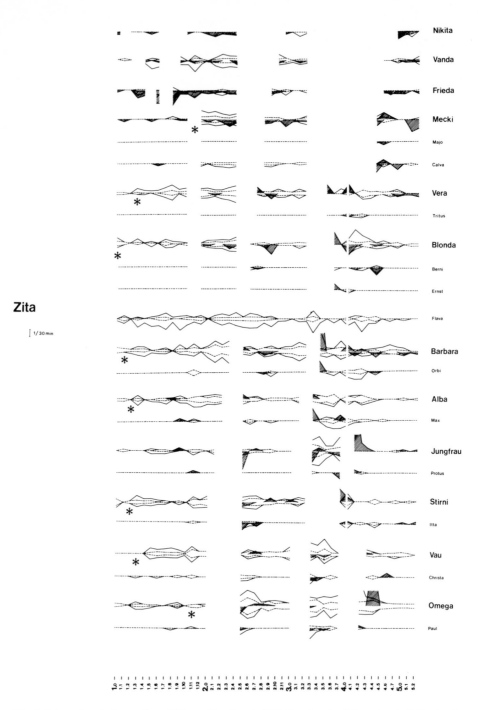

Fig. 3. Interactions between the middle-ranking female "Zita" and each of the other individuals of the group. For legend cf. Fig. 2

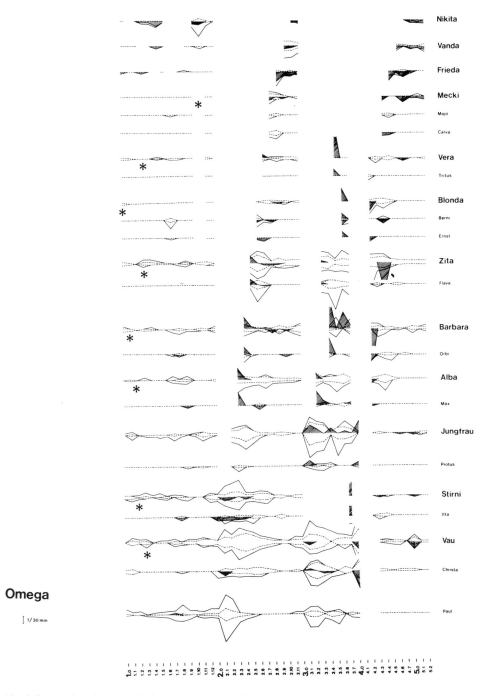

Fig. 4. Interactions between the low-ranking female "Omega" and each of the other individuals of the group. For legend cf. Fig. 2

Omega

| 1/30 min

At the beginning of our experiments we separated the alpha male (1.1), the alpha
female (1.3), and the beta female (1.5), respectively all three animals at the same time
(1.7), and later reintroduced them into the group (1.2, 1.4, 1.6, 1.8, 1.9, 1.10).
Thereby we were able to determine that the separation of these animals singly or all
of them together, as well as the separation of some clans (1.11), had no influence on
the rank of the other individuals of the group. It could be that one single behavior
pattern was responsible for these findings. So all females showed a tendency to
develop special connections to individuals of almost the same rank and to high-ranking
ones. So the social relations with the other females established in the last year could
be a factor making for group stability.

Therefore we separated the three lowest-ranking clans (2.0) and introduced to this
group successively the other clans in the contrary order (2.1 ff). By this arrangement
we wanted to give the lowest-ranking individuals a better starting position and to
make them by this procedure into artificially high-ranking individuals. It was evident
that these animals were able to keep their higher position against most of the newly
introduced females (Fig. 1). None of the later introduced females were able to recap-
ture their previous social position. Most of them showed a behavior which we called
"rank-securing behavior". They secured their rank against the previously introduced
individuals. This changed dramatically when we introduced the gamma female Mecki
together with her two children (2.8). Not only did Mecki achieve the highest-rank
position in the group, but also most of the other females developed a behavior which
we called "rank-improving behavior". They attacked the artificial high-ranking individuals one by one and achieved more or less their previous rank position in the group.
The introduction of the three highest-ranking individuals had no great influence on
the structure of the group (2.9, 2.10, 2.11). Individuals which are able to keep their
previous social position independent of the social situation we call "high-ranking
individuals". Animals which showed the "rank-securing" and the "rank-improving"
behavior we call "middle-ranking", and animals which showed none of these behaviors,
for example Alba and Jungfrau, we call "low-ranking".

But one reason for our findings could be that the highest-ranking female Stirni of
the three lowest-ranking clans was not a natural low-ranking individual, but perhaps
a natural high-ranking one, who had only a dependent low-ranking place in the hierarchy. To clarify this point, we started a control experiment. Again we separated the
three lowest-ranking clans, but this time without the Stirni clan (3.0). In this group
we again introduced the other females successively (3.1 ff). We got the same results;
none of them was able to get her previous position. Because the introduction of
Mecki brought the same results as before, we terminated this experiment. After
keeping the animals together for a longer period of time, we separated the three
highest-ranking clans of this group, which are the artificially high-ranking ones (4.0).
Then we introduced them successively into the group of females in which they had
previously held uncontested the highest-rank position (4.1, 4.2, 4.3). It was obvious
that they were not able to hold a high-rank position in this social situation. They
obtained only the lowest position in the hierarchy. Furthermore, they also failed to
show the rank-securing behavior which was typical for the middle-ranking ones. The
introduction of the gamma female Mecki (4.4) was now qualitatively different from
the previous introductions. Now she was not able to control the subadult male

children of Blonda and Barbara and lost her highest rank 6 hours after introduction. So Frieda's, Vanda's and Nikita's higher positions were uncontested when they were introduced; fights did not occur. Mecki got back her old position step by step (4.5 ff).

As an example of the social interactions which happened in the group we want to give the interactions of one high-ranking, one middle-ranking, and one low-ranking female.

The high-ranking female Vanda (Fig. 2) had mainly contacts with high-ranking individuals. Vanda's position was uncontested in each experimental situation, even when introduced in a group in which she was absent for a longer period of time (1.4, 1.9, 2.10, 4.6). During the whole experiment she was threatened only by Nikita, the alpha male, and was the active partner in all other agonistic interactions between her and any other individual of the group.

The middle-ranking female Zita (Fig. 3) had most relations with the individuals of almost the same rank. After introduction in the group of artificial high-ranking females (2.5, 3.3) she showed the rank-securing behavior against Barbara and Alba and tried to establish better relations with the artificially high-ranking ones (2.5: Stirni, Vau, Omega; 3.3: Vau, Omega, Jungfrau). By establishing special relations with the artificially highest-ranking female Stirni she even improved her rank and got a higher position than Vau, Omega, and Jungfrau (2.7). When introducing Mecki (2.8), Zita showed the rank-improving behavior against Stirni, at the same time Barbara, Blonda, and Vera showed the same behavior directed against Zita.

The low-ranking female Omega (Fig. 4) was able to hold the once-achieved position against the later introduced monkeys (2.2 ff, 3.2 ff). But Omega was not able to keep this position when Mecki was introduced (2.8). Omega did not even show rank-securing behavior or rank-improving behavior when she was introduced (4.2).

So the final position of each individual seems to be dependent on its behavior in the new social situation. Besides the natural rank which is designated as high-ranking, middle-ranking and low-ranking, our results (Welker and Lührmann, in prep.) indicate that the final rank position in one of these groups is dependent on relations with higher-ranking individuals.

Acknowledgments. Thanks are due to the German Research Foundation (DFG) for support (We 678/4), T. Fiegler, J. Friedrich, B. Kessel, W. Tiegel, and A. Siepmann for technical assistance, to Prof. Dr. H.O. Hofer and Dr. C. Johnson for reading the manuscript. Finally, I want to thank my co-workers B. Lührmann, M. Grebe, J. Hesse, U. Lingelbach, I. Sämmler, C. Schäfer, and L. Schindler who helped to gather the data.

References

Welker C, Lührmann B, Meinel W (1980) Behavioural sequences and strategies of female crab-eating monkeys, *Macaca fascicularis* Raffles, 1821, during group formation studies. Behaviour 73:219–237

Sexuality of Aging Monkeys (Macaca radiata)

G.D. Jensen, F.L. Blanton, and E.N. Sassenrath [1]

Limited reports of sexual behavior in older male monkeys are conflicting. Robinson et al. (1975) found reductions in ejaculations by older rhesus monkeys. Phoenix (1972) reported a reduction in mounting and increased latency to ejaculation in an older male rhesus monkey. Observations of Japanese macaques indicate that the older males may show considerable deficits or they may be as vigorous as younger males (Wolfe 1978, Eaton 1974). Few observations have been made on older female monkeys and no systematic data on socio-sexual behavior have been reported.

Descriptive Study

In our initial descriptive study, September, 1978, through February, 1979, we placed 26 older bonnets, mean age 15 years, into two separate social groups, each of 11 females and 2 males. We observed them for the first 5 months after group formation. The socio-sexual behavior that was observed appeared to be qualitatively like that described for mature bonnets (Kaufman and Rosenblum 1966). Ejaculatory mounts (N = 56) averaged 11.7 s in duration, slightly shorter than that reported for mature bonnets (Nadler and Rosenblum 1969). Considerable deficits were observed among the males. Only one of the four males was sexually vigorous; three showed little or no sexual behavior (Fig. 1). Two of them (Nos. 38 and 144 in Group A) turned out to have serious chronic diseases which eventually resulted in their deaths. An older male in Group B, second in rank, who was never observed mating, was found dead on a morning in December, grasping a female in a mount position. Post mortem examination indicated heart attack as the probable cause of death. A healthy male (No. 88) replacement in Group A mated actively. The two or three females of higher rank in each group were observed to copulate more frequently. Also, more copulations were observed during female mid-cycle than during the luteal phase.

---

1 Department of Psychiatry, School of Medicine, University of California, Davis, California 95616, USA

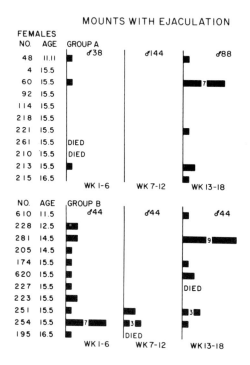

MOUNTS WITH EJACULATION

Fig. 1. Copulations with ejaculation during each six-week period of observations. In *Group A* – male No. 38 died week 6; male No. 144 died week 11, was never observed copulating; male No. 88 joined Group A between week 12 and 13. In *Group B* – male No. 10 died week 12, was never observed copulating

Experimental Study

A follow-up experimental study was aimed to determine if there are effects of aging on female socio-sexual behavior and hormonal correlates. This study, like the descriptive one the year before, was conducted during the breeding season. It utilized nine younger females, age 8 to 12 years, and seven older females, all over 16 years of age. The age groups lived in separate outdoor cages. The two males, one young, 10 years of age, and the other older, 19 years of age, were housed individually. All had visual access to each other. Each female was paired with each male for 15-min periods during the estrus and luteal phases of her menstrual cycle. Estrus and luteal phases were predicted for each female based on ongoing daily observations of menstrual bleeding to define regularity and duration of menstrual cycles. Cycle phases were subsequently confirmed by determination of plasma estradiol (E_2) and progesterone levels in blood samples taken from each female just prior to each pair-testing session. Estrus phase was defined by high estrogen and low progesterone; luteal phase by elevated progesterone and low estrogen.

The results showed significant differences between older and younger females (Table 1). The older females evoked fewer intromissions ($p < 0.01$) and only one of the eight was ejaculatory.

It was not possible to draw conclusions about the males in the experimental study because there were only two subjects. However, the results indicated that the aging male's sexual responsivity to older females was relatively less than the younger male's.

Table 1. Total intromissions and ejaculations with older and younger females

	Older females	Younger females	Mann-Whitney U
Total intromissions	8	51	p < 0.01
Total ejaculations	1	29	p < 0.01
Older male intromissions	2	29	–
Younger male intromissions	6	22	–

Specifically, the older male mounted the older females a total of two times, vs six times by the younger male (Table 1). However, the older male's responsivity to younger females was similar to that of the younger male, 29 and 22 intromissions, respectively.

In the young females, cycle phase appeared to affect sexual frequency (Table 2). The younger females engaged in more copulations during estrus than in the luteal phase (36 vs 15), whereas older females' copulations were equally frequent during the estrus and luteal phases of the cycle (3 vs 5).

The female cycle phase appeared to affect male function. The males ejaculated more frequently during estrus than during luteal phases (22 vs 8). The duration of ejaculatory mounts of both males was longer at estrus than at luteal phases (18.2 s vs 13.0 s). Duration of ejaculatory and nonejaculatory intromissions was significantly longer with younger females (p < 0.01).

Table 2. Intromissions and ejaculatory mounts during estrus and luteal phases

	Older	Younger	Mann-Whitney U	Older	Younger	Mann-Whitney U
	Estrus			Luteal		
Total intromissions	3	36	p < 0.01	5	15	n.s.
Ejaculatory mounts	1	21	p < 0.01	0	8	–
Nonejaculatory intromissions	2	15	p < 0.05	5	7	n.s.
Duration of ejaculatory mounts	8.0 s	18.2 s	p < 0.01	–	13.0 s	–
Duration of nonejaculatory intromissions	3.0 s	16.6 s	p < 0.01	5.0 s	8.1 s	n.s.

Circulating hormone levels were determined on only single test days during estrus or luteal phases of the menstrual cycle, and so did not consistently reflect peak values for that cycle. However, assuming an equal probability of sampling characteristic ranges for each hormone during these phases for each age sample, the data showed that older females had significantly lower mean estradiol levels during the estrus phase when estradiol levels are maximally elevated ($p < 0.025$). However, the two age groups showed no significant differences in mean progesterone levels during the luteal phase when progesterone levels are maximally elevated.

The changes in sexuality of these older female bonnets can be attributed to the aging process. Since the older females evoked significantly fewer intromissions and ejaculations compared with younger mature females, it can be said that their attractivity was diminished. This had not been previously reported in any mammal, although it is commonly believed that aging women have diminished attractiveness.

Our descriptive study was more naturalistic in contrast to our experimental study, which represented a highly artificial behavior situation. Possibly the aging effects found in the experimental study would be less evident under more naturalistic conditions. Further studies will be needed to clarify the nature of the complex interplay between social and physiological factors and aging in the socio-sexual interactions of older primates.

Summary

In a descriptive study, the sexual behavior patterns of healthy older bonnets appeared qualitatively similar to that of fully mature bonnets. Deficits in sexual behavior of two of four older males were associated with severe illness.

In laboratory tests older female bonnets did not copulate very frequently, much less than younger females. Younger females were more sexual during estrus than during the luteal phase. Ejaculations were more frequent and mounts were of longer duration during estrus compared with the luteal phase. Older females had lower levels of estradiol during estrus. Aging appears to be associated with a reduction in sexual responsiveness of females and their attractiveness to males.

References

Eaton GG (1974) Male dominance and aggression in Japanese macaque reproduction. In: Montagna W, Sadler WA (eds) Reproductive behavior. Plenum Publishing Corporation, New York, pp 287–297

Kaufman IC, Rosenblum LA (1966) A behavioral taxonomy for Macaca nemestrina and Macaca radiata: Based on longitudinal observations of family groups in the laboratory. Primates 7: 206–258

Nadler RD, Rosenblum LA (1969) Sexual behavior of male bonnet monkeys in the laboratory. Brain Behav Evol 2:482–497

Phoenix CH (1972) The role of testosterone in the sexual behavior of laboratory male rhesus. In: Montagna W (ed) Primate reproductive behavior. S Karger, New York

Robinson JA, Sheffler G, Eisile SG, Goy RW (1975) Effects of age and season on sexual behavior of plasma testosterone and dihydrotestosterone concentrations of laboratory-housed male rhesus macaque monkeys (Macaca mulatta). Biol Reprod 13:203–210

Wolfe L (1970) Age and sexual behavior of Japanese macaques (Macaca fuscata). Arch Sex Behav 7:55–68

Uses of Long-Range Calls During Ranging by Guinea Baboons

R.W. Byrne [1]

The Guinea Baboon *(Papio papio)* has so far been rather neglected, but at the Stirling African Primate Project site in Niokolo-Koba National Park, Senegal, it was studied from 1976 to 1979. The results are still being analysed, but preliminary findings show the Guinea baboon to be unusual in several ways. Day ranges are very long, and the baboons form large groups, often travelling in groups of 100–200 and aggregating at sleeping sites in numbers up to 700. Typically, they sleep in large kapok trees in the strips of forest found along permanent water (see Fig. 1), emerging onto the valley rim in the morning to groom, play, or socialise before setting off to forage.

HABITAT SECTION

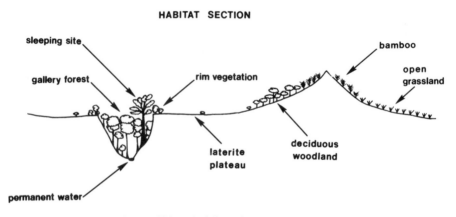

Fig. 1. Idealised section of part of Mont Assirik study area

Open, bare laterite plateaus are crossed with circumspection, usually in large groups, in silence and often after some hesitation. This may be to minimize predation risk, as leopards are frequent in the study area. In all other habitats, groups often fragment into a few or many small parties which rejoin into large groups several times in a day.

1 Department of Psychology, University of St. Andrews, St. Andrews, Fife, Scotland KY 16 9JU

This, along with the frequently dense vegetation, makes maintaining an accurate picture of their movements difficult, and habituation and individual recognition are hampered by the large numbers and extensive ranging. Despite these problems, study of these baboons' communication is particularly interesting, as they use vocalization extensively, unlike the rather silent East African baboons, and it may be the very factors which hinder research that *cause* this difference. So in 1979 I studied their vocal behaviour by means of check sheets, recording counts of each call in every 5 min interval during a "follow", along with situational variables such as habitat and whether parties were splitting or coalescing.

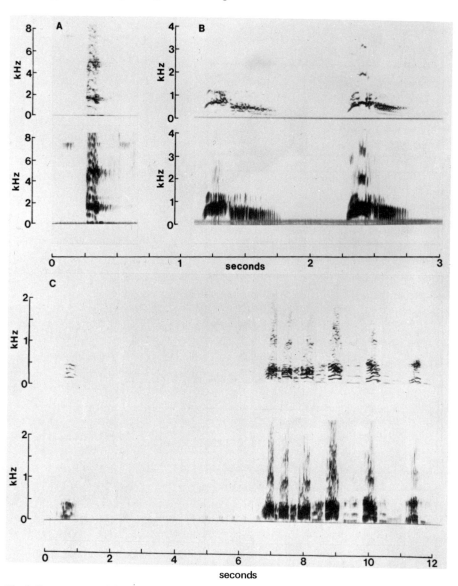

Fig. 2. Spectrograms of Guinea Baboon calls: A sharp alarm bark, B two examples of double-phase bark, C "roargrunt"

Using factor analysis to summarise the correlations between rates of use of the calls, it revealed six statistically significant factors. Four of these involve only the extensively graded close-range calls, such as grunts and squeals, and these will be discussed elsewhere. Relatively discrete and loud calls, on the other hand, have significant loadings only on the other two factors. Loud calls which I could readily distinguish by ear at most ranges were the double-phased *wahoo* bark (see Fig. 2), a Type 2 loud call in the sense of Gautier and Gautier (1977); a mixed bag of single-phased barks, which includes the shrill "alarm" bark of surprise, and others close to a *wahoo* in form but with the second phase absent or inaudible at any range (called "dog-like barks" by Hall and De Vore 1965); and the *roargrunt,* a strange call given only by adult males and consisting of a humming grunt, a pause of several seconds, and then

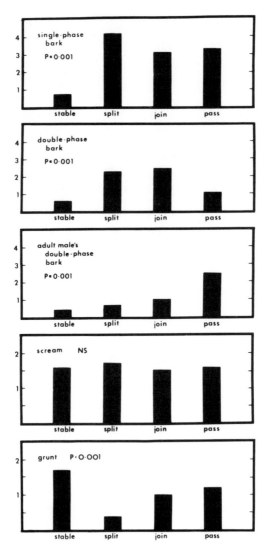

Fig. 3. Rates of occurrence of calls under different circumstances (see text for explanation)

a slow patterned series of loud roars. This call is apparently a Type 1 loud call (Gautier and Gautier 1977) and Waser (this vol.) argues that it is homologous to certain mangabey loud calls.

One factor groups the *roargrunt* with those *wahoo* calls which are given only by adult males. Nocturnal volleys of both these calls are common, in response to sounds of leopard, lion, or wild dog, so this factor is evidently related to "danger" (Rowell 1966 has pointed out that in Ugandan *Papio anubis* the *wahoo* is not an alarm call, elicited by initial perception of a major predator, but more a comment on its continued presence or movement).

The second factor involving discrete, long-distance calls has its highest loading on barks heard from groups of baboons other than the focal group: it apparently concerns intergroup contact. Rates of various calls can be classified according to whether the number of animals in the focal group seemed stable, or whether a detectable split or join was in progress, or another group was passing the focal one (Fig. 3). All rates of barking show highly significant increases during splits, joins, or passes, while rates of other calls are unaffected (e.g., screams) or may even show significant decreases (e.g., grunts). Adult male double-phase barks seem particularly correlated with contact with nonfocal groups, suggesting some association of danger with these occasions: nocturnal volleys of *wahoo* calls provoke answering volleys from animals in other sleeping sites, even 2–3 km away, so the same may happen in the daytime. The rates of barking recorded are in fact an excellent indication of the chance that a split, join, or pass is occurring (see Fig. 4).

Barking is evidently related to group fragmentation and agglomeration, but the way barks are used can be seen most clearly in an individual day's record. Figure 5 records a typical follow, in which at 0700 hours a group of about 150 baboons left many other animals still at the sleeping site, and by 1010 hours this group had reached a grove of trees, where they remained for some time. At first during their progression, the group travelled together, but at 0915 hours they began a slow movement across grassland, fanning out into columns and finally breaking into small parties, so that

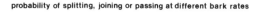

probability of splitting, joining or passing at different bark rates

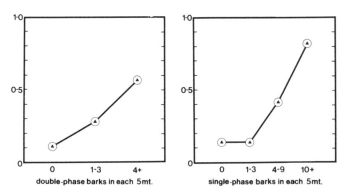

Fig. 4. Variation in the probability of independently recording a "split", "join", or "pass" with different rates of barking

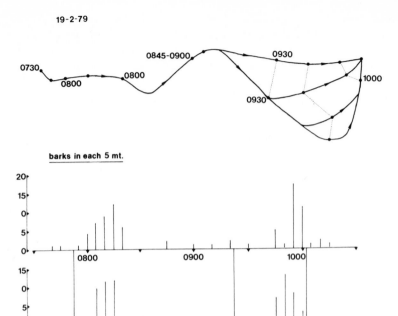

Fig. 5. Scale map of the route taken by a baboon group. Time is recorded by a *circle* on the line of progression each 15 mt; *below,* the rates of barking recorded in each 5 mt interval from focal and nonfocal baboon groups are plotted against time

I was left following a party of five, with no idea of the precise whereabouts of the others (whose routes of travel on the map are therefore very approximate). At 0945 hours the larger of two males in my party climbed to 4 m on top of a bush and began a deliberate, spaced series of *wahoo* barks. After a few minutes, "answering" barks came from the west, and the male descended and set off with the party towards these calls, still barking occasionally. Barks also began from at least two, probably more, other directions and gradually it became clear that parties from all over the grassland were converging on a group of trees, where the parties joined up and barking died away. This is shown on the trace of barks per 5 min interval (see Fig. 5), where a peak at 0945 hours in the focal group heralds a period of frequent barking from focal and nonfocal animals, which ceases at the reunion. Regrouping of scattered parties, under conditions of poor visibility, is not the only context of barking during ranging. When a group splits into two large parties which set off in different directions, as occurred earlier in the same follow when the 150 animals left others behind at the sleeping site, exchanges of barks are frequent and prolonged. If barks promote aggregation, then it would seem that in cases like this animals in the two large parties have differ- ent immediate needs and so require to travel to different areas. In some of these cases, the parties remain in auditory contact and later rejoin each other: in others, they separate fully. Often a group will meet another coming from another direction, and barks are normally exchanged; in some cases the two groups coalesce, and it may be that they had separated from each other earlier in the day or on a previous day. Another common context of barking is when a party becomes detached from the main group while travelling swiftly through forest, and they exchange barks with the main group until they catch up.

In summary, loud barks in *Papio papio* occur in two circumstances:

1. *danger,* with the shrill alarm bark denoting the initial perception of an alarming animal, and volleys of *wahoo* barks and *roargrunts* occurring in response to its continued presence, movement, or calling.
2. splitting up a group into *parties out of visual contact* with each other, when on the whole barks tend to promote aggregation, or prevent fragmentation. Typical cases of use are:

a) a party becomes separated during rapid travel in dense vegetation: barks are exchanged until they rejoin;

b) some of a large group set off to travel or forage in a certain direction, and do not *need* to forage as a small party because of the distribution of food: barks are exchanged with the rest of the group, leading to either the rest following, or the groups splitting into two;

c) parties sight or hear each other during ranging: barks exchanged between them lead to their either coalescing or continuing in different directions;

d) when a sparse and thinly spread food is being exploited, a group splits into many small parties despite the increased risk of predation: when they cease to feed on such food, or need to cross an open, exposed area, each small party barks to indicate its location, and this information is used to allow an efficient reunion.

In each case, it is assumed that aggregation into large groups is a mechanism of predator defence, which is employed except where the nature of food being exploited prevents it, and which is facilitated by vocal communication when visibility is poor.

Acknowledgments. Fieldwork in Senegal was supported by the Nuffield Foundation, and made possible by Drs W.C. McGrew and C.E.G. Tutin who generously allowed me to collaborate in the Stirling African Primate Project. Analysis was aided by advice from Drs P. Marler, D. Cheney, and R. Seyfarth and others at the Rockefeller University Field Centre, and my visit there was supported by the Royal Society. The paper benefited from helpful advice and criticism from Alison Conning.

References

Gautier J-P, Gautier A (1977) Communication in Old World monkeys. In: Seboeck TA (ed) How animals communicate. Univ Press, Indiana

Hall KRL, De Vore I (1965) Baboon social behaviour. In: De Vore I (ed) Primate behavior: Field studies of monkeys and apes. Hold, Rinehart and Winston, New York

Rowell TE (1966) Forest living baboons in Uganda. J Zool 149:344–364

On the Function of Allogrooming in Old-World Monkeys

C. Goosen [1]

Grooming behavior is a very common type of social interaction between adults of many species of Old-World monkeys. In this interaction, one individual appears to closely examine the coat or skin of his partner (allogrooming), while parting or plucking at hairs. This paper briefly considers various current hypotheses; a more extensive discussion is given elsewhere (Goosen 1980b). Hypotheses concerning the survival function can be divided into two groups: *clean and eat hypotheses* and *social bonding and tension reduction ones*. As discussed below, both types of hypotheses are incomplete; those in the first group are incomplete because removal or recovery of debris or vermin from the pelage being groomed is of only minor significance. Hypotheses of the second group are incomplete because they are too broad; the concepts of social bond or low tension are defined such that they cannot explain why grooming varies with the type of situation in which animals meet. An alternative hypothesis which combines several elements included in the others and which is in good agreement with the literature data is later presented here.

Clean and Eat Hypotheses

An obvious supposition following from the morphology of the behavior is that the groomer searches for vermin or other particles in the pelage of the *groomee*. This presumably leads to cleaning of the coat which reduces the risk of the groomee contracting dangerous infections (Watson 1908; see also Sparks 1967, Hutchins and Barash 1976). There are various indications that grooming does result in removal of ectoparasites such as ticks and lice. These indications are that socially living males appeared to have fewer lice and ticks in their pelage than solitary males (Washburn and DeVore 1961, McKenna 1978). Host-specific sucking lice, during their evolution, appeared to have adapted to the grooming dexterity of their host (Kuhn 1967). Nevertheless, it is doubtful that removal of ectoparasites is the only function of the act of grooming. Most monkeys, especially in captivity, are practically free of parasites. Yet, the animals eagerly solicit for and frequently submit themselves to grooming. Because monkeys can probably efficiently free each other of any parasites in a short

1   Primate Center TNO, 151 Lange Kleiweg, 2288 GJ, Rijswijk, The Netherlands

period of time, it seems likely that the amount of time the groomee spends in submitting to being groomed is far in excess of that needed for sanitary purposes.

The function of grooming to the *groomer* is also difficult to understand. One could
suggest that: (1) grooming occurs for reasons of "inclusive fitness" (Hamilton 1964)
when it is directed to a close relative, which is often the case; (2) grooming is a form
of "reciprocal altruism" (Trivers 1971) when it is reciprocated, which is often true.
But the two explanations are valid only if cleaning is a major function, which probably does *not* hold true. Another supposition is that the groomer finds and ingests
particles which are of high nutritive value (Zuckermann 1932; Ewing 1935). However,
the pelage is usually clean and the groomer shows no interest in any particles found
(Ewing 1935). Despite the first impression from the behavior, the fine coordination
of the movements during grooming are often at variance with effective harvesting
of any highly prized nutrients (pers. obs.). Therefore, it is unlikely that the function
of grooming is related only to removal or recovery of particles from the pelage.

Social Bonding and Tension Reduction Hypotheses

The idea that allogrooming between adult monkeys is closely related to the social life
of the animals was early expressed by Watson (1908). Various suppositions concerning the nature of that relationship have been advanced. Carpenter (1942) suggested
that grooming serves to strengthen social bonds. Sade (1965) considered it to be
useful for establishing, maintaining, and renewing peaceful relations. Both authors
also noted that grooming seemed to occur under different conditions with apparently
different effects, varying from not being noticeable to the observer to preventing
a pending attack by placating the expected aggressor. Lindburg (1973) was of the
opinion that grooming serves an important function in regulating certain aspects of
social life and thus promotes cohesiveness and persistence of groups. A suggested
mechanism in such promotion of cohesiveness is reduction of social tension or dissipa-
tion of aggression, effects postulated by several authors (e.g., Mason 1964, Poirier
1974, Rahaman and Parthasarathy 1969). A somewhat different view was expressed
by Oki and Maeda (1973), who regarded grooming as the result rather than a cause
of a strong social bond.

The above hypotheses, however, are not readily testable. They are used in a broad
reference to a wide variety of activities and related phenomena. As such, the hypotheses again emphasize the assumption that grooming is closely related to many
aspects of social life. When one attempts to pinpoint what is probably meant by a
strong social bond or low tension, it then becomes apparent that reference is made to
individuals which *stay close* to each other and which show relatively *little aggression*
towards each other. These two aspects are considered below.

Proximity

Throughout the literature, one finds a close relationship between proximity and
grooming which is consistent across a wide variety of social situations.

In rhesus monkeys, females appear to form the more stable core of natural groups, i.e., females are more likely to remain together in close proximity (Drickammer 1976, Altmann 1962). Males, on the other hand, maintain relatively longer distances between each other, do not generally form close associations with other individuals and are more likely to leave the group. This correlates with grooming: adult females show more grooming than do adult males (Kaufman 1967, Lindburg 1973, Drickamer 1976, Bernstein 1970, Rhine 1973, Chalmers 1968, Rahaman and Parthasarathy 1969).

Within the core of the group, genetically related individuals, especially females, generally maintain closer proximity to each other than do unrelated individuals. Grooming by females very often involves related individuals (Sade 1965, Kaufman 1967, Rosenblum 1971, Missakian 1974).

Rhesus males groom unrelated females mainly during the mating season (Vandenbergh and Vessey 1968, Wilson and Boelkins 1970, Drickammer 1973, Kaufman 1967). During that period, the males are also more frequently found in the vicinity of unrelated females. Grooming of an unrelated female by a male takes place especially during the fertile period of the female's menstrual cycle when the two form a so-called consort pair, i.e., they remain close to each other for a certain time period. During this consort period, the partners are frequently engaged in grooming in addition to sexual intercourse (Carpenter 1942, Conaway and Koford 1964, Drickammer 1976; see also Rowell 1968, Saayman 1970, Michael and Herbert 1963, Michael 1968).

Mothers of neonates are frequently approached by other females, apparently so that they can be near and touch or hold the newborn. These females often groom the mother, who usually attempts to avoid too much close interest in her offspring (Kaufman 1967, Lindburg 1973, Rowell et al. 1964, Rowell 1969, Bertrand 1969, Breuggeman 1973).

Differences in proximity could perhaps also account for amounts of grooming activity reported for different populations of rhesus monkeys. In natural groups comprising only a few males, grooming among the few adult males was practically non-existent (Lindburg 1973). More males were present in the populations on Santiago island, probably because the sea had discouraged most of them from leaving the area of their natal troop during adolescence. These males were found to frequently groom each other (Kaufmann 1967). The examples given mainly concern rhesus monkeys, but similar indications of a close relationship between proximity and grooming can also be found in other species.

In terms of causation, the close relationship between grooming and proximity can be interpreted in different ways: grooming leads to proximity, or proximity results in grooming. Laboratory experiments in pairs of stump-tailed macaques indicated that proximity to another individual elicited self-directed grooming (Goosen 1974a,b). When allogrooming was permitted, proximity appeared to increase but only in order to groom. There was no evidence that the close proximity was maintained after grooming was completed (Goosen 1980a). This supports the first interpretation, i.e., proximity causes grooming. Grooming probably enhances proximity only because this is an inevitable consequence of such activity and the act happens to be time consuming for some reason.

Aggression Reduction

The hypothesis that grooming reduces aggression requires some clarification. In this phrasing, one implicitly regards grooming as the result of a "tendency" for grooming which is independent of aggression and that, when grooming does occur, it affects a "tendency" for aggression. But grooming (or submitting to being groomed) and aggression are two activities which we already know are not performed at the same time by the same individuals; hence, measurements are almost certain to show a negative relationship. This returns us to a long-standing debate on the value of trying to explain relative increases or decreases in amounts of activities from the interaction between supposedly underlying "tendencies". These terms, however, can, in principle, be meaningful if "tendency for a certain behavior" is represented by the "probability per time unit of starting that activity", which thereby becomes quantifiable (Goosen and Metz 1980). The presupposition is that the behavior transitions occur randomly, the correctness of which can be formally tested.

A cursory review of the literature shows that there is no consistent correlation between grooming and the occurrence of aggression; see below.

Grooming often occurs during periods when the entire group is resting (Lindburg 1973), during which there is a conspicuous absence of aggression among the group members.

There is no correlation between grooming and aggression as measured by social rank (Varley and Symmes 1966, Kaufman 1967, Sade 1967, 1972, Rhine 1972, 1973, Lindburg 1973, Mörike 1973). The relative social rank of two individuals is determined by the ratio of wins and losses in the quarrels between the two and/or by the relative frequency by which one of the individuals can displace the other (Sade 1967, 1972; Kaufman 1967). Not all reports indicate that such a measuring procedure was employed, but it seems plausible that observations of this type were made.

Female rhesus monkeys are reported to groom more than males. However, there are no indications that females show different amounts of aggression than do males.

Grooming partners are frequently related individuals, but relatives have not been reported to be more aggressive toward each other than to nonrelated individuals.

In the situation in which the mother of a neonate is approached by females, grooming of the mother by the visitors is often observed. Although the mother often avoids too much attention, there is generally no mention of aggression by either the mother or the visitor.

The lack of a correlation between grooming and aggression does not, of course, rule out the existence of a causal relationship; it only indicates that a causal relationship, if existent, is not a simple one.

There are various indications in the literature that partners in a grooming relationship often support each other in frequent aggressive encounters with third parties. Related individuals are frequently grooming partners. They are not reported to be aggressive to each other but they do assist each other in aggressive encounters against third parties (Sade 1965, Kaplan 1977).

During the mating season, male rhesus monkeys primarily groom nonrelated females. During that season, the males are not aggressive to the females, but fight with other males which they do not groom (Kaufman 1967).

Grooming is frequently seen between the members of a consort pair. Again, the male and female are not aggressive toward each other. But they have been reported to be highly aggressive toward third parties (Lindburg 1973; see also Zumpe and Michael 1970).

The occurrence of aggression can be temporarily increased by introducing an unfamiliar individual into a group (Southwick et al. 1974). In such a period of increased aggression, most of it is directed to the newcomer. Shortly after this initial period, there is usually a period characterized by an increased incidence of grooming (Bernstein 1969, 1971). The grooming, however, is not primarily directed to the newcomer but to partners among the familiar group members (Vessey 1971, Wade 1976).

These observations suggest that grooming in one way or another possibly prevents aggression from being "misdirected" to the partner instead of to the opponent.

A Hypothesis: Avoiding Unnecessary Confrontations

The above discussion can be summarized as follows:

1. despite the appearance of being so, grooming is not primarily related to removal or recovery of small particles or vermin;
2. grooming is elicited by proximity in a variety of social situations;
3. grooming is often time consuming;
4. grooming possibly reduces aggression toward the partner, at least when third parties are involved;
5. grooming can probably have different effects.

In seeking to find an explanation for those phenomena, one must develop a clear picture of the intricacies of monkey social life. In an attempt to present such a picture, I will first consider encounters between pairs; encounters between three or more individuals will be alluded to afterwards.

Encounters Between Pairs

When a monkey encounters another individual of about the same size, there is a certain chance that it is regarded as an enemy and treated accordingly. The chance of being treated as an enemy can generally be presumed to be low, because it is of greater survival value to avoid hostilities than to seek them. However, the hazards inherent in being taken for an enemy are so great that one monkey cannot afford to completely ignore the other. Effective defence against hostility includes:

1. evasion of the assaulter or just his attack, so as to avoid becoming injured;
2. counterattack to be launched *before* the other's attack so as to prevent his assault or in *retaliation* to prevent a new attack.

As this holds true for both individuals, an encounter carries the risk of escalating into a fight due to sheer alertness without any survival benefits being gained by either party.

Grooming contributes to reducing unnecessary alertness because both partners indicate to each other that they are not preparing for hostilities toward each other, as follows from the following considerations:

1. grooming behavior is incompatible with aggressive behavior and, because of the close physical contact between the partners, it can not unnoticeably transform into aggression (as suggested by Marler 1965, 1968). Also the groomee often adopts postures which facilitate inspection of a certain skin area, while clearly avoiding postures or movements which could be interpreted as hostile;
2. there is little doubt as to the animal to which the behavior is addressed;
3. there is little cause for confusion about whether or not the partner spends the effort of participating in grooming for a purpose other than to indicate that hostilities are not intended (food items and ectoparasites are of only minor importance).

Assuming that the need for alertness and hence the chance of hostilities diminishes as time elapses, it would be expected that the animals would sooner or later proceed to other activities in order to cope with more urgent survival hazards. In doing so, each animal may go its own way or the two may team up. This may bring them into a new situation whch may again elicit grooming.

Encounters with Three or More Individuals

Monkeys live for almost all of their lives in social groups which are fairly stable in membership. Because the animals are familiar with each other, one would expect that there would be little uncertainty about the behavior of group mates, so that there would be little reason for the animals to groom each other. However, grooming still plays a prominent role because of the importance of support relations in social life, as explained below.

An individual monkey living in a group is likely to come into dispute with a competitor over a certain resource. His success in recovering that resource depends on whether or not he receives support from other individuals. Support can be given by close relatives for reasons of "inclusive fitness". But support can also be given by nonrelated individuals; for instance, if a resource is disputed by two or more individuals, two or more of them can increase their share by joining forces in chasing the other(s) away or by preventing themselves from being chased away.

Various reports indicate that monkeys do frequently assist each other in their disputes with third parties (Sade 1965, Varley and Symmes 1966, Kummer 1967, Kaplan 1977, Massey 1977, de Waal 1977), that serious wounding can occur (Kaufman 1967, Lindburg 1971, Rhine 1972, 1973, Bernstein et al. 1974, Bernstein and Gordon 1977, Estrada et al. 1977, Dittus 1977) and that changes in support coalitions can have dramatic consequences (see also Kaufman 1967, Vessey 1971, De Waal 1975, Bernstein and Gordon 1977, Estrada et al. 1977).

When three or more individuals meet over a certain resource, each individual may be mistaken about who is an opponent and who is a supporter. The kinds of mistakes an individual can make are:

1. a partner is falsely held to be an opponent; in this case, the individual first launches an attack on a possible partner, at the same time rendering himself vulnerable to an attack by the opponent;
2. an opponent is falsely held to be a partner; in this case, the individual first renders himself vulnerable to his competitor and probably attacks his true partner.

It is obvious that, in both types of error, an individual is likely to lessen the support he receives and to become vulnerable to attack by his opponent. And since support is of great survival value, errors involving support relations are to be avoided as much as possible.

Errors concerning support relations cannot be fully excluded for two reasons: (1) support relations do change with, e.g., changes in membership and strength of the support coalition or the opposition, and in the dependence on the survival resource disputed; (2) support relationships are the result of intricate interactions among a number of individuals, partners as well as opponents. It is difficult therefore, for a monkey to accurately predict how its relationship with another one is affected by the other group members and their relationships. In other words, support relationships are important but not completely reliable.

By grooming, both partners indicate that they are not preparing for hostilities against each other. When at the same time the situation involves a dispute with a third party over a certain survival resource, it is likely that the grooming partner reduces the risk of confusing partner and opponent in such a critical situation.

Corroborating Evidence

The above hypothesis is attractive because it can account for the phenomena mentioned in the foregoing section under 1 to 5 as explained below.

1. The hypothesis can be valid only in so far as the removal or recovery of particles is *not* of urgent interest. Otherwise, there can be confusion about whether the partner's interest is in those particles or in staying together for other reasons.
2. Grooming is time consuming because only under that condition is it a reliable indication to the partner that one is not preparing for hostilities and that alertness does not have to be maintained.
3. Grooming is elicited by proximity more or less independent of the kind of situation; in close proximity, the hazards inherent in mistaking a partner for an opponent or vice versa are greatest.
4. Grooming reduces aggression or tension in so far as this reflects a certain degree of alertness for defence. It does not reduce aggression or tension reflecting a preparedness to dispute a certain survival resource.
5. The effect of grooming can be characterized as *tension reducing* if one of the partners gives evidence of a greater alertness than the other. In general, the need for alertness is greater when third parties are involved than when they are not. In other situations, however, the effect of grooming could also be characterized as *probing the social interests* of the partner in other group members. As the partner is more seriously interested in another group member under the given conditions,

he is less likely to engage in grooming. Such probing of social interests can take place as a matter of routine monitoring. But it can also take place in situations in which a change can be expected, e.g., after the arrival of a newcomer to the group who is likely to have formed relationships with certain group members and thereby to affect relationships with others, or a neonate being born, the protection of which requires new alertness from the relatives. The testing of the partner's interests may lead to formation of a new support coalition. But the testing can also lead to breaking of a support coalition if the interests of the partners appear to be opposed.

The above hypothesis can also explain other observed phenomena. Animals of about equal social rank are frequently grooming partners because they are often in proximity with each other and frequently interact. This is a situation in which confusion of partner and opponent is most likely to occur and the inherent risks are greatest. Under such a condition, grooming is often performed by the animal of lower rank (Bernstein 1970). This is the individual which would probably incur the most damage in case of a dispute; hence, he or she puts more effort into reducing this risk.

The fact that grooming partners are frequently relatives (Sade 1965, Kaufman 1967, Rosenblum 1971, Missakian 1974) can also be accounted for. Confusing partner and opponent in a situation involving a relative constitutes, for reasons of "inclusive fitness", a greater survival hazard than when a relative is not involved. Therefore, it is understandable that relatives are more actively engaged in finding out when support can be expected and when not.

Inherent in the above described hypothesis is the possibility that an individual "cheats"; e.g., it participates in a grooming interaction while it actually plans to launch a surprise attack. However, an animal which is prepared to run the risk of a surprise attack after grooming in order to gain certain survival benefits is, by grooming the other, letting the opportunity pass to gain similar benefits in a less hazardous way. Such behavior has obviously not been promoted by natural selection. Therefore, although "cheating" might take place, it is to only a limited extent.

One could suggest that the function postulated for grooming can also be served by any other activity which is incompatible with aggression such as sitting or walking. However, these alternatives cannot serve the postulated function equally well as grooming can. In these alternative activities, it is: (1) less clear to the other individual(s) which particular individual is addressed by the performer; and (2) less certain to any adressed individual that the displayed activity prevents the performer from preparing for an attack or from pursuing some unexpected resource. In other words, although other activities may serve a similar function, resort to them involves a greater chance of misunderstanding the partner; this may be hazardous under certain conditions.

As a word of caution, it should be noted that the above hypothesis is based on a post hoc interpretation of published data. Therefore, it requires verification by systematic manipulation of the availability of certain survival resources to either or both individuals and of the presence or absence of a third party.

References

Altmann SA (1962) A field study of the sociobiology of rhesus monkey *(Macaca mulatta)*. Ann NY Acad Sci 102 (2):338–435

Bernstein IS (1969) Introductory techniques in the formation of pigtail monkey troops. Folia Primatol 10:1–19

Bernstein IS (1970) Primates status hierarchies. In: Rosenblum LA (ed) Primate behavior, vol I. Academic Press, London New York, pp 71–109

Bernstein IS (1971) The influence of introductory techniques of the formation of captive mangabey groups. Primates 12:33–44

Bernstein IS, Gordon TP (1977) Behavioural research in breeding colonies of Old World monkeys. Lab Anim Sci 27:532–540

Bernstein IS, Gordon TP, Rose RM (1974) Aggression and social controls in rhesus monkeys *(Macaca mulatta)* groups, revealed in group formation studies. Folia Primatol 21:81–107

Bertrand M (1969) The behavioral repertoire of the stumptail macaque. Bibliotheca Primatologica, no 11. S Karger, Basel

Breuggeman JA (1973) Parental care in a group of free ranging rhesus monkeys *(Macaca mulatta)*. Folia Primatol 20:178–210

Carpenter CR (1942) Sexual behavior of free ranging rhesus monkeys *(Macaca mulatta)*. J Comp Physiol Psychol 33:113–142

Chalmers RN (1968) Group composition, ecology and daily activities of free living mangabeys in Uganda. Folia Primatol 8:247–262

Conaway CH, Koford CB (1964) Estrous cycles and mating behaviour in a free-ranging band of rhesus monkeys J Mammol 45:577–588

Dittus WPJ (1977) The social regulation of population density and age-sex distribution in the Toque monkey. Behaviour 63:281

Drickammer LC (1973) Semi-natural and enclosed groups of *Macaca mulatta*. A behavioural comparison. Am J Phys Anthropol 39 (2):249–254

Drickammer LC (1976) Quantitative observations of grooming behaviour in free-ranging *Macaca mulatta*. Primates 17 (3):323–335

Estrada A, Estrada R, Ervin F (1977) Establishment of a free-ranging colony of stumptail macaques *(Macaca arctoides)*. Social relations I. Primates 18 (3):647–676

Ewing HE (1935) Sham louse-picking, or grooming, among monkeys. J Mammol 16:303–306

Goosen C (1974a) Immediate effects of allogrooming in adult stumptailed macaques *(Macaca arctoides)*. Behaviour 48:75–88

Goosen C (1974b) Some causal factors in autogrooming behaviour of adult stumptailed macaques *(Macaca arctoides)*. Behaviour 49:1–11

Goosen C (1980a) After-effects of allogrooming on proximity and locomotion in pairs of stumptailed macaques *(Macaca arctoides)*. Behaviour 74:1–21

Goosen C (1980b) On grooming in Old World monkeys. Dissertation, Univ Leiden, The Netherlands

Goosen C, Metz JAJ (1980) Dissecting behaviour: relations between autoaggression, grooming and walking in a macaque. Behaviour 75:97–132

Hamilton WD (1964) The genetical evolution of social behaviour. J Theor Biol 7:1–51

Hutchins M, Barash D (1976) Grooming in primates: implications for its utilitarian function. Primates 17 (2):145–150

Kaplan JR (1977) Patterns of fight interference in free-ranging rhesus monkeys. Am J Phys Anthropol 47:279–288

Kaufman JH (1967) Social relations of adult males in free ranging band of rhesus monkeys. In: Altman SA (ed) Social communication among primates. Univ of Chicago Press, Chicago, pp 73–98

Kuhn HJ (1967) Parasites and the phylogeny of the catarrhine monkeys. In: Chiarelli B (ed) Taxonomy and phylogeny of Old World primates with references to the origin of man. Rosenberg and Sellier, Torino, pp 187–195

Kummer H (1967) Tripartite relations in hamadryas baboons. In: Altmann SA (ed) Social communication among primates. Univ of Chicago Press, Chicago, pp 63–72

Lindburg DG (1971) The rhesus monkey in North India: an ecological and behavioural study. In: Rosenblum L (ed) Primate behavior, vol II. Academic Press, London New York, pp 2–106

Lindburg DG (1973) Grooming behaviour as a regulator of social interactions in rhesus monkeys. In: Carpenter CR (ed) Behavioural regulators of behaviour in primates. Buckwell Univ Press, Lewisburg, pp 124–128

Marler P (1965) Communication in monkeys and apes. In: De Vore I (ed) Primate behavior. Holt, Rinehart and Winston, New York, pp 544–584

Marler P (1968) Aggregation and dispersal: two functions in primate communication: In: Jay PC (ed) Primate studies in adaptation and variability. Hold, Rinehart and Winston, New York, pp 420–438

Mason WA (1964) Sociability and social organization in monkeys and apes. In: Berkowitz L (ed) Recent advances in experimental phychology, vol I. Holt, Rinehart and Winston, New York, pp 277–305

Massey A (1977) Agonistic aids and kinship in a group of pigtail macaques. Behav Ecol Socio-Biol 2:31–40

McKenna JJ (1978) Biosocial functions of grooming behaviour among the common Indian langur monkey *(Presbytis entellus)*. Am J Phys Anthropol 48:503–510

Michael RP (1968) Gonadal hormones and the control of primate behavior. In: Michael RP (ed) Endocrinology and human behaviour. Oxford Univ Press, London, pp 69–93

Michael RP, Herbert J (1963) Menstrual cycle influences grooming behaviour and sexual activity in the rhesus monkey. Science 140:500–501

Missakian EA (1974) Mother-offspring grooming relations in rhesus monkeys. Arch Sex Behav 3 (2):135–141

Mörike D (1973) Verhalten einer Gruppe von Diana Meerkatzen im Frankfurter Zoo. Primates 14:263–300

Oki J, Maeda Y (1973) Grooming as a regulator of behavior in Japanese macaques. In: Carpenter CR (ed) Behavioral regulators of behavior in primates. Bucknell Press, Lewisburg, pp 149–163

Poirier FE (1974) Colobine aggression: a review. In: Holloway RE (ed) Primate aggression, territoriality and xenophobia. Academic Press, London New York, pp 123–158

Rahaman H, Parthasarathy MD (1969) Studies on the social behaviour of bonnet monkeys. Primates 10:149–162

Rhine RJ (1972) Changes in the social structure of two groups of stumptail macaques *(Macaca arctoides)*. Primates 13:181–194

Rhine RJ (1973) Variation and consistency in the social behavior of two groups of stumptail macaques *(Macaca arctoides)*. Primates 14:21–35

Rosenblum LA (1971) Kinship interaction patterns in pigtail and bonnet macaques. Proc 3rd Int Congr Primatol, Zuerich, 1970, vol III, pp 79–84

Rowell TE (1968) Grooming by adult baboons in relation to reproductive cycles. Anim Behav 16:585–588

Rowell TE (1969) Intrasexual behaviour and female reproduction cycles of baboons *(Papio anubis)*. Anim Behav 17:159–167

Rowell TE, Hinde RA, Booth S (1964) Aunt-infant interaction in captive rhesus monkeys. Anim Behav 12:219–226

Saayman GA (1970) The menstrual cycle and sexual behaviour in a troop of free ranging chacma baboons *(Papio ursinus)*. Folia Primatol 12:81–110

Sade DS (1965) Some aspects of parent-offspring and sibling relations in a group of rhesus monkeys, with a discussion of grooming. Am J Phys Anthropol 23:1–18

Sade DS (1967) Determinants of dominance in a group of free-ranging rhesus monkeys. In: Altmann SA (ed) Social communication among primates. Univ of Chicago Press, Chicago, pp 99–113

Sade DS (1972) Sociometrics of *Macaca mulatta*. I. Linkages and cliques in grooming matrices. Folia Primatol 18:196–223

Southwick CH, Siddiqi MF, Farrooqui MY, Pal BC (1974) Xenophobia among free-ranging rhesus groups in India. In: Holloway RL (ed) Primate aggression, territoriality and xenophobia: a comparative perspective. Academic Press, London New York, pp 185–210

Sparks J (1967) Allogrooming in primates: a review. In: Morris D (ed) Primate ethology. Weidenfeld and Nicholson, London, pp 148–175

Struhsaker T (1967) Social structure among vervet monkeys *(Cercopithecus aethiops)*. Behaviour 29:83–121

Trivers RL (1971) The evolution of reciprocal altruism. Q Rev Biol 46:35–57

Vandenbergh JG, Vessey S (1968) Seasonal breeding of free-ranging rhesus monkeys and related ecological factors. Reprod Fertil 15:71–79

Varley M, Symmes D (1966) The hierarchy of dominance in a group of macaques. Behaviour 26: 34–75

Vessey SH (1971) The ranging rhesus monkeys; behavioural effects of removal, separation and reintroduction of group members. Behaviour 60:216–227

Waal F de (1975) The wounded leader: a spontaneous temporary change in the structure of agonistic relations among captive Java monkeys *(Macaca fascicularis)*. Neth J Zool 25 (4): 529–549

Waal F de (1977) The organization of agonistic relations within two captive groups of Java monkeys *(Macaca fascicularis)*. Z Tierpsychol 44:225–282

Wade TD (1976) The effect of strangers in rhesus monkey groups. Behaviour 66:194–214

Washburn SL, De Vore I (1961) Social behavior of baboons and early man. In: Washburn SL (ed) Social life of early man. Viking Fund, Publications in anthropology, no 31. Werner-Gren Foundation, New York, pp 91–105

Wilson P, Boelkins RC (1970) Evidence for seasonal variation in aggressive behaviour by *Macaca mulatta*. Anim Behav 18:719–724

Watson JB (1908) Imitation in monkeys. Psychol Biol 5:169–178

Zuckermann S (1932) The social life of monkeys and apes. Kegan Paul, Trench, Trubner and Co Ltd, London

Zumpe D, Michael RP (1970) Redirected aggression and gonadal hormones in captive rhesus monkeys *(Macaca mulatta)*. Anim Behav 18:11–19

Problems in Representing Behavioral Space-Time

D. Quiatt, J. Everett, S. Luerssen, and G. Murdock [1]

Two related models of spatial organization which dominated primate behavior literature in the 1960s and remain influential are the *oikean* or concentric circle model used by Imanishi to describe Japanese macaque troop organization (Fig. 1), and the baboon "march formation" put forward by DeVore (Fig. 2). It might be argued that properly speaking they are not models of physical spatial relations at all but, by intent, sociometric representations or geometric metaphors designed to convey ideas about hierarchical order and allied functional organization in primate troops. They do convey such ideas. They are loaded with implications about dominance relations, sexual behavioral dimorphism, functional organization of same-sex age classes, and, more generally, the purpose and meaning of primate group life, but what they communicate about spatial arrangements of individuals in time is debatable.

It is conventional in many disciplines and for a variety of purposes to represent individual entities as space-consuming "point-objects", with a position in space-time which is, at least in theory, exactly definable (Lenntorp 1976). When the temporal dimension is assumed to be insignificant, as in a single observation or a set of observations in a very thin slice of time, individuals may be depicted as stationary points on

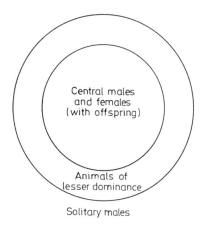

Fig. 1. Concentric circle model of Japanese monkey social organization. (After Imanishi 1960, 1963)

1 Department of Anthropology, University of Colorado at Denver, 1100 Fourteenth Street, Denver, CO 80202, USA

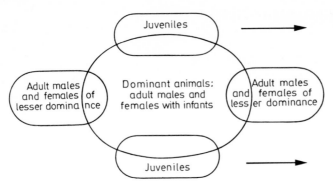

Fig. 2. Organization of baboons during group movement. (After Hall and DeVore 1965)

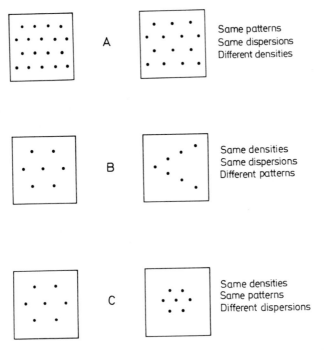

Fig. 3. Pattern, density, and dispersion of geographic facts. (Source: Dacey 1973). *Pattern* = Areal or geometric arrangement of geographic facts within a study area without regard to size of study area. *Density* = Overall frequency of phenomena within a study area relative to size of study area. *Dispersion* = Extent of spread of geographic facts within a study area relative to size of study area

an upended horizontal plane, the vertical dimension left out of account. Distribution of individuals in space is frequently so displayed by ecologists, geneticists, demographers, and, for that matter, ethologists. Figure 3 provides a generalized example of this practice and illustrates also three aspects of spatial distribution which it is sometimes useful to distinguish: pattern, density, and dispersion.

We may also be interested, especially when examining the distribution of *animals* in space, in questions of regular vs irregular distribution, and in whether individuals are more likely to be found in relative isolation or in groups (Fig. 4). Clustered distribution of course is not the same kind of logical alternative that regular and irregular distribution are for each other; clusters of individuals can be distributed on either a regular or irregular basis, as can individuals.

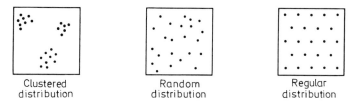

Clustered distribution   Random distribution   Regular distribution

Fig. 4. Clustered, random, and regular spatial distributions. (Source: Dacey 1973)

While such representations of entities as point-objects in *timeless* space has its uses, e.g., to show how the distribution of organisms may be affected by that of food specie, they provide little information about behavior per se or about ongoing relations between individuals. Primates are mobile organisms with strong affinities for particular others, and it is almost always of interest to behaviorists not just whether, at a given moment in time, they happen to be distributed regularly or irregularly, and in isolation or in clusters, but whether regular patterns may emerge from irregular distribution, whether clusters may form or break up, and whether clusters more or less constant in number will be similarly constant in membership.

Such questions are related to practical geographic concerns for "packing" or "budgeting" space (Hägerstrand 1973). The geographic facts of distribution such as those in Fig. 4 may consist of a number of individuals whose locations are fixed by an observer at one time, of a time sample of one individual with several fixes of location, or, similarly, of a time sample of more than one individual. Intuition suggests that for most species of mobile organisms, including primates, the three sampling procedures would produce different results. We know of no practical studies of this sort of thing, but it is unlikely for instance that a sample over time of the same individual's locations in space would show either a random or a very evenly spaced distribution — for an individual displaying preferential use of space the distribution must be clustered. For a social group of individuals with similar but not identical patterns of preference, a series of locations over time would yield a pattern which contained larger clusters (as compared with a series for one individual member of such a group) with irregular shading: dense cores, more gray areas, fewer white spaces.

A variation of Galton's problem is involved here: overlapping preferences in use of space cannot be considered wholly apart from preferential association of individuals; and if nothing else directed our attention to the question of how interactional and spatial associations are linked in time — that is, if we were unaccustomed to thinking of individuals as anything *more* than point-objects in space — a consideration of these

sample differences would do it. Of course, we know that primates show preferences of
many sorts in their behavior. What we want to get at eventually, for a thorough
understanding of the social dynamics of primate groups, is how preferential associations (and the converse) are maintained over time and how individual-individual associations link up in a systematic way to provide continuity to larger group structure.
An appropriate tool to begin with, to assess in a general way the use of space by individuals and groups, and to compare that of individuals *in* groups, is cluster analysis of
time-sampled individual locations.

    Quiatt, in an early study of rhesus monkeys in a 1/4-acre enclosure on Parguera
Island, P.R., obtained positional fixes at regular intervals and made a conventional
comparison of use of space by individuals in a group of ten. Figure 5 shows overlapping use of space by a mother and two of her offspring, a 2-year old female and
a 3-year old male in that group. Overlaying use patterns of all ten individuals (not
shown) provided a picture of use of space by the group as a whole, and overlaying
smaller combinations of individuals afforded comparison of greater and lesser degrees
of overlap.

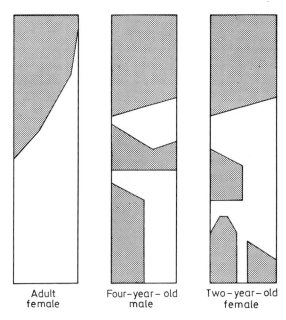

Adult   Four-year-old   Two-year-old
female   male   female

Fig. 5. Overlapping use of space by
three individuals (a mother and two
of her offspring) in a ten-member
group of rhesus monkeys, *Macaca
mulatta* (Quiatt 1966). *Shaded area*
indicates heavy use of 6' x 24' surface of a pole-and-wire structure in
a 1/4-acre outdoor enclosure,
Parguera, P.R.

    In such a comparative procedure the object is to generate statements about temporal
duration, to pick apart the strands of association in time which make up the fabric of
ongoing group life, from simple spatial data. We note below (in connection with a
suggestion by C. Ray Carpenter) the limited utility of such statements, but it will be
useful here to draw a distinction between "relative" and "absolute" measures of
spatial relationships. Relative spacing is appropriate for unbounded sites, for natural
or open settings for which there may be no conveniently fixed dimensional axes

(except the vertical). In the absence of these, one is reduced to estimating an individual's distance from (or noting his position with respect to) fixed or floating features of the environment, including other individuals. Spatial data from repeated sightings can then be summarized in several ways, e.g.:

1. Proportion of instances in which an individual was observed within or without some radial area around feature A or individual B (or, by setting a radius around a focal subject, as is more usual, one can obtain an index to individual spatial associates by counting "ins" and "outs").

2. Mean distance over time between subject and feature A or individual B. This is a useful measure, but difficult to obtain in natural settings and, even in circumstances which permit its use, too cumbersome to be practical for groups larger than dyads or triads in a relative spacing situation where coordinates cannot be obtained.

3. Grouping patterns as in the older models of social space (e.g., those of Imanishi and DeVore), but we suspect that those are not so much the products of systematically collected and routinely summarized spatial data as they are impressionistic, idealized representations with biases that are difficult to isolate and correct for.

Absolute spacing affords much the same data as do relative spacing measures, but, in the bounded and frequently rectilinear world of enclosures, where coordinate grids permit quick and accurate fixes of individual locations, spatial data can be recorded easily and more efficiently; and distances between individual locations fixed on a scale plan can be measured at leisure. For the ten-individual group from which were derived the clusters in Fig. 5, Quiatt obtained mean distances between all group members under various circumstances and noted the effect of time of day, removal of individuals, addition of new members by birth, etc., again generating statements about process from simple spatial data. In this paper, we are more concerned with what such data do *not* reveal.

Carpenter long ago suggested that mean distance between individuals can be treated as an operational measure of strength of attachment, i.e., "positive interactional motivation and conditioning" (Carpenter 1952). He also suggested that the standard deviation of such measures provides a measure of stability of individual-individual attachment. It seems to us that this is pushing simple spatial measures about as far as they will go, probably further. It is at this point, extrapolating from strictly spatial information (albeit derived from time samples) to statements about the quality of ongoing interactional relations, that one risks overworking two-dimensional point-distributional data. Whether we regard space-time as the context in which behavior occurs or as properties of extension and duration that are for many purposes better considered as congruent with behavior processes, we need the temporal dimension in our models of primate use of space, and we need it as much for description as for analysis, to secure for record and for heuristic organization of data descriptive access to the processual nature of the activities, social or otherwise, of mobile, decision-making organisms.

A simple way of building (smuggling?) time into graphic models of spatial deployment is to substitute the temporal for the vertical dimension in diagrammatic representations. In popular accounts of relativity theory there is a long-standing convention of so depicting the movements of heavenly bodies and atomic particles in space-time (Fig. 6). More recently, the geographers Torsten Hägerstrand, Bo Lenntorp, and

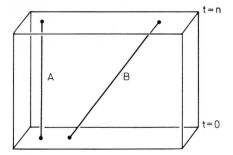

Fig. 6. Diagram of two particles in space *(vertical lines)* and time (an unspecified number of horizontal planes between $t = 0$ and $t = n$ representing instantaneous "position readings"). Particle A is at rest. Particle B is moving at a constant velocity. (After Geroch 1978)

Tommy Carlstein, in their association with the Lund school of geography, have been studying human actors and human decision-making in the transformation of geographic systems in a way that seems to us directly relevant, from a methodological view, to more general questions of animal use of space. They have taken the individual as their focal unit, looking at individual behavior "as an unbroken sequence of actions", at the "connections between large-scale . . . expressions of human action and . . . the microspaces of individual technology and face-to-face cooperation", and at "the give and take of social costs and benefits", which they suggest are "so strongly associated with minute locational acts that it is necessary for spatial analysts to apply the best magnifying glass in order to detect them" (Hägerstrand 1972).

Lenntorp, studying sequences of individual activity without concern for social interactions, has followed the convention of substituting time for the vertical dimension to depict individual paths through three-dimensional space-time (Lenntorp 1976). We quote Hägerstrand again: "If the individual does not move in space, this path is parallel to the time axis. Movement in space gives rise to an angle between the time axis and the path — the higher the velocity, the wider the angle". Lenntorp's work provides the fullest presentation of this approach in geography that we know, but it centers on the individual in the absence of other individuals and is not designed to provide information about social behavior. In ethology, Fischer's discussion of phases of the animal path (Fischer 1971), though somewhat of tour de force, touched on some analogous concerns, and Ted Grand has been assessing the sensory input and decision junctures associated with his route to work at the Oregon Primate Center, using independently much the same conceptual approach as Lenntorp and Hägerstrand but not the same notation or time-space structure (Grand, pers. comm.).

Recently, we conducted a short-term study of orangutans in a small indoor enclosure at the Denver Zoo, in which observers working simultaneously and employing different "clocks", one chronological and three behavioral, recorded locations of individuals in a group that contained one adult male and two adult females, one with an offspring aged 1.5 years. In several series of 20-min and 1/2-h observation periods, one observer recorded locations of every individual in the enclosure every 30 s, while a second observer recorded locations of all individuals each time the mother changed her location (moved more than one foot and then remained within a one-foot radius for more than 5 s), a third keyed the fixing of locations to similar changes by the infant, and a fourth keyed to changes in location by any member of the group.

All observers recorded locational fixes at 2 1/2-min intervals as a test of interobserver.

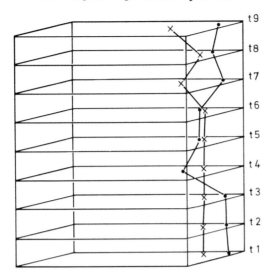

Fig. 7. Locations of orangutan mother *(X-line)* and offspring at 2 1/2-min intervals over a 20-min observation period

reliability and to integrate the clocks on an ongoing basis. Our analysis of these observations is far from complete, but we present a simplified representation of integrative chronologically keyed records from one series (Fig. 7), for the mother-offspring dyad only, just to give an idea of what space-time paths of individuals in this group look like when velocity is constant over time. In this projection the X-axis is rotated considerably and the Y-axis is tilted slightly from the recorder's standpoint. For purposes of comparison, perspective can be manipulated with finer control, and we remind the reader that different behavioral clocks may generate different paths for both mother and offspring between, e.g., *t7* and *t8* in Fig. 7. While physicists and geographers, in their use of a representational space-time structure of three dimensions, assume a constant velocity in time, it is not at all clear that that is an appropriate assumption for behavioral scientists to make. It seems to us that for a given individual time asleep is not the same as time awake, as far as constancy of relationships with others goes, nor, perhaps more obviously, is time spent quietly resting the same as time spent grooming or fighting. Students of behavior may prefer to tie observations of individual movement in space to activities, so that the velocity measured is variable instead of constant (and it is likely, in any event, that we will *see* it as variable).

We assume, further, that observers of groups of primates bring to their projects different cognitive structures deriving from different theoretical bases, and that these cannot help but affect the allocation of attention to specific individuals within the group. Thus, even slightly different assumptions concerning the role of mother, for instance, with respect to offspring, might be expected to bias an observer toward one or another apperception of how individual relations and activities are organized in the group in time and space. Is the mother viewed primarily as a source of food and stimulation necessary to normal development of her infant, a sort of subsistence station to which the young individual, active in his own right, must return from time to time? Is the infant viewed as, at least initially, a more passive recipient of information about the environment, much of it filtered through the mother? Or is a mother a more dynamic mediator of environmental stimuli, an integrator rather than a filter?

Difficult questions of meaning are embedded in issues such as these, and we cannot expect to deal with them as rigorously as we might wish. The representational technique with which we are experimenting is not a predictive model but a device for setting down relationships concretely and in temporal extension. It has its most obvious application in enclosed settings where, as we noted earlier, the use of coordinate grids allow absolute fixes of location to be recorded with easy efficiency. The cost of that efficiency is well known and heavy — we refer to those general limitations associated with results derived from small, unnaturally formed groups of primates in artificial enclosures with predominately flat surfaces. But one benefit of absolute spacing is that, apart from the question of whether it may afford greater or less insight than relative spacing into the behavior of subject animals, it lends itself as a tool for examining the behavior of the observer. Using it, we have become more conscious of something which no doubt everyone knows to begin with, and which is that (to quote Tommy Carlstein) "the way in which the real world is chopped into entities for sampling is intimately related to how the same pieces can be put together again in order to make generalizations about the workings of the system as a whole . . . . In its essence, all sampling entails cutting the real-world cake into some kind of slices and there are many implications of slicing a compound total reality in different ways." (Carlstein and Thrift 1978). If we are to understand those implications and have confidence in the generalizations we make about the workings of social behavior systems, it is of first importance to question the various ways in which we go about slicing up the "real-world cake".

Acknowledgment. This paper derives in part from studies conducted in the Primate House of the Denver Zoo. We thank Clayton Freiheit, Zoo Director, for use of facilities.

References

Carlstein T, Thrift N (1978) Towards a time-space structural approach to society and environment. In: Carlstein T, Parkes D, Thrift N (eds) Timing space and spacing time, vol II. Human activity and time geography. John Wiley and Sons, New York

Carpenter C (1952) Social behavior of nonhuman primates. Colloq Int Centre Nat Rech Sci, vol 34. Reprinted in naturalistic behavior of nonhuman primates. Pennsylvania State University Press, University Park

Dacey F (1973) Some questions about spatial distributions. In: Chorley RV (ed) Directions in geography. Methuen, London

Esser AH (ed) (1971) Behavior and environment, the use of space by animals and men. Plenum Press, New York

Fischer F (1971) Ten phases of the animal path-behavior in familiar situations. In: Esser AH (ed) Behavior and environment. Plenum Press, New York

Geroch R (1978) General relativity from A to B. University of Chicago Press, Chicago

Hägerstrand T (1973) The domain of human geography. In: Chorley RV (ed) Directions in geography. Methuen, London

Hall KRL, DeVore I (1965) Baboon social behavior. In: DeVore I (ed) Primate behavior: field studies of monkeys and apes. Holt, Rinehart and Winston, New York

Imanishi K (1960) Social organization of subhuman primates in their natural habitat. Curr Anthropol 1:393–407

Imanishi K (1963) Social behavior in Japanese monkeys, *Macaca fuscata.* In: Southwick CH (ed) Primate social behavior. Van Nostrand, Princeton NJ

Lenntorp B (1976) Paths in space-time environments, a time-geographic study of movement possibilities of individuals. Lund Stud Geogr Ser B. Human Geogr No 44

Quiatt D (1966) Social dynamics of rhesus monkey groups. Ph D Dissertation, Ann Arbor, Univ Microfilm

Courtship and Mating Behavior of Wild Orangutans in Sumatra

C.L. Schürmann [1]

All field studies describe the orangutan as an animal with a predominantly solitary life style and a low frequency of social interaction. It is not really surprising therefore that, despite all the field work in the past 15 years, literature still provides little factual knowledge about the social behavior and the reproductive behavior of this species. It is especially remarkable that previous field studies contain very few observations of copulations. Copulations by subadult males have been reported by MacKinnon (1974) and Rijksen (1978). Matings by adult males have been seen by Galdikas (1978) and by myself. Between June 1975 and April 1979 I studied a wild orangutan population in Ketambe in the Gunung Leuser Reserve in Sumatra. The study focused on the animals' social behavior and as part of this study I was extremely lucky to have the opportunity in the field to make an extensive detailed observation of courtship and mating behavior. So far only part of the data has been worked out, so I shall restrict myself in this paper to giving a qualitative account of the courtship and mating behavior.

Subjects and Method

In the course of my study I encountered altogether 34 different individuals in the research area, which covered 5 km^2. From this population I studied 17 animals intensively by following each individual for several days (2—40) in succession and making a continuous and detailed sequential protocol of their behavior. The field data, consisting of 4200 h of observation, are recorded partly in small notebooks and partly on tape. Perhaps I should remind the reader that the Sumatran orangutan is almost completely arboreal. Therefore, all the described behavior took place up in the trees.

1 Laboratory of Comparative Physiology, State University of Utrecht, Jan van Galenstraat 40, 3572 LA Utrecht, the Netherlands

Adult Male-Female Relationships

A few members of the population, namely the adult male Jon, two subadult males and three females, were frequently involved in social and sexual interactions for several months. One of these females is the young female Yet. From my study and from the data of my predecessor Rijksen (1978), I have a record of the socio-sexual development of this female from adolescence into adulthood over the past 7 years. This was a slow and very gradual process of developing relations between this maturing young female and several males. Young subadult males were the first to show interest in Yet in that they tried to form a consort with her. A consort is a relationship in which the male and female travel together and show coordination in their behavior for several days. Such consorts have been described previously by MacKinnon (1974) and Rijksen (1978). The purpose of a consorting subadult male seems quite obvious. The male often tries to induce the female to copulate. Characteristic is the repeated touching and smelling of the female's genitals. In response to this the female may present to the male who then usually mounts and copulates with her.

In other occasions subadult males initiate copulations more forcefully. These "rapes", as they have been called by MacKinnon (1974), typically occur in short encounters, whereas cooperative copulations are observed during consorts. The female Yet was involved in a considerable number of consorts. During my study period her partners included at least four subadult males. She showed a clear preference for the bigger males, in particular for the biggest one in the area: the adult male Jon. From adolescence onwards Yet was already keenly interested in the adult male Jon, but it took a long time, namely at least 5 years, for her to build up a relationship which involved consortship and mating with him. As an adolescent female, Yet often tried to attract the attention of Jon by using various kinds of soliciting behavior. She moved about in his vicinity, looked at him, approached him and touched him. At first Jon avoided all these advances, but gradually he began to show more tolerance towards her. In view of the reported solitary attitude and the supposed intolerance of particularly the adult male towards his conspecifics, this tolerance was remarkable. Yet would often feed very close to Jon and sometimes she was allowed to pick some pieces of fruit directly out of his hand. Gradually, during many encounters in the course of several years, Yet's soliciting behavior increased, turning into more overt proceptive behavior. She often presented in front of Jon, but initially Jon merely looked at her. She touched Jon more often, investigating his genitals manually and sometimes orally.

It was not until the last year before Yet conceived that Jon started to react to Yet's proceptive behavior with "male presenting", which can be described as follows: Jon from an upright sitting position usually extended his arms and legs and bent backwards till he almost lay on his back. This particular pattern of presenting was only observed in the adult male Jon; it was never seen in subadult males. In response to this male presenting Yet would touch Jon again, look at him and position herself in a hanging posture above or in front of him and lower herself on his penis, often aiding intromission with her fingers.

Female Yet not only took the sexual initiative in most copulations with Jon (of which I saw about 40), she also was the active partner and did all the pelvic thrusting, whereas Jon remained completely motionless and looked away. Most copulations

Fig. 1. The female Yet *(left)* mounts the adult male Jon who performs "male presenting"

Fig. 2. Female Yet *(left)* mates with the adult male Jon in a ventro-ventral position. Jon is quietly sitting on a branch, while Yet is active in copulation

took some 15 min or more. Positions varied greatly. Most frequently seen was the ventro-ventral position, but often latero-ventral and dorso-ventral positions occurred during the same copulation.

Although Jon remained inactive even during his later copulations, he nevertheless became more interested in Yet, as was evident from his more active role in maintaining coordination. They formed a consort for two periods and in each showed an extremely high level of mutually coordinated behavior. These consorts lasted about 15 and 20 days respectively and occurred in consecutive months. During these consorts many copulations occurred, up to 24 in 10 days, reaching a peak in the middle of the consort periods. These mid-consort multiple copulation days of the two consort periods were 30 days apart. This fact and the progress of the consorts suggests a cyclicity in the behavior of the female which is most probably related to her ovulatory cycle.

Three weeks after the last copulations I noticed a swelling of Yet's nipples and vulvae. She was obviously pregnant. She became more solitary and avoided contact with males. About 9 months later this conception resulted in the delivery of a healthy infant.

Discussion

Despite 20 man-years of field work, the available literature provides few facts about orangutan reproductive behavior in the wild. The early data from the field suggested that copulations were forceful and were performed by subadult males. This even led MacKinnon (1974) to doubt the reproductive function of the adult male. Rijksen (1978) did observe cooperative copulations but only in semiwild subadult males and these were during consort relationships. I too recorded forceful copulations, but I found that the majority of sexual interactions were cooperative and occurred in a consort relationship. A close social relationship built up during consorts seems to be of importance for cooperative and probably also for successful copulation.

In previous field studies there has been a lack of observations of copulations of adult males. Consort formation and mating of adult male orangutans in the wild have now been observed, in Borneo by Galdikas (1978) and in Sumatra by myself. Although there appear to be many differences between the studied Borneo and Sumatran populations, the observed mating behavior patterns of the two subspecies show many similarities and seem comparable.

In my study it appeared that the adult male Jon did indeed have reproductive success where four subadult males had been unsuccessful. The lack of success of the subadult males is all the more remarkable because we know that female Yet was already menstruating 5 years before she conceived and she mated dozens of times with subadult males before she mated with Jon. But obviously none of these copulations with subadult males resulted in conception. This is really surprising and cannot yet be fully explained. The difference in success may partly be due to the longer duration of the copulations of the adult male, the higher frequency and the more adequate timing compared with the copulations of subadult males.

The adult male Jon is unquestionably the most dominant male in the area, the "alpha male". Although he may be able to exclude other adult males from the area, he certainly does not exclude the subadult males. Also, he cannot prevent subadult males from forming consorts with females in the same area. His dominant position allows him to maintain a consort, whereas subadult males may be forced by bigger males to give up a consort. Thus the reproductive success of the adult male is probably mainly the result of the female's preference. The female selects the adult male as her sexual partner and she chooses when to consort and mate with him. Since female orangutans show no visible estrus signs, it must be the changes in their behavior and, additionally, probably their genital smell which instigate the male to mate or at least to cooperate.

The well-known "long call" of adult male orangutans seems to serve as a means for the receptive female to locate the alpha male.

The observations on Yet and on a second young female show that such females display a great amount of proceptive behavior in their sexual contacts with the adult male. I observed Jon's copulations with an older multiparous female and she showed considerably less proceptive behavior.

The above information may suggest that the adult male is very reluctant to mate with young females. Males appeared much more interested in older females with offspring. It seems that the young female has to invest a lot of energy in order to induce the adult male to consort with her and to motivate him to mate with her. However, such strong reluctance on the part of the male to mate with a willing female seems hard to explain in terms of the optimal reproductive strategy of the male.

A second possibility is that the adult male's behavior reflects a strategy that minimizes the chance that a potentially willing female will be prematurely frightened off. In that case his reluctance is not so much a lack of motivation as cautious reservation, allowing the female to overcome her fear of the much bigger male. Nadler's recent investigations (this congress) seem to point to the second alternative. Whereas in conventional zoo test conditions male sexual behavior tends to resemble the forceful rapes in the wild situation, a simple change in the captive situation can drastically alter the male's behavior pattern. As Nadler's experiments demonstrate, if the female is given the opportunity to regulate her access to the male, she will avoid his forceful approaches but will take the initiative when the male adopts a waiting attitude. The "male presenting", as described above, can then be seen as restrained soliciting behavior on the part of the male, which may induce the female to venture upon further proceptive behavior. In previous studies there has been doubt about whether the adult male has a reproductive function at all. I conclude that indeed he has and is selected by the female to serve this function. This selection may partly explain the evolution of the marked sexual dimorphism in the orangutan.

Acknowledgments. This study was supported by a grant given by the Netherlands Foundation for the Advancement of Tropical Research (WOTRO) to Prof. Dr. J.A.R.A.M. van Hooff, to whom I am greatly indebted for supervising this study and criticizing this paper. I should like to thank the Indonesian Nature Conservation Service (PPA) and the Indonesian Institute of Science (LIPI) for giving me permission to do orangutan research in Sumatra. I am grateful to Dr. Westermann and the Netherlands Gunung Leuser Committee for their support and interest. I owe special thanks to Mrs. Sulaiman of Universitas Nasional in Jakarta and the biology students who participated in the field work.

References

Galdikas BMF (1978) Orangutan adaptation at Tanjung Puting Reserve, Central Borneo. Ph D Thesis, Univ California, Los Angeles

Horr DA (1975) The Borneo orang-utan: Population structure and dynamics in relationship to ecology and reproductive strategy. In: Rosenblum LA (ed) Primate behavior, vol IV. New York, pp 307–323

MacKinnon JR (1974) The behaviour and ecology of wild orang-utans *(Pongo pygmaeus)*. Anim Behav 22:3–74

Nadler RD (1977) Sexual behavior of captive orangutans. Arch Sex Behav 6:457–475

Rijksen HD (1975) Social structure in a wild orang-utan population in Sumatra. Contemp Primatol 5th Congr Primatol Nagoya 1974. Karger, Basel, pp 373–379

Rijksen HD (1978) A field study on Sumatran orangutans *(Pongo pygmaeus abelii* Lesson 1827). Ecology, behaviour and conservation. Ph D Thesis, Commun Agric Univ Wageningen

Rodman PS (1973) Population composition and adaptive organization among orang-utans of the Kutai Reserve. In: Michael RP, Crook JH (eds) Comparative ecology and behaviour of primates. London, pp 171–209

Responses of Wild Chimpanzees to Potential Predators

C.E.G. Tutin, W.C. McGrew, and P.J. Baldwin [1]

This paper reports the responses of wild chimpanzees *(Pan troglodytes verus)* to the presence of potential predators at Mt. Assirik, in the Parc National du Niokolo Koba, Senegal. Many field studies of wild chimpanzees have been made in the last 20 years but only a few reports have appeared on the responses of chimpanzees to potential predators (Gandini and Baldwin 1978, Izawa and Itani 1966, Itani 1979, Kano 1972, van Lawick-Goodall 1968, Nishida 1968, Pierce, unpubl.). The scarcity of such reports is due largely to the absence or rarity of predators large enough to present a threat to chimpanzees, in the majority of study sites. For example, at both Gombe and Kasoje in Tanzania where chimpanzees have been studied for 20 and 15 years respectively, leopards are the only potential predator and they are extremely rare.

At Mt. Assirik, four species occur which can be considered as potential predators of chimpanzees. These are lion *(Panthera leo)*, leopard *(Panthera pardus)*, spotted hyaena *(Crocuta crocuta)*, and wild dog *(Lycaon pictus)*. Not only is there a wider range of species than at any other chimpanzee field study site, but also the frequency of contacts is relatively high.

No confirmed report exists for predation on wild chimpanzees by any of these four species, but all are known to be capable of killing prey larger than chimpanzees. There is circumstantial evidence of leopard predation both on chimpanzees (Rahm 1967) and mountain gorillas (Schaller 1963). Rijksen and Rijksen-Graatsma (1975) reported that a clouded leopard *(Neofelis nebulosa)* killed seven orangutans at a rehabilitation centre. Leopard, which are adept at tree climbing, probably present the greatest threat to chimpanzees. However, given the extremely open nature of the habitat at Mt. Assirik, where less than 3% of the study area is gallery forest (McGrew et al. 1981), the terrestrial predators (lion, wild dog, and hyaena) must also constitute a considerable threat to the chimpanzees, since they are sometimes obliged to cross areas where trees are absent or sparse.

1   Department of Psychology, University of Stirling, Stirling FK9 4LA Scotland

Methods

The data were collected over a 44-month period on 1976–79 as part of a synecological study of the four species of diurnal primates *(P.t. verus, Papio papio, Cercopithecus sabaeus,* and *Erythrocebus patas)* at Mt Assirik. The climate of the area is characterised by a dry season (November–May) with maximum temperature of about 40°C and minimum of about 25°C; and a wet season (June–October) in which maximum is about 32°C and minimum around 22°C. Annual rainfall averages less than 1000 mm, making Mt. Assirik the driest and hottest site in which chimpanzees have been studied (McGrew et al. 1981).

The vegetation of the area has been described in detail by Baldwin (1979). Gallery forest of almost continuous canopy ranging in height from 10 to 40 m occurs in the steep-sided valleys of water courses and covers 2.7% of the study area. Woodland with discontinuous canopy and trees of 5–15 m covers 37%; bamboo and grassland with scattered trees, 32%; and open lateritic plateaux with scattered bushes cover the remaining 28%.

The chimpanzee population of Mt. Assirik is an isolated group of 26–35 individuals with a home range of between 278 and 333 km^2 (Baldwin et al. 1980a). They had not been studied prior to February 1976 and were, at first, very shy of humans. No artificial provisioning was employed and progress towards habituation to the presence of human observers was slow.

The response of chimpanzees to vocalizations or visual contact of the four species of potential predator were recorded throughout the study. Sightings of all large mammals were recorded systematically for 37 months, November 1976–November 1979, as were vocalizations of the four species of large carnivore.

Results

During the 37 months the four species of potential predator were seen or heard on 245 occasions: 29 of these were sightings and in the remaining 216 cases the predators were heard but not seen. Of the sightings 97% occurred in daylight, while 87% (188 of 216) of the vocalisations were heard during the night. The contacts are separated by species in Table 1.

Table 1. Contacts with four species of predators during 37 months (November 1976–November 1979)

Species	Sighting	Vocalizations	Total
Spotted hyaena	5	92	97
Lion	5	83	88
Leopard	9	39	48
Wild dog	10	2 [a]	12
Totals	29	216	245

a   Underestimated, as vocalizations not recognised reliably until June 1979

Table 2. Interactions between chimpanzees and potential predators during 37 months

Species	Response	No response	Total
Spotted hyaena	0	12	12
Lion	8	4	12
Leopard	6	5	11
Wild dog	1	0	1
Totals	15	21	36

The responses of chimpanzees to the presence of potential predators were recorded on 36 occasions (see Table 2). Of the 36 interactions 30 occurred during the hours of darkness when the chimpanzees were in their nests. All of these nocturnal and 4 of the 6 daylight interactions involved one or more bouts of vocalization by the potential predator(s). Visual contact between the chimpanzees and potential predator(s) was highly probable in 4 of the 6 daylight interactions. On 15 of the 34 occasions, potential predator vocalizations provoked an immediate response of loud calls (*wraaahs*, *waa barks*, and *pant hoots*, after van Lawick-Goodall 1968) from the chimpanzees.

Hyaena calls never provoked vocal response from chimpanzees. Only one close-range interaction occurred, when a group of vocalizing hyaenas passed below the nests of chimpanzees. In addition, more distant hyaena calls were heard on 11 occasions when chimpanzees were known to be nested within earshot.

On 6 of the 11 occasions that a leopard vocalized within earshot, chimpanzees responded with loud calls to some or all of the leopard's vocalizations. Leopard calls failed to provoke a vocal response from chimpanzees if the distance between them was greater than approximately 200 m (N = 6), although in three such cases chimpanzees did respond vocally to subsequent or earlier closer calls in the same series. On two occasions leopard calls within 100 m of chimpanzees produced no vocal response: In the first case, during daylight, four chimpanzees fled silently following leopard calls; and in the second case, a family group of an adult female and her two dependent offspring, who had nested alone, remained silent when a vocalizing leopard passed below their nests. On all of the six occasions that leopard calls did produce a vocal response, the distance between chimpanzees and leopard was estimated to be less than 100 m.

Responses to lion calls were less consistent. In the four occasions that lion roars failed to provoke a vocal response, the distance between lion and chimpanzees was twice greater than 1 km and twice 100 m or less. One of these latter cases involved the same family group mentioned above: Later on the same night a lion passed within 100 m of their nests but its roars provoked no vocal response. The other case involved a nested group of 15 chimpanzees who did not respond vocally to repeated lion roars less than 50 m from their nests. On the eight occasions when lion roars did provoke a vocal response, the distance between chimpanzees and lion(s) ranged from less than 50 m (N = 6 within 200 m) to greater than 1 km (N = 2).

Two prolonged daylight interactions were observed, one with a lion and the other with a group of wild dogs. The two interactions were very similar. Both began with calls from the potential predator(s) which were approximately 100 m from the chimpanzees. The chimpanzees, in both cases groups of mixed age-sex class composition including several adult males, responded with loud calls, following which the potential predator(s) moved closer to the chimpanzees. Subsequent responses by the chimpanzees included charging displays and a variety of loud vocalizations. With the continued approach of the potential predator(s) the chimpanzees climbed high in trees where they remained, uttering frequent loud vocalizations, until the potential predator(s) left the area.

Discussion

Previously published reports and the data from Mt. Assirik show that there is variation in the way that chimpanzees respond to the presence of large carnivores. The present study indicates that one important variable is the species of carnivore; for example hyaenas never provoked a response while three other species did, at least in a proportion of encounters. Another important factor seems to be the distance between the carnivore(s) and chimpanzees. In general, chimpanzees were more likely to respond vocally to leopards and lions if they were within 200 m. The loud vocalizations of chimpanzees may communicate to the carnivore that it is detected and induce it to move elsewhere in search of food. The data suggest that there are times when chimpanzees are too vulnerable to announce their presence and exact position, for example when group size is small or when no adult males are present; or, if the carnivore is very close when detected. In these cases, as when carnivores are a considerable distance from the chimpanzees, perhaps the best strategy is to remain silent.

This assumes that the large carnivores, with the possible exception of hyaenas, do represent a danger to chimpanzees: But how great a threat do they present to the chimpanzees of Mt. Assirik? While there is no definite evidence of predation, there can be little doubt that all four species are technically capable of killing chimpanzees. However, the threat would appear to be limited as, at Mt. Assirik, two of the predators (hyaena and leopard) are almost completely nocturnal and lions largely so. This is reflected by the high proportion of vocalizations which occur at night and by the comparative scarcity of sightings.

During the hours of darkness chimpanzees are in their nests and of the potential predators only leopards possess the ability to climb trees with any degree of skill. Gandini and Baldwin (1978) reported an arboreal encounter between a leopard and an adult female chimpanzee with an infant of 15 months. The chimpanzee, on discovering the leopard, approached it and chased it aggressively and quickly from the tree. This might indicate limitations on the arboreal abilities of leopards and no reports exist of leopards actively hunting in trees.

The ability of chimpanzees to climb and move through trees is an excellent protection against predators. However, the extremely open nature of the habitat at Mt. Assirik (McGrew et al. 1981), with less than 3% being forest, means that trees provide a refuge but rarely the possibility of escape. In the 28% of the habitat comprised of lateritic plateaux, trees are rare or absent. In the remaining 65% (woodland, grassland, and bamboo) trees can be sought for refuge, but a determined predator could follow a chimpanzee and wait below the tree. This situation would disturb the activity budget of a chimpanzee to a greater extent than that of a large carnivore whose normal pattern involves up to 20 h/day resting (Schaller 1972).

Thus, while tree-climbing does not provide complete protection it does give primates an advantage over other potential prey. Seven species of ungulates were common in the study area. In 4 years we discovered no evidence of predation on any primate but found adult ungulates killed by carnivores on six occasions. So, while it seems unlikely that the large carnivores actively hunt chimpanzees, they might be expected to take advantage of an easy opportunity to kill, arising from any lack of vigilance by the chimpanzee.

The two cases at Mt. Assirik when potential predators approached groups of chimpanzees, and reports of similar instances elsewhere (Itani 1979; Pierce, unpubl.), indicate that chimpanzees have a healthy respect and fear of large carnivores encountered in daylight. Thus, while carnivore vocalizations heard during the night present no great threat, close-range contacts during the day, especially in the open habitat of Mt. Assirik, are potentially very dangerous.

There are indications that coexistence with a varied and substantial population of large carnivores may have affected other aspects of the behaviour of the Mt. Assirik chimpanzees. Baldwin et al. (in press) found that chimpanzees at Mt. Assirik build nests higher in trees than those of Equatorial Guinea where there are no large carnivores. McGrew (in press) compared the meat-eating behaviour of different populations of chimpanzees and found that the Mt. Assirik population never prey on young ungulates or diurnal primates, in contrast with the chimpanzees of Gombe and Kasoje. He concluded that this difference might be a result of competition at Mt. Assirik from specialised predators, i.e., the large carnivores, which are extremely rare at the other two sites.

Acknowledgments. The authors are grateful to B. Alexander, J. Anderson, R. Byrne, S. Chambers, S. Hall, M. Harrison, S. Harrison, C. Henty, N. McBeath, M. Sharman for data collection; La Délégation Générale à la Recherche Scientifique et Technique and Service des Parcs Nationaux for permission to study in the park in Senegal; American Philosophical Society, Carnegie Trust for the Universities of Scotland, L.S.B. Leakey Foundation, Science Research Council, and Wenner-Gren Foundation for Anthropological Research for financial support of the field work in Senegal.

References

Baldwin PJ (1979) The natural history of the chimpanzee *(Pan troglodytes verus)* at Mt. Assirik, Senegal. Ph D Thesis, Univ Stirling

Baldwin PJ, McGrew WC, Tutin CEG (1980a) Wide-ranging chimpanzees at Mt. Assirik, Senegal. In prep

Baldwin PJ, Sabater PiJ, McGrew WC, Tutin CEG (in press) Comparison of nests made by different populations of chimpanzees *(Pan troglodytes)*. Primates

Gandini G, Baldwin PJ (1978) An encounter between chimpanzees and a leopard in Senegal. Carnivore 1:107–109

Itani J (1979) Distribution and adaptation of chimpanzees in an arid area (Ugalla Area, Western Tanzania). In: Hamburg DA, McCown ER (eds) The great apes. Benjamin/Cummings, Menlo Park, pp 55–72

Izawa K, Itani J (1966) Chimpanzees in Kasakati Basin, Tanganyika. Kyoto Univ Afr Stud 1: 73–156

Kano T (1972) Distribution and adaption of chimpanzees on the eastern shore of Lake Tanganyika. Kyoto Univ Afr Stud 7:37–129

Lawick-Goodall J van (1968) The behaviour of free-living chimpanzees in the Gombe Stream Reserve. Anim Behav Monogr 1:161–311

McGrew WC (in press) Animal foods in the diets of wild chimpanzees: Why cross-cultural variation? Carnivore

McGrew WC, Baldwin PJ, Tutin CEG (1981) Chimpanzees in a hot, dry and open habitat: Mt. Assirik, Senegal, West Africa. J Hum Evol 10:227–244

Nishida T (1968) The social group of wild chimpanzees in the Mahali Mountains. Primates 9: 167–224

Pierce A (unpubl.) An encounter between a leopard and a group of chimpanzees at Gombe National Park

Rahm U (1967) Observations during chimpanzee captures in the Congo. In: Starck D, Schneider R, Kuhn HJ (eds) Neue Ergebnisse der Primatologie. Gustaf Fischer, Stuttgart, pp 195–207

Rijksen HD, Rijksen-Graatsma AG (1975) Orang-Utan rescue work in north Sumatra. Oryx 13: 63–73

Schaller GB (1963) The mountain gorilla: Ecology and behavior. Univ of Chicago Press, Chicago

Schaller GB (1972) The Serengeti lion. Univ of Chicago Press, Chicago

Piagetian Assessment on Cognitive Development in Chimpanzee (Pan troglodytes)

M. Mathieu and G. Bergeron [1]

Many authors have stated that intelligence should be the main focus of comparative research, but even a few years ago we knew very little about the intelligence of non-human primates and we knew even less about species differences. We had access to many data on learning, delayed response, tool using in nonhuman primates but these data were not integrated in a comprehensive view of intelligence in man and animal (Bouchard and Mathieu 1976, Mathieu et al. 1980).

In the seventies a few researchers have started to study animal intelligence using Piaget's model of the development and organization of intelligence in humans. This model seemed the most appropriate for comparative study. Piaget considers intellectual functioning as a special form of biological activity and the basic principles of cognitive development (assimilation, accomodation, and adaptation) are the same as those of biological development. Piaget also gives a comprehensive description of cognitive development from the simplest behaviors like reflexes to the more complex intelligent behaviors. He gives clear behavioral criteria for the different stages, which is extremely important for comparative studies. Also it is true that no other developmental model offers insight into virtually all aspects of behavioral organization. Piaget provides not only a theoretical framework but also an objective method, focusing on behaviors, to observe development of intelligence in a comparative perspective.

As most studies on primate intelligence have focused on the sensorimotor period, this first period of cognitive development will be briefly outlined. Piaget (1936, 1937) describes six stages from almost complete lack of differentiation between the child and the external world to symbolic activity or mental representation. The child progressively constructs reality through his own actions. He constructs object permanence, causality, space, and time. He also adapts through imitation. Piaget also describes certain behavioral units typical of the sensorimotor period: the schemata, and the circular reactions. The capacity of representation characteristic of stage VI makes it possible for the child to take into account the invisible displacements of a hidden object, to infer a cause given its effect and foresee an effect given its cause. At this stage the child is able to invent new means through mental combinations. He can also imitate new behaviors with exact matching the first time and is capable of delayed or deferred imitation.

---

1 Département de Psychologie, Université de Montréal, Montréal, Québec, C.P. 6128, Succ. "A", H3C 3J7, Canada

Object permanence has been studied in chimpanzee (Mathieu et al. 1976), stump-tailed macaque (Parker 1977), gorilla (Redshaw 1978), and rhesus monkeys (Wise et al. 1974). Chimpanzee, rhesus monkey, and gorilla do attain stage VI. Although Parker (1977) and Redshaw (1978) did observe development of causality in the macaque and the gorilla, they did not assess stage VI, a very important stage linked to mental representation. Attainment of stage VI of causality was observed only in chimpanzee (Mathieu et al. 1980). In most of these studies only a psychometric approach was used and none has followed the full course of sensorimotor development.

The aim of the present study is to observe the cognitive development of four infant chimpanzees from the first weeks of life. This extensive longitudinal study implies the use of both the psychometric approach and the observation of spontaneous behaviors so as to get a clear picture of intelligence of nonhuman primates in a piagetian framework.

Method

Subjects

Four nursery reared chimpanzees served as subjects: two females (Sophie, now 4.6 years old, and Maya, 3 years old) and two males (Spock, 4.6 years old and Merlin, 3.6 years old). They were born in captivity and were brought to our laboratory soon after birth. The chimpanzees live in a mobile home on the campus of Université de Montréal. The older subjects, Sophie and Spock, were given surrogate mothers for the first 18 months. A full time caretaker and the members of the research team raised Merlin and Maya as well as Sophie and Spock after the surrogate mothers left. The chimpanzees spend most of their time in a large playroom equipped with monkey bars and with a large number of toys usually found in nurseries. In the other studies the subjects were zoo animals. Our subjects received more stimulation from their physical and social environment and, in this respect, they could more easily be compared to human infants.

Procedure

There are two main ways of assessing cognitive development: formal testing and direct observation of spontaneous behaviors in a freeplay situation.

Formal testing implies the use of tasks inspired by Piaget, systematized by Gouin-Décarie (1965), Goulet (1972), and Uzgiris and Hunt (1975) and, when needed, adapted to the chimpanzee. This approach could be called a psychometric approach. Scales have been devised for object permanence, causality, imitation, and space. Although this method is suitable for the assessment of the development of these four concepts, it does not permit to observe the emergence of the other important behavioral components described by Piaget (schemata, circular reactions, coordination of schemata). The observation of spontaneous behaviors in a freeplay situation allows for a more complete description of the organization of intelligent behaviors during a given stage. We feel that this coupling of methods provides the most accurate tool for the study of the development and organization of intelligent behaviors in different species.

Results and Discussion

The results of this study should answer the following questions: Do chimpanzees pass through the same developmental stages as human infants? If they go through the same stages, do they do so in the same order? At each stage do they show the same behavioral patterns? Do they show in the course of their development the main concepts described by Piaget? Do they all progress at the same rate?

Formal Testing

Chimpanzees pass through the same stages in the same order on the way to developing concepts of object permanence, causality, imitation, and space. They do show attainment of stage VI of object permanence and imitation, that is they are able to follow multiple invisible displacements and are capable of delayed imitation, behavior typical of stage VI. Although they do master some stage VI items of causality some of their responses differ from what is usually observed in human infants. Chimpanzees as well as gorillas (Redshaw 1978) do not often use other individuals as agents of action. The human infant does this with great facility but it was not frequently seen in the chimpanzee and never in the gorilla. Chimpanzees seem to center most of their attention and efforts on the toys but not always in a "causal" way. The items that were not mastered and that lead to noncausal responses (hitting, pushing, biting) dealt with the functioning of the toys. Chimpanzees succeeded with items involving a social agent or getting access to food or preferred objects (support, stick, rope). They showed little or no interest (or a different interest!) in understanding how to activate a windmill or how to have a firetruck go out of a firestation.

In summary, chimpanzees do attain stage VI of the four main concepts described by Piaget.

Observation of Freeplay Behaviors

Chimpanzees show the same order of acquisition as human infants and attain stage VI. In the first stages they develop the same schemata (hand waving, shaking, hitting, etc.). They also show primary and secondary circular reactions. The observed primary circular reaction were mostly related to sucking and locomotion. Secondary circular reactions are very numerous and quite similar to those observed in human infants.

Obs. 29. At 0:3 (13) Spock holds a rattle in his hand and waves his arm in many directions thus making noise. He stops, looks at the rattle, smiles (play face) and waves his arm again, stops, looks at the rattle, starts again . . . (11 times).

We also observed typical stage VI behaviors: differentiation of means and ends, use of known schemata in new situations.

Obs. 35. At 0:6 (7), Sophie, when Spock passes nearby holding a small plastic toy in his mouth, tries twice to touch the object, while remaining seated on the floor. As she does not succeed she stands up, grabs Spock's neck with one hand and pulls vigorously; Spock opens his mouth, dropping the toy on the floor. Sophie takes it and runs away.

Obs. 44. At 0:11 (12), Sophie, while the surrogate mother is out of the room, takes a "forbidden" diaper in the drawer and applies to it almost all her schemata: she drops it on the floor many times, folds and unfolds it a few times, rubs it around her on the floor in a repeated circular movement, puts her fists on it and walks rubbing the diaper on the floor, steps on it, jumps on it, hits with the hand and then the foot, puts the diaper on her head, climbs to the monkey bars and falls on the diaper, and has not finished when the videorecording is stopped (the whole incident has lasted 20 min).

Although we did observe many stage V and VI behaviors, they were less frequent and less varied than in the first stages. Chimpanzees do show tertiary circular reactions (active experimentation) but mostly with the "dropping" schema. They do not experiment on their environment as much as human children do. Again they do not seem much interested in the functioning of mechanical toys; most often they will not do more than serial application of known schemata which is typical of stage IV, or will simply give rough treatment to these toys.

However, we did observe many means-end coordination behaviors in order to get food or to go out of the room. Sophie, for example, could spend hours trying to unlock a very carefully locked door (and she would unfortunately succeed sometimes), or trying to open a purse. We also observed our subjects using pieces of furniture as support for reaching the window or the doorknob. Sophie would pull the heavy "monkey bars" structure for a distance of 2 or 3 feet in order to climb on it, thus being able to play with the light. In a few instances these new means were found by mental combination which is present in stage VI. But one has to be very cautious in assessing stage V and especially stage VI behaviors: it is very hard to know if it is real mental combination or if this means was acquired by trial and error (active experimentation) a few days before.

Finally some of the clearest and most interesting stage VI behavior involved a social agent.

Obs. 251. Sophie 2:6 (5) plays outside with the other chimpanzees and two human observers. At one point she heads toward a forbidden area, but comes back quickly. (At that time they showed fear when alone too far away from us.) She then goes to Spock who plays quietly (as usual) with grass, and grabs him from behind. He screams and quickly holds Sophie who can then lead him directly to the forbidden area.

Sophie 3:6 (0) is in the playroom with the other chimpanzees and one human adult while the caretaker cleans the floor, the door being opened. At one point Sophie takes the adult by the hand and leads him to a tunnel (4 foot high). When they have reached the end, she quickly goes out of the tunnel, goes out of the room, directly to the refrigerator (the tunnel being only 4 foot high the adult could not follow her rapidly).

These behaviors were more frequent than interactions with objects.

It is interesting to note that use of social agents, although infrequent in formal testing, was observed very often in freeplay behavior, but at a later age.

As far as time of attainment of the stages is concerned the psychometric and free-play results agree with a margin of 2 weeks which indicates the complementarity of these two modes of assessment of cognitive development. With both methods we also observed important individual differences, the two females showing many stage VI behaviors as early as 12 months, whereas the two males had a much slower development rate attaining stage VI as late as 24 months.

Conclusion

We can conclude that the piagetian model is useful in the description of development and organization of intelligent behaviors in nonhuman primates. It allows for a much finer comparison between species especially if both the psychometric and the observational approaches are used.

This study allows for relatively firm conclusions on development of human and chimpanzee infants. There is close similarity in the cognitive development of the two species: they both attain stage VI with the same number and the same order of stages, most of the behavioral patterns are similar (schemata, circular reactions, active experimentation) and, in the Piagetian framework, we can conclude at the existence of the beginnings of mental representation. The main difference lies in the scope of the repertoire, which suggests quantitative rather than qualitative differences between the two species.

In conclusion, the chimpanzee gives evidence for mastery of Piaget's stage VI representational skills, which are believed to be the critical foundation for symbol use in human infants (Bates 1976). The major contribution of our study is to show the spontaneous appearance of these skills in the chimpanzee.

References

Bates E (1976) Language and context: The acquisition of pragmatics. Academic Press, London New York

Bouchard MA, Mathieu M (1976) Analyse critique de la réponse différée on fonction de la notion d'objet chez Piaget. Can Psychol Rev 17:22–28

Gouin-Décarie T (1965) Intelligence et affectivité chez le jeune enfant. Delachaux et Niestlé, Neuchatel

Goulet J (1972) Notion de causalité et réaction à la personne étrangère. in: Décariel T (ed) La réaction du jeune enfant à la personnne étrangère. Presses Univ Montréal, Montréal

Mathieu M, Bouchard MA, Granger L, Herscovitch J (1976) Piagetian object-permanence in *Cebus capucinus, Lagothrica flavicauda* and *Pan troglodytes*. Anim Behav 24:585–588

Mathieu M, Daudelin N, Dagenais Y, Decarie T (1980) Piagetian causality in two house-reared chimpanzees *(Pan troglodytes)*. Can J Psychol 34:179–186

Parker ST (1977) Piaget's sensorimotor period in an infant macaque: A model for comparing unstereotyped behavior and intelligence in human and nonhuman primates. In: Chevalier-skolnikoff S, Poirier FE (eds) Primate bio-social development: Biological, social and ecological determinants: Garland, New York

Piaget J (1936) La naissance de l'intelligence chez l'enfant. Delachaux et Niestlé, Neuchâtel
Piaget J (1937) La construction du réel chez l'enfant. Delachaux et Niestlé, Neuchâtel
Redshaw M (1978) Cognitive development in human and gorilla infants. J Hum Evol 7:133—141
Uzgiris IC, Mc V Hunt J (1975) Assessment in infancy: Original scales of psychological development. Univ of Illinois Press, Chicago
Wise KL, Wise LA, Zimmerman RR (1974) Piagetian object permanence in the infant rhesus monkey: Dev Psychol 10:429—437

Brain, Sociobiology, and Evolution in Primates

H. Hemmer [1]

Socialization in primates can be understood essentially as a function of the information processing ability of the CNS, which can be roughly measured in terms of relative brain size in closely related species groups. Both the cephalization constant (Hemmer 1971, 1974) and the extra neuron number (Jerison 1964, 1973) may be used for relevant quantification, as there is a highly significant correlation of both parameters in primates (7 ape species: $r = 0.97$, 20 Old World monkey species: $r = 0.99$; Hemmer 1978). The author has shown in a previous paper (Hemmer 1979) close negative correlations of relative brain size and the social organization as expressed in troop size ($r = -0.92$) and of relative brain size and reproductive success in captivity ($r = -0.90$) in the genus *Lemur*. This has been discussed as reflecting changes in the level of sensibility to stressing influences (psychosocial tolerance) that is caused in over 80% by the informations processing ability. The lemur example led to the conclusion that the sociobiological place of each primate species may be seen as resultant from two opposite processes, both of them depending on progressive cephalization, i.e., decreasing psychosocial tolerance and increasing social learning plasticity, paired with aspiration to social ties. This resulted in an oscillation concept of social group evolution in primates. For progressive primate cephalization a continual change has been postulated between zones of high social tolerance, large social group size, high population density in relatively open habitats and relative evolutionary stability, and zones of low tolerance, small group size, low population density mostly in forest habitats and high evolutionary lability.

If this oscillation concept, which has been developed on the lemur basis only, really has the predicted general validity and importance for primate evolution, the basic social oscillation must be detectable in the whole primate cephalization series.

Methods

A first analysis of the original brain and body weight data in primates, as given by Bauchot and Stephan (1966, 1969), showed that the standard deviation of the cephalization constant that has been used here (for discussion see Hemmer 1971, 1974, 1978)

1 Institut für Zoologie der Johannes Gutenberg-Universität, 6500 Mainz, Saarstraße 21, Postfach 3980, FRG

scatters in the whole range from lemurs to apes around 10% of the mean cephalization values. The existence of this fixed ratio points to the necessity of logarithmic analysis of the whole cephalization series to bring out a periodic cycle of an oscillating variable. The logarithms of cephalization values in the primate series to be analyzed were arranged in classes with 0.05 intervals.

Two types of analysis, mostly known from studies of biological time series, have been used, i.e., autocorrelograms and power spectra (for the methods see, e.g., Strumwasser et al. 1967, Orlick and Mletzko 1975). These methods allow detection of cycles even if they are obscured by a high noise component. The two identical data sets necessary to compute the autocorrelation function were shifted half a unit out of phase. The power spectrum was calculated in unsmoothed and smoothed form. Significance was set as the double mean noise value.

The analyses were done for the frequency distribution along the cephalization constant axis of the primate species with an average feeding group size lower than four, i.e., small one-male, and mostly one-female families, and with an average feeding group size higher than ten, i.e., large and mostly multi-male groups. The data used here are those compiled by Clutton-Brock and Harvey (1977). The two sets were chosen to represent the minimum and the peak regions of the predicted oscillation. This oscillation should be found by the analysis in the same magnitude of values in both series if really present. The first series contained 25 species, the second 27 species for which both cephalization constants and feeding group size were known.

Results

The results of both autocorrelogram and power spectrum analysis confirm the basic postulation. There are significant periodic oscillations in both data sets. The calculated periods are given here as cephalization constant ratios by retransformation of the logarithms:

Analysis type	Autocorrelogram	Power spectrum
Feeding group size		
< 4	1:1.46	1:1.30
> 10	1:1.41	1:1.47
mean ± standard error	1:1.41 ± 0.04	

Extrapolations with the two values marking the ± range of the standard deviation of the mean (1:1.37 and 1:1.45) were done over the whole range of living primates starting with the cephalization values of the *Lemur* cycle used to establish the concept of oscillations. The *Lemur catta* value (3.8) was set as the starting point for calculating peaks, and the *Lemur variegatus* or *Lemur rubriventer* value (5.0) for foot points of the curve.

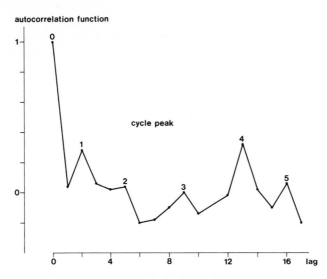

Fig. 1. Autocorrelation function plotted against the lag steps along the cephalization constant axis of primate species with an average feeding group size <4. This shows the autocorrelation cycle peaks

Extrapolated	Minima of psychosocial tolerance	Maxima	Minimum-maximum transition zones (overlapping)
at cephalization constant values:	0.8– 1.0	0.9– 1.1	0.9– 1.0
	1.1– 1.4	1.2– 1.5	1.2– 1.4
	1.6– 1.9	1.8– 2.0	1.8– 1.9
	2.4– 2.7	2.6– 2.8	2.6– 2.7
	3.4– 3.6	3.8	3.6– 3.8
	5.0	5.2– 5.5	5.0– 5.2
	6.9– 7.3	7.1– 8.0	7.1– 7.3
	9.4– 10.5	9.8– 11.6	9.8– 10.5
	12.9– 15.2	13.4– 16.8	13.4– 15.2
	17.6– 22.1	18.3– 24.4	18.3– 22.1
	24.1– 32.0	25.1– 35.3	25.1– 32.0
	33.1– 46.5	34.4– 51.2	34.4– 46.5
	45.3– 67.4	47.1– 74.2	47.1– 67.4
	62.0– 97.7	64.6–108	64.6– 97.7
	85.0–142	88.5–156	88.5–142

The extrapolated values near the *Lemur* basis, where the extrapolation inaccuracy is small, show that a minimum is followed here immediately by a new peak. The oscillation obviously follows not the type if a sinusoid, but rather of a sawtooth wave, as it was already indicated theoretically by Hemmer (1979: Fig. 13).

We always have to keep in mind in the following comparison of these theoretical extrapolated values with the mean cephalization values of primate species over their

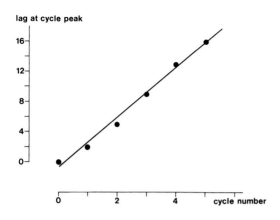

Fig. 2. Regression analysis of auto-correlation peaks of Fig. 1. r = 0.995

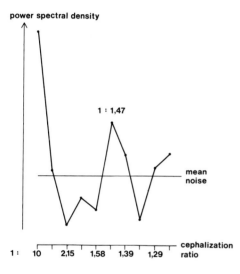

Fig. 3. Power species (unsmoothed values) on the basis of autocorrelation analysis along the cephalization constant axis of primate species with an average feeding group size > 10. The signficance limit at double mean noise is surpassed by the cephalization constant ratio 1:1.47

whole range that the same value in difference species need not mean the same biological situation, due to different sensory organ and brain organization. Thus exceptions to the predicted peaks and foot points must be expected to some extent. This is also the reason to restrict the comparison at first to the diurnal species.

Cephalization values of the monogamous callitrichids scatter between 2.5 and 2.7 in the genus *Saguinus*. They fit exactly an extrapolated minimum of social tolerance. The same also is true of *Callimico goeldii* (value 2.4). *Leontideus rosalia* (3.2) ranges toward the end of the next higher cycle, also in accordance with low social tolerance. *Callicebus moloch* (3.4) as well as the nocturnal species *Aotes trivirgatus* (3.4) fit the minimum of the same cycle, both species with very small one-male, one-female groups. *Saimiri sciureus* (4.9) approaches the end of the following, the diurnal lemur cycle, whereas *Saimiri oerstedii* with larger multi-male troop size than the former has a cephalization value (5.4) in the peak range of the next cycle. In the descending part of this cycle (maximum-minimum about 5.3 to 7.1) ranges the genus *Alouatta*

with the more tolerant species (largest troop size) *A. villosa* (6.6) in the middle zone
and *A. seniculus* (7.0) with lower troop size at the end. The multi-male troop species
of the genus *Cebus* (11.2–11.6) fit the peak range in a higher cycle, whereas the
connecting cycle seems not to be filled by recent cebids. *Ateles paniscus* (13.3) is
known for its breeding group, but not for its feeding group size. Assuming a similar
situation as in the other *Ateles* species with small feeding groups within larger breeding or population groups, this would also fit its cephalization place at the minimum
of the *Cebus* cycle. *Lagothrix lagotricha* (14.1) with larger troops fits the transition
zone to the next cycle peak.

The lowest cephalization rank in the cercopithecids is taken by *Cercopithecus
(Miopithecus) talapoin* (8.0). This species with very large multi-male troops just falls
in the peak level of the first cercopithecid cycle. In this cycle range some other *Cercopithecus* species, some *Presbytis* species and *Colobus guereza*. The mean feeding
group size decreases from *C. talapoin* (70) over the species with cephalization values
between 9.0 and 9.5 *(Presbytis obscurus, P. cristatus, P. melalophos, Colobus guereza:*
mean ± standard deviation = 17.5 ± 8.5) to the species with values between 9.6 and
9.9 *(Presbytis rubicundus, Cercopithecus mona, C. ascanius:* 9.5 ± 3). Thus they fit
exactly this extrapolated cycle. They are followed by a species with very small troops
(Cercopithecus cephus, 10.1), species with medium-sized troops *(C. mitis* / 10.1,
Macaca fascicularis / 10.2) and a species with large troops *(Colobus badius* / 10.2).
Thus the transition to a new cycle peak obviously is placed just in this range, quite
in accordance with the extrapolated transitional span. Next are species with large to
low troop size, multi- or single-male social structure and cephalization values between
10.6 and 11.5 *(Cercopithecus nictitans, C. aethiops, C. lhoesti, Colobus polykomos,
Nasalis larvatus).* The small-troop species *Cercopithecus lhoesti* and *Colobus polykomos* fit not this peak zone. Another fitting problem arises with *Presbytis entellus*
(12.9) ranging near the foot point of the extrapolated cycle. Transitional or peak
position is taken by the multi-male structured species *Cercocebus albigena, C. torqua-
tus, C. galeritus* (all 13.2), and *Macaca mulatta* (13.9). *Erythrocebus patas* (14.9)
with its large troops also joins here. The highly social species *Macaca nemestrina*
(15.6) and *Theropithecus gelada* (16.6) range at the end of this peak zone or at the
descending slope of this cycle. The genus *Papio* with species-specific single- or multi-
male troop structure and large to very large groups fits well in the transitional or
peak zone of the final cercopithecid cycle (cephalization values 19.8–20.2).

A main fitting problem is given in the apes by the genera *Hylobates* and *Symphalangus.* The cephalization values in *Hylobates* range from 12.0 *(H. agilis,* 12.8:
H. moloch) to 13.8 *(H. lar).* Cephalization in *Symphalangus syndactylus* reaches 15.5.
The essentially homogeneous social structure in all these species of lesser apes shows
no consistency with the extrapolated cycle minima. The predicted social situation
is given on the other hand in the larger apes, where the psychosocially low tolerant
Pongo pygmaeus fits a cycle minimum or a minimum-maximum transition zone
(cephalization value 28.4 calculated on the basis of the original adult weight speci-
mens as cited by Bauchot and Stephan, 1969, thus somewhat differing from the
earlier given value 30.1); the highly tolerant species *Gorilla gorilla* ranges more cen-
trally in the assumed peak zone (31.3), and *Pan troglodytes* reaches the downward
slope of this peak (35.5).

This comparison shows that there are only few exceptions that are not yet understood by the oscillation concept of social group evolution in primates. The best fitting to the real species data obviously is realized with the oscillation ratio 1:1.40, leading to the following extrapolated peak and foot points:

1.0\ /1.4\ /1.9\ /2.7\ /3.8\ /5.3\ /7.4\
   \1.3/ \1.8/ \2.6/ \3.6/ \5.0/ \7.0/ \9.8

  /10.4\ /14.5\ /20.6\ /28.6\ /40.0\ /56.0\
9.8/ \13.7/ \19.2/ \26.9/ \37.6/ \52.7/ \73.8

  /78.5\ /109.9
73.8/ \103.3/

Discussion

The results confirm the basic oscillation concept. It shows the never well understood distribution of group size across primates (see Clutton-Brock and Harvey 1977) in a new light. Progressive cephalization means progression of curiosity (Hemmer 1971), progression of childhood and youth span with more and more capacity and time for general (and especially social) learning (Hemmer 1974), thus progression of basic family size by an increasing number of juveniles from successive births, but also progression of sensibility to environmental, especially social cues. This should lead to a progressive increase of stress, as stress may be described as a function of environmental cues, and psychosocial stress of social cues. Thus progressive cephalization should result in progressive social intolerance to lower psychosocial stress, if social learning could not periodically stop and reverse this process by creating more elaborated social rules, social structures, social filters, that have to be passed forward as social traditions. Thus progressive cephalization necessarily results in a cycling process of declining social tolerance within each cycle and overcoming this decline by the rise of refined social rules and filters, to reach a new peak level on the basis of this learned behavior. This type of evolution demands increasing possibilities of social communication and thus derives differentiations in the morphological basis of facial expressions, signalling, vocalization etc.

The oscillation in social evolution produces primate species that aspire to social ties and are extremely tolerant to conspecifics. These join closely to large troops. The real size and structure of these groupings are surely governed by the environmental resources, as discussed by several authors (e.g., Crook and Gartlan 1966, Jolly 1975, Clutton-Brock and Harvey 1977). There are other primate species produced by this cycling process of evolution also aspiring to social ties but being rather nervous and extremely intolerant to conspecifics. Such species in forced groups suffer from social stress and live under natural conditions in some sort of everlasting social conflict holding a fairly large breeding population together in a large area, but hindering social grouping of more than a heterosexual pair at most. All other combinations of social tolerance and tie aspiration range specifically for individuals, populations, and species somewhere between these poles.

The system of balanced social grouping should be increasingly susceptible to disturbance of the social structure in the progressive sequence of cycles, especially for species ranging between the extremes on the cycle's slope. Outbursts of social aggression after serious disturbances of the social order, the habitual social filter, may be the result of the basic uncompensated intolerance in such situations. This may provide better explanations for strange-looking events in primate behavior, as, e.g., infant killing in langurs, than given by some current sociobiological ideas (for the langur example see Vogel 1979).

Man is also a primate. Thus man's sociobiology has its place within the cycling of primate social evolution. If large-brained primates must learn in their youth a wide range of social mechanisms allowing social life (also in psychosocially low tolerant species), the more this must be true for man. Thus if man is not forced by his social environment or has not the opportunity or is even prevented from learning in his youth, the elaborate filter mechanisms that allow him low aggression and low-stress social life, as they are postulated by the different systems of social rules, then aggressive reactions toward the conspecifics must be preprogrammed by his top position in primate progressive cephalization (cephalization value 104).

The broad brain variability (cephalization constant standard deviation about 10%) in primate populations gives each a pool of tolerance variability reaching over the whole span of a cephalization cycle. This provides the basis for selection in progressive cephalization, if it is not counteracted by social disqualification reactions of the groups toward their social outsiders. Thus progressive cephalization may be promoted best if habitat changes are possible, if new ecological niches can be gained by progressive outsiders. Less gregarious primates may be forced into the protection of better sheltering habitats, if they lose the social shield of large troops living in open habitat types. More gregarious primates may be turned out of the dense forests by their own multiple tie aspiration, as communication within large groups becomes easier in less dense habitats. The development of special adaptations to an ecological niche, to a special habitat type, hinders a later new change and thus may stop or delay further progressive cephalization in the evolutionary line in question. A part of all phyletic branches running through each cycle of progressive evolution therefore is filtered out from further brain progression by adaptive specializations. Thus the number of branches reaching higher cycles will be progressively smaller, if new radiations do not create new bases.

Conclusion

The oscillation concept of primate sociobiological evolution first deduced by the author on the basis of lemur sociobiology is verified using autocorrelogram and power spectrum analysis methods. It easily explains the distribution of social group size in the whole primate range and points to a close evolutionary network of a species' place in progressive cephalization, its habitat, its means of social communication and its troop size and social tolerance.

Acknowledgment. The author thanks Bernd Rosenbaum who did the programming and computer operations.

References

Bauchot R, Stephan H (1966) Données nouvelles sur l'encephalisation des insectivores et des pro-
simiens. Mammalia 30:160–196
Bauchot R, Stephan H (1969) Ecephalisation et niveau évolutif chez les simiens. Mammalia 33:
235–275
Clutton-Brock TH, Harvey PH (1977) Primate ecology and social organization. J Zool London
183:1–19
Crook JH, Gartlan JS (1966) Evolution of primate societies. Nature (London) 210:1200–1203
Hemmer H (1971) Beitrag zur Erfassung der progressiven Cephalisation bei Primaten. Proc 3rd Int
Congr Primatol Zürich 1970, vol I. Karger, Basel, pp 99–107
Hemmer H (1974) Progressive Cephalisation und Dauer der Jugendentwicklung bei Primaten,
nebst Bemerkungen zur Situation bei Vor- und Frühmenschen. In: Bernhard W, Kandler A
(eds) Bevölkerungsbiologie. Fischer, Stuttgart, pp 527–533
Hemmer H (1978) Socialization by intelligence: Social behavior in carnivores as a function of
relative brain size and environment. Carnivore 1:102–105
Hemmer H (1979) Beobachtungen zur Soziobiologie madagassischer Lemuren. Z Kölner Zoo 22:
43–51
Jerison HJ (1964) Interpreting the evolution of the brain. In: Garn SM (ed) Culture and the direc-
tion of human evolution. Detroit, pp 45–73
Jerison HJ (1973) Evolution of the brain and intelligence. Academic Press, London New York
Jolly A (1975) Die Entwicklung des Primatenverhaltens. Fischer, Stuttgart
Orlick M, Mletzko H-G (1975) Auswertung biologischer Zeitreihen mittels Fourier- oder Auto-
korrelationsanalyse. Biol Rundsch 13:265–276
Strumwasser F, Schlechte FR, Streeter J (1967) The internal rhythms of hibernators. In: Fisher
KC et al (eds) Mammalian hibernation, vol III. Oliver & Boid, Edinburgh London, pp 110–139
Vogel C (1979) Der Hanuman-Langur *(Presbytis entellus),* ein Parade-Exempel für die theoreti-
schen Konzepte der „Soziobiologie"? Verh Dtsch Zool Ges Jahresvers 72:73–89

A Case of Male Adoption in a Troop of Japanese Monkeys (Macaca fuscata fuscata)

L.D. Wolfe [1]

During the past few years interest among primatologists in male parental care has increased. In this paper I will describe a series of events which occurred in the Arashiyama B troop of Japanese macaques in the spring of 1978 that resulted in the third highest ranking male, Ran63, becoming the primary caretaker of two sisters — one 10 months of age and the other 22 months of age at the time of the adoption — and another unrelated male infant also 10 months of age at the time of the adoption. The term primary caretaker is being used here to define a situation in which (1) the mother is no longer available to be the caretaker, (2) the adoptee(s) maintain close proximity to the male while traveling, foraging or eating provisioned food and may even be carried by the male (although Ran63 did not in this case carry any of his adoptees), (3) the male protects the adoptee(s) from the aggression of other troop members, and (4) the male and the adoptee(s engage in grooming and huddling while resting and sleeping. Following the description of the adoptions, a series of questions involving altruism, kin selection, and reproductive strategies will be explored. It is hoped that by exploring these questions the behavior of Japanese macaque males toward motherless infants and juveniles will be better understood. Because of the rarity of such adoptions, the data are necessarily anecdotal. As an aside, adult Arachiyama females have not been observed adopting motherless infants.

The troop — the Arashiyama B troop — is a habituated, free-ranging tourist troop provisioned in a park located at Arashiyama near the west end of Kyoto, Japan. The troop has been under study by Japanese primatologists since 1954 and the genealogy is, therefore, over 20 years old. The observations described here were made by myself during a 1977—1978 study of the socio-sexual behavior of the troop and Yukio Takahata, a University of Kyoto primatologist, between 1975 and 1978. The observations are based on 50 h of a focal group study on Ran63 and the adoptees, and numerous ad lib observations.

Troop records on Arashiyama indicate that the adoption of a motherless infant or young juvenile by an adult male is not an unknown act. On the contrary, the records indicate that two other adoptions similar to the ones to be described here have occurred in the past. The first recorded adoption occurred in August, 1964, when an adult migrant male named W adopted a female infant named Shiro64 whose mother died. The second occurred in November, 1975, between Kusha63 (an adult male) and

1 Department of Anthropology, University of Florida, Gainesville, FL 32611, USA

Blanche58·73 (a 1 1/2 year old female) when the mother of Blanche58·73 died (B. Grewall, pers. comm.).

Moreover, adoptions have occurred in other troops of Japanese monkeys. For example, Alexander (1970) reported such an adoption in the Oregon troop of Japanese monkeys between a motherless female named Gamma and an adult male named Boris. There was also a paternal relationship in the Arashiyama West troop of Japanese monkeys between an adult male, Kojiwa59, and a motherless female named Kujiro65·70 (Linda M. Fedigan, pers. comm.) whose mother died in 1971. Interestingly, in all these cases the relationship carried over into adult life and mating avoidance was observed between the male adoptor and the female adoptee when the female reached adulthood (cf. Alexander 1970 for the case of Boris and Gamma; Wolfe 1979 for the case of W and Shiro64, and for the case of Kusha63 and Blanche58·73, and Kojiwa59 and Kujiro65·70; unpublished personal field notes). On the other hand, Arashiyama B adult males have only occasionally been observed carrying and caring for year old infants upon the birth of siblings, a form of male parental behavior which has been described as common among adult males in the Oregon troop (Alexander 1970) and the Takasakiyama troop of Japanese macaques (Itani 1959).

The Adoptions

One of the three adoptions of Ran63 involved an infant named Ai59·72·77, an offspring of a low-ranking female. In December, 1977, Ai59·72·77 was injured and lost the ability to support his weight on his forelimbs. Prior to the injury, he was almost weaned and quite independent of his mother. Following his injury, he was incapacitated and his mother allowed him to nurse again. Because he was unable to walk or to ride ventrally, he rode on his mother's back in an awkward jockey style. By the beginning of April, 1978, Ai59·72·77 had recovered to the extent that he was no longer nursing and could walk in a seemingly normal manner. He was, however, smaller than his age-mates and less capable of climbing and jumping (personal observation). On 12 April, Ai59·72·77's mother was captured at the base of the monkey park and subsequently sent to a medical research laboratory. From the time of the capture of Ai59·72·77's mother, Ai59·72·77 was to be found in the vicinity of Ran63 and the two young sisters whom Ran63 had adopted the previous month. Under the protection of Ran63, Ai59·72 ·77 was able to consume quantities of provisioned food he ordinarily would have been excluded from because of his low rank. By July he was the same size as his peers and appeared to have no visible locomotive handicaps. In addition to being groomed by Ran63, he was also groomed by the adopted sisters. The adoption of Ai59·72·77 will be further discussed after the events which led to the adoption of the two sisters are described.

For reasons unknown, in the fall of 1977, 17 members of the mid-ranking Kusha matrifocal unit and Kusha, the aged primogenitrix, began to spend their days toward the periphery of the troop and in the company of the Rakushi matrifocal unit and a semicentral adult male named Solitary76-1. By the end of February, the Kusha matrifocal unit had completely severed its relationship with the rest of the troop including the Rakushi matrifocal unit and was named Arashiyama C. On 18 March, two sisters of the Kusha matrifocal unit — one 10 months old named Kusha59·71·77, and the other 22 months old named Kusha59·71·76 — appeared at the feeding station with Arashiyama B monkeys. It is not known how or why these two sisters left their mother and the other members of Arashiyama C. For example, on 17 March 1978, the day before the sisters appeared at the feeding station, I observed Kusha59·71·77 being carried ventrally by her mother and the interactions between her and her mother seemed to be normal mother-infant interactions. Furthermore, the mother lived in apparent good health until her capture in July, 1978.

When Kusha59·71·76 and Kusha59·71·77 were first observed among Arashiyama B monkeys on 18 March 1978, they were following the Rakushi matrifocal unit and Solitary76-1. They were, however, chased and threatened. The next morning, 19 March, they were observed in the vicinity of Ran63. By the end of the day, Ran63 was grooming, huddling, and protecting them as they ate provisioned food. Both sisters followed Ran63 wherever he went. This association between Ran63, the two sisters, and Ai59·72·77 was still intact when I completed my observations in July, 4 months after the onset of the association.

Another 10-month old female member of Arashiyama C — Kusha69·77 — joined Arashiyama B in mid-April for 3 days and followed the Rakushi matrifocal unit and Solitary76-1. However, after being chased and threatened, she returned to Arashiyama C and her mother.

Altruism, Kin Selection and Reproductive Strategies

Altruism is one possible aspect of the parental care of Ran63 that needs to be considered. As for endangering the life of Ran63, I observed nothing besides the ordinary threats and chases that would indicate that the life of Ran63 was threatened by the presence of the adoptees. Furthermore, because the adoptor/adoptee relationship depends to a great extent on the following and approach behavior of the adoptee(s), there are no promiscuity costs to Ran63 as the adoptions do not interfere with his ability to mate with as many or as few females as might accept him. For these reasons, I do not believe that the actions of Ran63 can be considered altruistic, even though his actions were of benefit to the young monkeys.

Before questions concerning kin selection and reproductive strategies can be explored, it is necessary to discuss the genetic and social relationships between Ran63, his adoptees, and the mothers of the adoptees. In the case of Ai59·72·77, his mother can best be described as a submissive follower (as defined by Itiogawa 1973). That is, the mother of Ai59·72·77 was often in the vicinity of Ran63 and he protected her during aggressive interactions with other females. According to previous Arashiyama B researchers, Ai59·72·77's late grandmother had been a submissive follower of another male who is now dead (Y. Takahata, pers. comm.).

What then are the possible genetic relationships between Ran63 and Ai59·72·77? Because Japanese macaque females lack sex swellings and estrous cycles (Hanby et al. 1971, Wolfe 1979) and mate promiscuously, nothing is known of paternal relationships.

However, it is known that Ran63 and Ai59·72·77 are not matrilateral relatives. Because adult males generally do not mate with females as young as the mother of Ai59·72·77 was at the time of his conception (Wolfe 1979) or with their submissive followers (Y. Takahata, pers. comm.; personal unpublished field notes and also see Itiogawa 1973 on the submissive followers of the Katsuyama troop of Japanese macaques), Ran63 can be ruled out as the father of Ai59·72·77. Certainly, Ran63 and the mother of Ai59·72·77 were not observed copulating during the 1977–78 breeding season. It is quite possible, however, that Ai59·72·77 is a grandson of Ran63.

If, in fact, Ran63 and Ai59·72·77 are a grandfather-grandson dyad, are the actions of Ran63 toward Ai59·72·77 to be explained by kin selection? Unless one believes that related individuals can innately recognize one another as such (however, see Wu et al. 1980 for positive evidence) and/or that Ran63 could remember a mating with Ai59·72·77's grandmother 6 years previous to the adoption of Ai59·72·77 amid the 20 or so other females he has mated with each year since, the case for kin selection is not particularly strong. However, kin selection cannot be definitely ruled out.

In the case of Kusha59·71·76 and Kusha59·71·77, neither their mother nor their grandmother was a submissive follower of Ran63 and they shared no matrilateral relatives with him. Mating records, however, indicate that while the mother of the sisters was not a consort of Ran63, he has in the past mated with members of the Kusha matrifocal unit and could, therefore, be distantly related to the sisters as a grandfather or a great uncle (Y. Takahata, pers. comm.). No matings between Ran63 and the mother of the sisters were observed during the 1977–78 breeding season.

To what extent, therefore, can the behaviors of Ran63 toward the sisters be explained as examples of kin selection? As in the case of Ai59·72·77, kin selection can only be accepted as an explanation of the adoptions if Ran63 and either or both of the sisters are actually relatives — for which there is little evidence. If Ran63 and the sisters were shown to be relatives, however, one would still have to demonstrate that Ran63 and the sisters could innately make that judgment before kin selection could be fully accepted as an explanation of the adoptions. Interestingly, the sisters did have two high ranking great maternal uncles — Kusha63 and Kusha65 — in the Arashiyama B troop, neither of whom approached the sisters and the sisters were not observed approaching them.

There is another manner in which the adoptions of the sisters might be viewed as a reproductive strategy of Ran63; perhaps by adopting the sisters he is providing himself with loyal mating partners in the future. This prospect seems unlikely because if this adoption follows the behavioral pattern of past adoptions described at the beginning of this paper, there will be mating avoidance between Ran63 and the female adoptees.

Lacking unambiguous evidence that the actions of Ran63 can be explained as either kin selection or a reproductive strategy, the most parsimonious explanation is that the adoptions by Ran63 — and adoptions by other adult male Japanese macaques — are an epiphenomenon; an epiphenomenon of the sociality of Japanese monkeys.

Epilogue

An interesting paper on the evolution of male parental care by Werren et al. (1980) has just recently come to my attention. In that paper, by taking a mathematical approach derived from population genetics, the authors concluded that "only in mating systems where a parental male 'sacrifices' promiscuous matings (which parental Japanese macaque males do not) can paternity (i.e., parental confidence) influence the evolution of male parental care" (Werren et al. 1980, p. 619). In other words, Werren et al. found that systems of male parental care can develop which are not based on kin selection and parental confidence as long as that care does not interfere with the ability of the parental male to mate promiscuously. This finding of Werren et al. supports the above conclusion based on the available data on Ran63 and the adoptees that the parental care given to motherless infants by adult Japanese macaque males is probably not based on kin selection.

References

Alexander BK (1970) Parental behavior of adult male Japanese monkeys. Behaviour 36:270–285

Hanby JP, Robertson LT, Phoenix CH (1971) The sexual behavior of a confined troop of Japanese macaques. Folia Primatol 16:123–143

Itani J (1959) Paternal care in the wild Japanese monkey *Macaca fuscata fuscata*. Primates 2: 61–93

Itiogawa N (1973) Group organization of a natural troop of Japanese monkeys and mother-infant interactions. In: Carpenter CR (ed) Behavioral regulators of behavior in primates. Bucknell University Press, Lewisburg, p 229

Werren JH, Gross MR, Shine R (1980) Paternity and the evolution of male parental care. J Theor Biol 82:619–630

Wolfe L (1979) Behavioral patterns of estrous females of the Arashiyama West troop of Japanese macaques *(Macaca fuscata)*. Primates 20:525–534

Wu H, Holmes WG, Medina SR, Sachett GP (1980) Kin preference in infant *Macaca nemestrina*. Nature (London) 285:225–227

Parasitic Selection and Group Selection: A Study of Conflict Interference in Rhesus and Japanese Macaque Monkeys

C. Boehm [1]

Macaques, like baboons, regularly exhibit third party interference in dyadic conflicts. These most hierarchical primates are well known for forming alliances and coalitions, so presence of interference is not surprising. But as a risky helping behavior which prevents damage to other individuals and also reduces levels of agonism in a group, interference does present some special problems for explanation.

First, what are the selection mechanisms which foster such helping behavior, in cases in which interference entails obvious costs to interferers? Arguments of genetic selfishness including parental investment and kin selection do not fit with most data on interference; nor does the reciprocal altruism model. So, alternative selection routes must be considered, including parasitic genetic selection, a concept to be developed here, and group selection at the genetic level, which is to be discussed in conjunction with parasitic selection. Cultural selection at individual and group levels, while pertinent to the complete understanding of interference, is treated only with reference to future research.

A second problem for explanation is the "motivation" of monkeys which interfere to control conflicts of other monkeys. Elsewhere (Boehm 1979), in discussing the selection basis of "altruistic" behavior in humans, I have emphasized the need to consider not only overt behavioral outputs but *motives,* as well. After examining the various types of interference found in macaques, I shall apply a similar mode of analysis to this nonhuman species, differentiating between what I shall call "genetic altruism," and "psychological altruism." In venturing to discuss the motivation of monkeys without any very precise experimental operationalization of the psychological assumptions required, I shall be following Griffin's (1976) suggestions that the question of psychological awareness in nonhuman animals must not be avoided, as a bona fide issue for scientific ethological study.

By devoting attention to such speculation I hope to demonstrate that an advantage is obtained in more fully explaining the genetic selective basis for certain more complicated helping behaviors in macaques. For example, in the case of conflict interference, are we dealing with a highly preprogrammed *protective impulse?* With a genetically rather well-prepared *intolerance of social disruption?* With a conscious *sense of reciprocity* in forming political alliances? Or, perhaps, even with something

1 Department of Anthropology/Sociology/Philosophy, Northern Kentucky University, Highland Heights, KY 41076, USA

like a *sense of social responsibility to the group?* Any of these "motives" could result in interference behaviors helpful to other individuals. But while certain behaviors would be so strongly prepared by genes that in a human frame of reference they would be labeled "innate" or "instictive" or "compulsive", others would involve rather careful calculation, selection among alternatives, and the option not to interfere at all. I hope to demonstrate that even in macaques, such differences in "motivation" exist, and have large implications for selection process.

Social Control in Macaques

Interference is different from alliancing, in that interference serves as a social control, reducing agonism levels before individuals are injured in fights. Hall (1968) is one ethologist who uses explicitly the language of social control as applied to humans, to discuss social behavior of nonhuman primates. But Scott (1974) has pointed out, correctly, that human uses of agonistic behavior for very complicated control purposes are absent in other animals. His example is forced labor. Without making direct comparison with humans, Reynolds (1976) has discussed "control animals" on their own merits, using a characterization originally suggested by Bernstein's (1970) studies of captive macaques. It is clear that alpha males not only selfishly control other animals in terms of obtaining preferential access to resources (Popp and DeVore 1979), but also interfere impartially in conflicts in such a way as often to diminish agonistic levels, and occasionally "herd" other animals to safety by threatening them (Kurland 1977). The subtle role of dominant animals in controlling the direction of travel is also important, as is the role of alpha males in coordinating aggression in intertroop encounters.

Less dominant macaques, including females, also control the behavior of other animals. This is most notable when animals in the mother role control their charges, interceding in sibling conflicts which become more than playful. But macaque females (and less dominant males) also may control the behavior of animals dominant to them, by interfering in dyadic conflicts among adults. Altogether, a rather wide range of social control behavior is exhibited by this species.

In the interest of focusing on interference behaviors as a particular area of control, a typology is developed below to deal with the various forms of interference found in macaques. I shall concentrate chiefly on the Japanese and rhesus species, whose interference behaviors are best reported in a free-ranging condition.

Existing Typologies of Interference Behavior

The typology I have designed is based on a number of typologies in the literature of primate ethology. Van Hoof and de Waal (1974) found 17 types of triadic interactions in captive *Macaca fascicularis,* of which 11 occurred more than five times. The most frequent triadic events were:

1. *actor alliances:* the third party shows aggression in the same direction as the first aggressor;
2. *reactor alliances:* the third party shows aggression toward the first aggressor, in a protective role;
3. *retaliation:* the aggressee of the initial dyad passes on aggression to a third party (this also has been called "redirected aggression").

Later de Waal (1978) analyzed actor and reactor alliances, to find that in captive *fascicularis* (two groups), females form alliances which tend to help kin, while alpha males form alliances twice as often as the next group of animals, and help the victim 60% of the time in doing so. When alpha males intervene in actor alliances to help the original aggressors, this almost never brings the conflict to a rapid termination. Rather, the conflict ebbs until new, extra aggressors join in, when it becomes worse. Behaviors out of which this typology is built are similar to those of rhesus and Japanese macaques.

In the Japanese macaque, Kurland (1977, pp. 83—84) calls agonistic bouts in which a third party intervenes on behalf of the victim "defensive bouts," but he identifies as well a type of intervention by an animal dominant to the combatants, which "simply terminates the fight without preferential aid to either participant of the agonism" (1977, p. 92). He calls these "policing bouts." On the other hand, Kaplan (1976, p. 40; 1977, p. 282) emphasizes that interfering animals nearly always aid one of the original combatants against the other one, and distinguishes three roles: *interferer; beneficiary* of the interference; and *target* of the interferer's aggression. On the basis of these roles, he identifies "policeman" behavior, in which the interferer is dominant to the animals in the original dyad, and "alliancing" interference, in which the interferer is subordinate to one or both of the original agonists (1976, pp. 3—4).

Bernstein and Sharpe (1965, p. 101) indentify three patterns of interference in a captive rhesus group by the alpha male. Fights were broken up and quickly terminated:

1. by his attacking any animal involved agonistically with certain favored animals;
2. by his substituting himself for an aggressor, to turn the attack into a quickly terminated token aggression;
3. by his attacking another animal in the vicinity of the agonistic dyad, creating a distraction which terminates the agonism.

The authors also report that adult females served to "check . . . the aggression of the dominant male who, when aroused, is capable of seriously maiming an animal" (1965, p. 102). Such interferences by females came when the alpha male was acting not as interferer, but as aggressor.

As is usually the case with typologies, each has its purposes and merits. Van Hoof and de Waal are interested in the relation of rank to interference, while Kurland is interested in whether preferential aid is given to kin because of an interest in kin selection. Kaplan, on the other hand, focuses on the role of females in social control, a role he feels has been neglected in other studies due to ethological preoccupations with the power end of dominance hierarchies, as would appear to be the case with Bernstein and Sharpe. Since the present paper is focused on the related issues of mode of selection and motivational mechanisms for conflict interference, it will be useful to incorporate all these prespectives into the broadest possible view of interference.

Five Types of Conflict Interference

The typology set up below is designed to faciliate simultaneous analysis of rank, sex, age, and relatedness of aggressors, victims, and interferers, and to provide a frame of reference within which five different contexts of interference may be analyzed separately.

1. Alliancing Interference of Females. Adult females subordinate to one or both combatants in the original dyad may come to the aid of the victim, either distracting the aggressor while the victim escapes, or joining in an alliance with the victim against the aggressor in which power is balanced; both strategies are subsumed under this category.

2. Impartial Policing Interference. When an adult dyadic agonistic bout is interfered with by another animal without showing preference to either combatant, that animal invariably is dominant to both combatants, and is a leading male or the alpha male in the group. It is possible that several different strategies are subsumed under this heading.

3. Preferential Policing Interference in Favor of Victims. When a dyadic agonistic bout is interfered with by an animal dominant to the combatants with favor shown to one particular combatant, such policing is preferential. Interference preferential to the *victim* is practiced by males in adult or juvenile conflicts, and by females in conflicts among infants or young juveniles.

4. Preferential Policing Interference in Favor of Aggressors. When preferential policing favors the aggressor, it is usually leading males which enter in. There are differences of opinion as to whether such interference serves as a mechanism of either temporary or permanent pacification. If the original aggressor does not bow out, two-against-one ganging up effects may increase agonistic levels. There are also scapegoating episodes which sometimes develop, in which additional animals join in with the policeman and agonism is even more intensified. These last are treated separately below.

5. Scapegoating Interference. In certain cases of policing interference in favor of aggressors, after initial diminution of the agonism level other animals enter in on the side of the original aggressor and interferer, to do serious harm to the victim. Such behavior is also initiated in the form of gang attacks in the absence of interference. While such attacks are not very well explained at present, they tend to be directed only at certain individuals, and therefore superficially resemble "scapegoating" in humans, rather than conflict resolution. Interference which turns into scapegoating probably should be viewed as a combination of interference behavior and a particular form of alliancing behavior.

These five types will facilitate making distinctions among different interference acts, rather than lumping them into one or two categories. All these behaviors are to be treated as analytically separate from coalition and alliancing behaviors so widely reported for macaques. However, in addition to the ambiguity with scapegoating interference, the distinction between "interference" (other than impartial) and "alliancing" is necessarily somewhat artificial, even though interference is presumably oriented to stopping a fight and does tend to have that effect, while alliancing seems to be oriented to helping another animal win a fight. I shall now examine each type of interference in detail, to provide the descriptive basis for assessing motivational and selective mechanisms which make interference possible.

Alliancing Interference

In a physically dimorphic species, alliancing interference enables a female (or sometimes a subordinate male) to help another animal against larger males, including alpha males. Among adult macaques, alliancing interference may be difficult to distinguish from alliancing in general, although early termination of agonism is a criterion for interference, as a form of social control. Ontogeny suggests alliancing interference could be based on maternal protective intervention to help younger siblings attacked by older siblings, although such interference consists in *policing,* since the mother is dominant to her wards. Alliancing interference is similar, in that the underdog is assisted. But it is differerent, in that the interferer is subordinate to the aggressor, and therefore is put a greater risk in the process of helping.

Kaplan (1976, 1977, 1978) has carefully analyzed alliancing interference, as a neglected form of social control. In a Cayo Santiago rhesus group, he finds (1978) that in severe fights males preferentially aid victims or aggressors with equal frequency, while females aid victims ten times as often, and very frequently these females are subordinate to the aggressor. As one might expect, in such alliancing interference risks are greater than when a dominant animal interferes by policing. In preferential policing (both types), Kaplan reports that only in 3% of the cases does the aggressor attack the interferer, and of these attacks only a third are escalated to the biting level. However, when interference is by alliancing, interferers receive attacks nearly half the time, and biting is involved 5% of the time. Kurland (1977) finds 63% of all interference behavior to be of the alliancing type, while less detailed information is provided for other macaques (e.g., Eaton 1976).

Kaplan (1976, 1977) emphasizes that female alliancing interference is more efficacious in terminating agonistic episodes than are the various forms of policing interference practiced chiefly by males. On the other hand, Bernstein and Sharpe (1965) see the alpha male's interferences (in captive rhesus groups) as highly useful in reducing levels of injuries, and see female alliancing against the alpha male as useful in preventing him from maiming his victims when he enters combat as a aggressor rather than as an interferer. These differences of opinion between Kaplan and several other authors partly result from healthy differences in theoretical bias. But I believe these differences have been exacerbated by the use of relatively crude typologies for sorting out different forms of interference behavior exhibited by alpha males, which fail to separate out scapegoating interference and impartial interference as types of behavior different from preferential interference.

Impartial Policing Interference

It is only ranking males which terminate fights by interfering impartially, directing threats or attacks simultaneously at both original agonists. Probably because primate ethologists have concentrated so heavily upon consistently coding relatively less ambiguous dyadic relations, reports of impartial policing tend to be inconsistent and ambiguous. For example, Kaufman (1967) refers to provisioned Cayo Santiago dominant rhesus males breaking up fights, without separating preferential and impartial strategies. And Kaplan (1976, 1977, 1978), who focuses upon interference by rhesus females at the same research site, does not analyze the few interferences he implies may be impartial. On the other hand, Kurland clearly identifies impartial interference as a salient behavior in the provisioned Japanese macaques he studies (1977, p. 92), and finds that the group's most dominant male performs 74% of such policing actions, and in nine cases out of ten the original antagonists are immature animals from different matrilines. Kurland judges such interference to be positive in promoting social harmony, and notes that such social control sometimes took place by "shorthand", in that once the dominant animal made his beginning move toward the pair in conflict, they immediately drew apart.

In a group more directly comparable to Kaplan's, Lindburg reports in India that males often intervene in conflicts without taking sides, while when females intervene, they always side with either the victim or the aggressor (1971, p. 168). In these provisioned rhesus monkeys, Lindburg states that the leading male performs various functions important to group maintenance, including mobilization for protection from external dangers, and frequently policing intragroup squabbles, while other adult males may sometimes undertake such functions, but usually just support their leader (1971, p. 91).

Two behaviors reported for captive rhesus monkeys by Bernstein and Sharpe (1965) may belong with impartial policing. One is diversionary attacks by the alpha male, made on animals not far from the combatants. Neville (1968) also observed this behavior in free-ranging Indian macaques. This might represent an alternative impartial policing strategy, or a path chosen by a leader unsure of himself, or perhaps even a learning stage in the acquisition of the alpha male role behavior. The other behavior takes place when the alpha male first substitutes himself for the aggressor, then once he has taken over immediately terminates the attack. This strategy is somewhat difficult to fit into one type exclusively, because it appears that the alpha male first threatens the aggressor in order to displace him, then assumes his role only momentarily to threaten the victim and terminate the agonistic encounter. If this interpretation is correct, such interference is closer to impartial than to preferential, since the threats in two directions are all but simultaneous.

An atypical case of impartial policing must be mentioned, one which pertains to an adult rhesus pair which took up long term residence with a langur group in India. When langurs engaged in noisy squabbles, the rhesus male made a threatening move at them and as a group they immediately quieted down (Dolhinow 1972). The interference was not triadic, because an entire group was involved. Since Dolhinow also reports that langur females similarly threatened young langurs en masse when agonism developed, it seems possible that the male rhesus was adapting the normal rhesus impartial policing interference response to "another culture," perhaps "inventively" or perhaps through observational learning from langur mothers. In any event, there is no clear report of such simultaneous mass sanctioning of adults in normal rhesus groups.

Since normal macaque triad-based impartial policing interference has not been singled out for intensive study on its own in free-ranging groups, its exact effects are less well known than with preferential interference or alliancing interference. However, whenever impartial policing is mentioned, it is in the context of social control which results in early termination of agonism with positive effects upon group social dynamics, and it does not appear to be very risky to the dominant interferers.

Preferential Policing Interference in Favor of Victims

In Kaplan's rhesus monkeys, inferences may be drawn from his data as to what the effects are from policing in favor of victims, where a dominant animal intervenes to create a balance of power rather than to fight. In 268 cases of interference by males in milder fights, victims are helped 158 times while aggressors are helped 110 times. The interference is successful in protecting the victim about 80% of the time. In more serious fights (defined by presence of biting), males interfere on behalf of victims and aggressors equally, but when victims are helped, the interferer is successful in reducing agonism almost 90% of the time (Kaplan 1978, p. 244). Kaplan's findings jibe with more intuitive findings of other ethologists, although it seems possible that in some cases he may be interpreting impartial interference as preferential, or that they may be doing the opposite. In any event, it appears that preferential interference in favor of victims has a positive effect on social equilibrium through restoring a balance of power, and that it curtails damage to victims and possibly to aggressors as well.

Preferential Policing Interference in Favor of Aggressors

Preferential policing in favor of aggressors is also practiced mainly by males, and, as we have seen above, in Kaplan's rhesus group such aid is more frequent than aid to victims in milder fights; but in biting fights both types of interference occur equally (Kaplan 1978, p. 243). Kaplan (1976, pp. 5–6) emphasizes the disruptive effects of policing in favor of aggressors, especially compared with female aid to victims through alliancing interference. He emphasizes that the peacemaker role of alpha males has been overperceived.

When the original aggressor withdraws from combat, agonism does appear to be ameliorated. Substitution of the interferer for the aggressor mentioned in the last section may conceivably be a variation along this theme, and such behavior is visually documented by Eaton (1976) for Japanese macaques. However, Van Hoof and de Waal (1975) agree with Kaplan (1976) that dominant males may exacerbate agonism, and agree with Kaplan (1978) that policing attempts of dominant males do not necessarily control aggression. But later de Waal (1978) makes a finer distinction.

In certain cases, he believes alpha male interference preferential to aggressors does initially weaken the aggressor's attack, but then if new aggressors join in, the agonism is intensified. In two different captive groups of *fascicularis* macaques, he observed that in 41% of such interferences the aggressors did stop or weaken their aggression. But if new aggressors joined in, the same attacks could become unusually severe, with biting, Since such attacks were leveled against two particular victims, the behavior in question probably belongs with scapegoating.

Scapegoating Interference

Situations in which dyadic conflicts lead to ganging up of many individuals against one may begin along interference lines discussed above. However, once gang-style agression comes into play, it has an entirely different air about it. Kurland (1977) discusses a scapegoating episode in which the victim might well have lost its life, and other authors discuss this phenomenon as well (Lindburg 1971, Southwick et al. 1975, Van Hoof and de Waal 1975, Eaton 1976, de Waal 1978). A few thoughts have been offered on the causes of scapegoating, including tensions between different groups, and on its functions, in terms of tension reduction. But this behavior basically remains a mystery.

The exact boundary between policing in favor of aggressors and scapegoating is difficult to define, but it does appear that some intervention of leading males in favor of aggressors may be intended to reduce the level of agonism, since that is the immediate effect, but that frequently this strategy leads to group attacks which are not inhibited by the leader. However, it is of interest that while alpha males continue to attack victims once scapegoating develops against adult males, when a more vulnerable female or juvenile is mobbed the alpha male may come in to break up the gang aggression (de Waal 1978). This would be one case in which interference becomes more than triadic, but there exists no description adequate to determine whether such interference is preferential or impartial, or whether the interference is directed at more than one aggressor at a time.

Social Control Effects of Interference

Policing in favor of aggressors, if taken as a single type of interference, appears ambiguous in its effects as a social control, and policing which leads to scapegoating results in immediate disruption and grave danger to the scapegoat. However, impartial interference, and both kinds of interference in favor of victims, clearly serve to reduce agonism levels and physical damage to individuals.

More generally, dominance hierarchies in macaques have obvious functions which facilitate adaptation (Popp and DeVore 1979). Basically, they regulate individual access to resources. In terms of emergent effects, they also set up groups to be territorial without having to devote too much time and energy to coping with conspecific neighbors, and set them up to mobilize defensively against predators with a marked and efficient division of labor.

Without interference, one dangerous by-product of macaque dominance behavior would be fights in which ambiguity exists in a dominance relation and both animals decide to fight. Another dangerous by-product comes when a subordinate animal, by submitting, is unable to release a cessation of dominance behavior on the part of its aggressor. Without the inhibition provided by interference, these by-products might produce outcomes adverse for adaptation. First, excessive rates of wounding and killing could push population dynamics into an "abnormal" range. Second, disruption resulting from serious fights could affect social stasis adversely; for example, uncontrolled agonism could lead to dangerously premature fissioning of groups, leading to territorial disadvantages.

These broad assumptions are largely speculative. But there do exist rather specific data which provide a picture of the kind of damage macaques actually do to one another, given the fact that they are geared for dominance and submission, and given the fact that third parties do sometimes help to control agonistic interactions. Compared with other nonhuman primates whose dominance interactions may be quite ferocious-appearing (e.g., Hall and DeVore 1965) in terms of vocalizations and posturings. It appears that macaques actually suffer a relatively high rate of wounds and deaths. When macaque agonism involves biting (Kaplan 1976), severe damage is possible. And while such wounding and killing is seldom observed directly (Symons 1978), in surviving animals it is evident in the form of wounds and scars from old wounds, in the occasional discovery of an animal dead of wounds, or in certain disappearances of healthy animals.

Over 9 months Lindburg (1971) observed 2000 agonistic events in provisioned rhesus monkeys in India, of which 13% resulted in physical contact of some form. Lindburg noticed 93 wounds on 115 animals, and 8 wounds were judged to be severe. But none of these severe wounds was witnessed when inflicted. Over the same period, adult males received an average of 1.56 wounds, while adult females received 1.35 and younger macaques received only 0.29 wounds per animal. 61% of all wounds, and the majority of the 8 severe wounds, were inflicted during the three months' mating season. So it would appear that both serious agonism and, presumably, the interference which helps to control such agonism, were heightened during that period. In Japanese macaques, Kurland (1977) notes 5 severe wounds, all inflicted by aggressors on distant kin or on nonkin belonging to low-ranking matrilines, who did not fight back. This suggests that in macaques, submissive posturings lack effectiveness at times in releasing a cessation of aggression. Apparently, interference is a secondary or backup mechanism which achieves the same effect through a radically different means.

Precise measurement of benefits of interference would be very difficult. However, in the opinion of many primate ethologists interference does reduce levels of agonism and physical damage due to agonism. One must always be suspicious of such statements. They can be both tautological and meaningless, when one makes them in the spirit of taking any pattern of behavior which might be construed to be adaptive in some general sense, and asserts that the behavior therefore must contribute positively to adaptation, without specifying the precise mode of selection. But above I have demonstrated that rates of physical damage among macaques are substantial even with the presence of interference, which enhances the inferential case that interference reduces death and maiming. I have tentatively suggested some ways in which reduction of agonism levels could be adaptive both for individuals, and for groups of individuals. Following an assessment of the psychological mechanisms which lead to interference taking place, and of the implications of these findings for selection process, I shall attempt to be more definitive in proposing hypotheses about how and why interference is selected.

Motives for Interference

Interference behaviors have been discussed so far with only oblique reference to "motives," as is traditional in a behaviorist tradition which has brought primate ethology the scientific respectability it deserves. However, motives are to be explored here as ethologically usable data. Before specific motives are hypothesized, several preliminary questions arise, which require that the term "motive" be defined as it is to be used below:

1. Is an act of interference set in motion by something motivationally closer to a fixed action pattern, or more like the well-calculated decisions made by humans?
2. Is interference based on as many different motives as there are different strategies for interference, or upon some overarching motive or set of motives?

I take the term "motive" in its broad, commonsense aspect, as referring to the reason, conscious or less than conscious, that an animal decides to perform an action. The "reason" may be that a preprogrammed response is released by some very specific signal, in a way which is "stupid" to the extent that the animal is caught in a compulsion which leaves it little room for calculated choice. At the opposite end of the continuum is the highly labile animal which banks upon learning from past experiences and makes highly calculated but utterly intuitive decisions, choices among alternatives, to reach desirable goals. (Indeed, many human choices are so "intuitive" that they fit with this definition.) Lorenz (1966) has helped to clarify the differences between such polar types of behavior, as has Eibl-Eibesfeldt (1970).

In keeping with this well-founded distinction, I differentiate helping behavior which is preprogrammed from helping behavior which results from deliberate calculation based on past experience, as polar types of behavior with a continuum lying between them. "Genetic altruism" is the label I use for helping behavior which lies at the preprogrammed pole; "psychological altruism" is helping behavior which lies at the deliberate calculation-from-past-experience pole. Such helping behaviors should be labeled "altruistic" only if, for the individual helper, such behaviors are self-sacrificial or at best selectively neutral, in terms of individual relative fitness.

This distinction between genetic and psychological altruism requires further clarification. In labile macaques, even rather well-preprogrammed behaviors like bonding, protecting, and dominating/submitting may be assumed to be relatively unstupid, in terms of both the variety and subtlety of stimuli which "propel" such behaviors, and the presence of sophisticated, calculating motivational processes. For example, female protection of infants surely contains a heavy dose of preprogramming, but is enacted rather flexibly. This suggests a mixture of genetic and psychological altruism. Greater motivational complexity may be assumed when still more flexible behaviors such as interference develop, since the increased dependency upon previous experience (often through observational role learning) results in a larger role for calculation. At such a point, altruism becomes quite psychological.

It may be hypothesized that the interferer *cares* about the beneficiary, and/or that the interferer tries to help in order to reduce social tension or enhance social stasis. These are two hypotheses which might explain the motivational basis of interference. They depend, however, on assumptions which would be difficult to test through experimental procedures which operationalize mental processes. Given the overtly discernible strength of bonding behavior, it would not be surprising if an emotional concomitant existed, in the form of something like sympathy or caring. Whether some interferences are motivated by a crude sense of appreciation for social harmony, or an aversiveness to social disruption, is obviously a more complicated question. These and other motives will be tentatively explored, in the interest of better explaining the selection basis for interference.

When macaques interfere in conflicts, it is certain that the motives are not always uniform. For example, it is obvious that aiding certain allies and scapegoating result from divergent motives. However, in more predominant patterns of interference, many different tactical approaches are taken to achieve one and the same effect: to control a conflict by forcing its termination. If this behavior were heavily prepared by genes, one would expect a different preparation to underlie each tactical strategy as a discrete fixed action response. In this case, the motives would be a series of different genetically altruistic responses. However, when many different tactical strategies converge to accomplish a single result, and also the behavior is labile, then one must consider the possibility of a single predominant *psychological* motive.

Because such monkeys' general capacity for deliberate social calculation is invariably described as great, this leads one to say that the majority of interference control actions are highly deliberate, well-calculated, and relatively uniform in motivation, even though basic, nonaltruistic genetic preparations for dyadic dominance and submission are utilized emergently, as a means to this end. Why is it, then, that animals want to stop conflicts so often, and in so many contexts and ways? I now advance more specific motivational hypotheses for the various types of interference behavior, looking to both genetic and psychological altruism as potential sources.

1. For males, the *basic protective orientation,* which is closer to genetic altruism, underlies not only impartial interference and policing in favor of victims, but policing in which the interferer benignly substitutes himself for the aggressor. Possibly due to *basic bonding capacity,* some kind of affective warmth may be operative, with sympathetic calculation of probable consequences such as individual pain or psychic distress. Female interferers may well generalize the same *basic* orientations (by which they protect weaker offspring by preferential policing in favor of victims) into an *emergent* behavior in which they favor adult underdogs rather generally, and resourcefully employ alliancing tactics to do so. Motives would be similar to males, but tactical calculations are different because policing of other adults by females is less often feasible, due to dimorphism.

2. A *sense of reciprocity* might motivate the few interferences in which specific "friends" are helped by alpha males regardless of their structural positions in quarrels. A sense of reciprocity also may help to motivate the frequent alliancing interferences practiced in favor of matrilineally related adults by females, since such animals tend to be strongly bonded. But in neither case is there documented any very strong tendency of beneficiaries to reciprocate over time, so Trivers' (1971) reciprocal altruism hypothesis remains weak (see Kaplan 1978).

3. It is possible that observation of a socially disharmonious scene like fighting releases a genetically rather well-prepared, basic frustration reaction which places the observing animal under tension, and results in *hostility directed to the source of disturbance.* Such "intolerance" could be closely linked to the basic aesthetic sense so prominent in great apes as well as in humans, which also has been identified experimentally in certain monkeys (E.O. Wilson 1975). The action of the rhesus male to make an entire group of agitated langurs calm down in the absence of serious fighting is highly suggestive in this respect.

4. Alternatively, it is possible that leading male macaques develop a rudimentary, yet rather sophisticated, *positive appreciation of social harmony* in terms of predicting social dynamics, as a far more psychologically motivated behavior built upon the same basic aesthetic sense. They assess fights cognitively as injurious to a social equilibrium which they intuitively understand, and which they feel capable of manipulating in certain contexts.

5. If interference motives become this sophisticated, we may be speaking of something similar to a *sense of social responsibility,* based upon an appreciation of social harmony combined with a generalized tendency to be sympathetically protective to members of the primary group.

The sheer variety of strategies followed to terminate conflicts suggests a complicated, generalized motive of social responsibility, rather than a narrower, genetically well-prepared motive of intolerance of social agitation. Either motive seems possible, and both could work together. But social responsibility evident in macaque males' flexibly enacted group-protective vigilance and herding, or in their threatening or attacking of predators or external conspecific groups, supports the argument that a similar sense of social responsibility motivates impartial interference and most preferential policing as well, and that this sense of responsibility comes through learning the role of "control animal." Bernstein's experiments (e.g., 1970) are highly suggestive in this respect.

This completes the list of putative motives for interference, based by homological possibility on known human emotions. I must, however, remark on some possibilities for sex differences. Given the pronounced *physical* dimorphism of macaques and baboons, sexual dimorphism in genetic preparations for social behavior is not unlikely. Since macaque females mainly protect their offspring, while males look to group defense, genetic preparations for basic altruistic behaviors may well be somewhat dimorphic. However, while genetic preparations may differ by sex, role learning could either intensify or mitigate such effects. In any event, it is possible that certain of the motives discussed above may be more applicable to male than to female interference, and the differences may be due to genetic preparations and/or role-learning differences, but probably both.

Selection Mechanisms

Interference always requires some investment of time and energy. In terms of physical damage, risks always exist for interferers, but these vary according to fighting ability, dominance position, and the particular tactical strategies pursued in interfering. For these reasons, it makes sense to place interference in the "altruistic paradox" category, so far as mechanisms of selection are concerned. The paradox is most easily resolved when parental investment (Trivers 1972) or kin selection models (E.O. Wilson 1975) seem applicable.

At first glance, this would appear to be the case for alliancing interference of females, since this type of interference predictably helps the victim, and it entails the highest costs for interferers, in terms of physical damage. However, Kaplan (1978) finds that the more severe the aggressor's attack on the victim, the less likely it is that a close kin relation will exist between the interfering female and the victim. When males interfere impartially or preferentially, the risks diminish, but so do kin connec-tions with victims or aggressors, compared with alliancing interference. And of course if a nonnatal male assumes group leadership, kin selection will be entirely negligible for a time, although from the start protection of actual or potential breeding partners may still be at issue, as a mechanism favoring selection through inclusive fitness.

One quick solution to the altruistic paradox would be to assume that interference releases tensions and so provides a tonic for the body, as it were, or that frequent interferences strengthen or make less ambiguous the interferer's position in a social dominance hierarchy. There may, indeed, be some truth in both such imprecise hypotheses. However, they are eminently unsusceptible of falsification, and I believe there are better, more specific hypotheses for the explanation of selection mechanics which maintain interference behaviors.

One such alternative hypothesis concerns what I have called the "fallacy of genetic overspecification" (Boehm 1979, p. 18), in criticizing the sociobiological assumption that each altruistic behavior has its own gene and vice versa. Once this fallacy is dis-pelled, it is logical to posit that a single set of genes might prepare simultaneously: (1) an eminently selfish behavior, relatively well prepared by genes, which brings large benefits in terms of individual relative fitness, and (2) a similar but functionally quite different and more labile behavior, which results in modest genetic losses due to altruism. In such a case, as we shall see, the altruistic losses can be sustained "para-sitically," without any benefit from inclusive fitness effects. A second alternative hypothesis is derived from a new model for group selection proposed by D.S. Wilson (1980), which suggests that helping behaviors which are selectively neutral in terms of individual relative fitness may be extremely sensitive to selection at the interdemic level.

Parasitic Selection

Elsewhere (Boehm 1979), I have criticized the too-simplified "one-gene, one-behavior" arguments used to model kin selection as an explanation for genetic and even for psychological altruism (e.g., E.O. Wilson 1975). The problem lies in the well-known fact that genes and polygenes may be pleiotropic. Where less complicated "fixed action" sequences are at issue, such arguments may be only moderately oversimplified, but in humans, apes, and monkeys, many helping behaviors are quite flexible and complicated. This means routes for genetic selection would be far more complex and circuitous, so a more sophisticated assessment of possible selection mechanisms is required.

I propose that labile helping behavior which weakly reduces a donor's relative inclusive fitness could be selectively *parasitic* upon a genetically selfish but similar behavior, prepared by precisely the same genes. This selfish behavior must be strongly selected through classical Darwinian inclusive fitness effects, namely through direct individual benefits, combined with parental investment and kin selection benefits, if it is to support the self-sacrificial behavior which does not benefit from classical inclusive fitness benefits. I shall call the selfish behaviors "basic," and the more labile, altruistic behaviors which are parasitic upon basic behaviors "emergent." A simplified case of parasitic selection is seen in the relation between macaque females' protection of very young monkeys attached to them, and alliancing interference practiced by the same females in favor of other adults.

A female macaque rather predictably will defend her infant charge against any adult conspecific interloper, regardless of size and dominance status. In combination, the predictability of this altruistic compulsion, the potentially high risks, and the high likelihood of defending her own offspring, make it likely that strong parental investment effects could be maintaining relatively strong genetic preparations which make the response compulsive and basic. On the other hand, when females riskily attack more dominant animals to assist other adults as victims, this emergent, altruistic response occurs far less predictably. The emergent behavior is optional, rather than compulsive.[2]

The parasitic hypothesis assumes that exactly the same genes prepare both of these protective responses, but the emergent response depends much more upon careful calculation from prior experience. There exists a very obvious selection explanation for basic protection of one's own offspring, but none for the emergent pattern, in which females favor non-kin in more severe fights. Since the emergent response appears to be a similar but more generalized version of the basic response, it is logical that the emergent behavior is parasitic on the basic one. Its continued existence therefore

---

2 This basic characterization is partially implicit in Kaplan (1978), whose work served as the original stimulus for writing this paper. Kaplan sees female aid to juvenile kin as altruism perpetuated by parental investment, a behavior I would call *basic.* Female aid to adult peers, a behavior I would call *emergent,* he views as a means of "ensuring reinforcement of bonds within the wider social group" (1978, p. 247). Kaplan suggests (1978, p. 248) that a biosocial approach to explanation must be taken, advice which has been heeded in this paper in spite of the heavy focus on genetic selection. He also suggests that "classical (individual) selection rather than group selection or kin selection" is the mechanism operating, as interfering individuals improve their own affiliations and strengthen their social membership in the group. This Darwinian explanation is logical, but perhaps mechanically insufficient to explain the riskier forms of interference, in particular. I should point out that there is nothing incompatible between Kaplan's selection hypotheses and those advanced in the present paper. Both sets of hypotheses offer alternative routes for explanation, which could reduce the present overdependency upon kin selection arguments

poses no altruistic paradox, even though the question remains as to exactly how emergent, parasitic biocultural behavior is *shaped* by variation and selective retention.

Two points must be emphasized, before this simplified exemplification is complete. First, if on the average the emergent behavior becomes more costly to individual relative fitness than the basic behavior is beneficial, then neither behavior can be maintained at a high level in a breeding population. The second point is obvious, but deserves to be stressed: by definition, a self-sacrificial helping behavior cannot be genetically maintained in the absence of a parasitic relationship, unless it is profiting strongly from inclusive fitness effects, and/or from improbably strong group selection effects (E.O. Wilson 1975, 1978) which more than compensate for relative fitness deficits of altruists.

Now that the basic principle of parasitism is established, this form of explanation may be applied to macaque conflict interference in its full complexity. Interference as a parasitic emergent behavior surely involves basic responses other than protection. It appears that all forms of interference which result in bona fide assistance to combatants are based on basic *dominance/submission* and *bonding* responses, as well. In each case, a specific set of genetic preparations sets up the basic behavior, and simultaneously contributes to the emergent behavior. Where an emergent behavior is parasitic upon several basic behaviors, this may be termed "multiple parasitism".

By the time the three basic behaviors I have hypothesized for macaques have been assessed for possible relations to five or more emergent strategies of interference, and also to several kinds of emergent group-protective activity, a rather complicated analysis is required. My claim is that it is useful to the development of ethology as a science, to face this complexity squarely. The alternative is to indulge in "one-gene one-behavior" speculations on selection which introduce a misleading and premature degree of parsimony into the analysis of altruism as an effect of genetic preparation.

The notion of parasitic selection fits neatly with the complicated and variegated behaviors of macaques, and provides an alternative to the often overworked notion of kin selection, as a key to altruism puzzles. Parasitic selection will be more difficult to "quantify," compared with measuring the proportion in which self-sacrificial helping behavior goes to close kin, as opposed to distant kin or non-kinsmen. But for explanation, the advantage of parasitic selection is that it accounts for self-sacrificial assistance to non-kin and kin alike, and is logically compatible with kin selection arguments where they do become convincing.

This introduction to the notion of parasitic selection provides a hypothesis as to how certain "altruistic" behaviors may avoid being culled from a behavioral repertoire. However, it does not fully explain how flexible, emergent, group-beneficial helping behaviors are *shaped* by selective forces. With respect to the biological basis for such behaviors, such explanation will be made easier by consideration of group selection possibilities. After the relation of parasitic selection to group selection is clarified, I shall treat interference in more detail as a product of genetic selection.

Group Selection Effects

Group selection offers an additional explanatory dimension, one neglected because most ethologists (e.g., Gadgil 1975, Popp and DeVore 1979) have chosen to limit themselves to parsimonious but necessarily limited "Darwinian" explanations. These are based on what geneticists (e.g., E.O. Wilson 1975) presently are capable of modeling in terms of single behavior-genes, when they analyze behaviors which have a very complex genetic basis. Since Wade's (1978) interdemic extinction experiments do not apply to the more enduring groups formed by macaques, dramatic rates of group extinction cannot explain selective maintenance of group-beneficial behaviors which are sacrificial in terms of individual relative fitness. A more logical place to begin is with D.S. Wilson's (1980) recent arguments in favor of group (interdemic) selection as a force which shapes gene pools.

The once widespread assumption that "characteristics of organisms are designed to benefit the species or the ecosystem" is a philosophical bias which accepted Darwinian principles appear to falsify (D.S. Wilson 1980, p. 2). But Wilson suggests that when an organism behaves not in its own self-interest, but in the interest of the community in which it lives, this may involve an "emergent property" (1980, p. 2) which is positively selected without any altruistic paradox. The genetic algebra is complicated, but the basic arguments are fairly simple. Selective possibilites for group advantage follow two courses:

1. An "altruistic" pathway: an "individual voluntarily sacrifices personal fitness for the good of the group" (D.S. Wilson 1980, p. 84). As E.O. Wilson (1975) makes clear, this requires very high variation between trait-groups, as well as extremely frequent extinction events. It is therefore unlikely to be found in nature.

2. A "neutral" pathway: "traits which are neutral in terms of individual selection within trait-groups become perfectly responsive to the between trait-group selection in structured demes" (D.S. Wilson 1980, p. 84). Criteria for such selection depend not upon extreme isolation of demes, nor upon their improbably frequent extinction, but simply that traits be selectively neutral in terms of individual relative fitness, and that populations be structured into trait-groups. More technically, this is stated as follows:

> In traditional models a trait can be selected only if it provides a direct advantage to its bearer. Natural selection is insensitive to any trait whose advantage accrues through indirect effects. However, in structured demes with binomial trait distribution, natural selection does not discriminate between direct and indirect effects. The trait is selected whenever its net effect on fitness, both direct and indirect, is positive for the individual manifesting the trait (D.S. Wilson 1980, p. 96).

Wilson's theory more simply stated holds that if I help someone else without actually reducing my own relative fitness, this trait is selectively *neutral* for individual relative fitness, rather than self-sacrificial. If so, it will be extremely sensitive to interdemic selection, assuming the population is divided into textured trait groups such as those of macaques. This provides an alternative to Popp and DeVore (1979) to help in explaining the existence of social dominance hierarchies and particularly some of their emergent features.

This new explanatory route should stimulate reappraisal of behaviors identified as "altrustic", to see if they may be in fact selectively neutral in terms of individual relative fitness. For example, on the average animals giving warning cries might neither increase nor decrease their personal genetic advantage, directly. Or dominance interactions involving unprotectable resources (D.S. Wilson 1980) may be neutral, in that they require the same time and energy of both aminals.

Relation of Parasitic Selection to Group Selection

Earlier I suggested that, even without the benefit of parasitic selection effects, interference by leading macaque males in conflicts might be selectively neutral for them rather than genetically self-sacrificial. Tension release could contribute to mental and therefore physical health, and losses of time and energy, or bodily damage sustained in interference might be compensated because dangerous status ambiguities in the dominance hierarchy are reduced by practicing interference.

There is also Kaplan's (1978) hypothesis that interference enhances individual group affiliation. Such arguments may be moderately plausible for male interference, and possibly for male leadership in intertroop encounters, but they are too difficult to substantiate by empirical data, to consider any further. They are also clearly inadequate to account for predator defense of males, or alliancing interference of females, where risks would be much higher. In the case of female alliancing interference, such hypotheses are particularly unlikely due to well-documented, very high rates of physical damage to interferers. This very high rate of self-sacrifice suggested a kin selection explanation to Kurland (1977), but since the highest risks are taken for more distantly related animals, and the greatest benefits are delivered to them, Kaplan's (1978) doubts about the operation of kin selection seem justified. On the other hand, D.S. Wilson's brand of interdemic selection could not account for a behavior which apparently is so risky that it could not be selectively neutral, at least when it is viewed in isolation from other behaviors. It is only when a parasitic selection explanation is relied upon that female alliancing interference becomes logical, in terms of genetic selection.

A further question must now be asked, as to whether parasitic self-sacrificial emergent behaviors, including both male and female forms of interference, are susceptible to the kind of interdemic selection outlined above. For such selection to work, it is required by the theoretical model that the behavior be selectively neutral for the individual, in terms of its direct effects. For purposes of genetic selection analysis, a parasitic behavior should be just as selectively neutral as any other behavior which is selectively neutral, since the issue is whether or not the behavior, in the *absence* of interdemic selection, would be eliminated from the gene pool due to Darwinian selection effects. With parasitic behaviors, this is emphatically not the case; I propose for this reason that they be counted as eligible for interdemic selection.

This means that when an emergent behavior is being sustained through parasitic selection effects, it can be simultaneously selected interdemically, if it benefits the group and therefore benefits the individual indirectly. Such selection effects would be weak, but they apply to all types of interference which make positive contributions to adaptation either through protection of group members or through furthering an adaptive degree of social stasis, so long as interferers are reaping indirect benefits of their altruistic actions.

If these assumptions are correct, when parasitic selection renders an emergent behavior viable in terms of individual relative fitness, interdemic selection effects may be operating as well, to shape the behavior in question, and to cull other emergent behavioral variants. Since the behaviors we are speaking of are emergent ones involving a very heavy dose of learning, it makes sense that this selection process operates at both the genetic and the cultural level. Above, I have discussed only the genetic side of this selective process.

Given the slim possibility that any form of interference in adult macaque conflicts is based exclusively on kin selection, it would appear that all types of interference judged to be helpful to individual beneficiaries or to group functioning are best explained by a combination of parasitic selection and interdemic selection. This would include impartial policing interference, alliancing interference of females and preferential policing interference in favor of victims. These forms of interference, including all the optional strategies employed, are parasitic upon the three basic responses referred to earlier. It might be best to include preferential policing interference in favor of aggressors with scapegoating as a special form of alliancing behavior rather than a form of interference until it is better studied.

Conclusions

I have attempted a substantive analysis of interference which may be interesting in its own right, but has been taken as a means of making a theoretical point about genetic selection contributions to labile altruistic behaviors. I have argued that emergent, psychologically altruistic interference behaviors in macaques may be founded on basic *bonding, protective,* and *dominance/submission* mechanisms. These basic responses of course involve some calculation, and presumably are based upon appropriate emotions of affection, possessiveness, anger, fear, and possibly sympathy, if human counterparts may be cited. The point is that basic responses are more closely prepared by genes than are emergent responses, and involve less calculation and choice.

It is assumed that emotional elements like those listed above combine emergently, to produce well-calculated helping behaviors. These are based on psychological altruism which involves rather sophisticated assessments of social dynamics. It may seem farfetched to suggest that alpha males exhibit a sense of social responsibility, and have some insightful appreciation of social dynamics and of the negative effects of escalated levels of agonism. But something of this sort may be going on in their heads, as they make decisions as to which fights merit intervention. More conservatively, it may well be that a generalized sense of sympathy similar to that developed out of bonding behavior in humans (Wispé 1978) operates in both male and female interference in conflicts within the macaque group. But even with a far more conservative estimate of what is going on motivationally, there still can be no doubt that interference behavior is highly labile.

I must emphasize that it is not just on the basis of these speculations about motives that I have assumed interference is a product of great lability. To the contrary, the best evidence for lability is the fact that a similar pacification effect is achieved through such a large number of tactical approaches, involving considerable differences of strategy with respect to the structural position of the animal(s) to be attacked, and the exact method of interference. Also, the momentary predisposition of the animal apparently determines whether or not it will choose to intervene. This already solid evidence for lability is consonant with the speculations about motives. And when many different strategies result in the same effect, namely, termination of the agonistic episode, similarity of motive becomes quite logical if not necessary, so long as the behavior is labile.

As a matter of theoretical interest, conflict resolution in macaques has been analyzed to try some new ways of explaining a type of genetic puzzle which has received sustained attention over the past several decades. Interference is not well explained through the inclusive fitness or reciprocal altruism models which have received so much attention. Such models have been contrived to explain not only self-sacrificial helping behavior highly prepared by genes, but more labile varieties of such behavior as well (E.O. Wilson 1975, 1978).

The parasitic selection model developed here is obviously genetically imprecise. But when it comes to speaking of behavior genes, imprecision is what we must realistically face. This model is designed to take into account gross differences in degree of genetic preparation, for functionally different behaviors which nevertheless bear a marked similarity to one another. It also deals with the fact that one behavior may be prepared by many genes, and one gene may prepare many behaviors, since parasitic selection effects can be multiple.

Conflict interference has never been focused on, exclusively and in advance, in a study of a free-ranging macaque group. Therefore, the available data are not ideal for a synthetic study such as I have undertaken. However, by assuming that most of these data hold for macaques in general, or at least for Japanese and rhesus monkeys, I have patched together a tentative analysis which hopefully will encourage ethologists to give more attention to triadic interactions, as Kummer has done for baboons (1967). With less than definitive data, it still seems likely that most types of interference do make a contribution to social stability, and that stability itself is good for adaptation, so long as social flexibility is available in coping with environmental changes. Availability of a flexible mode of social control such as conflict interference obviously contributes to the overall flexibility of the social group in adaptations.

I must hasten to emphasize that this statement is not premised on species selection principles long discredited by ethologists, but on interdemic selection principles suggested by D.S. Wilson (1980) and elaborated above with respect to macaque interference. I have argued that in effect parasitic selection makes apparently self-sacrificial behaviors selectively neutral, and this means that genetic group selection may operate on the structured demes inherent in macaque social organization.

D.S. Wilson (1980, pp. 82–84) does specifically include conflict interference in his scheme, citing Eaton (1976). But I emphasize that even if Wilson's theory did not apply very well to macaque interference, parasitic selection still could explain the continuing presence of interference. To fully explain selection among variant emergent behaviors *within* the group, however, one would have to look to cultural selection (Pulliam and Dunford 1980) and possibly to rational decison making at the micro-level (Boehm 1978), as well as genetic selection.

In this synthetic study, a number of interlocking hypotheses have been built, some of which are speculative and others *highly* speculative. My purpose, in pushing sound ethological data to its outer limits, has been to create a model which might better explain highly labile helping behavior and its selective basis. If I have limited my hypotheses to selection at the genetic level, the capacity of macaques for technological invention, and for incorporating such inventions into group tradition, are too well known as protocultural phenomena even to require citation. Surely, observational learning of complex social roles also plays an important part in cultural transmission with these animals. But I have not tried to account for the cultural side of selection, since this will be done in a different paper.

Very general cultural selection principles outlined by Pulliam and Dunford (1980) could easily be applied here, although for macaques data are lacking to make any definitive case for the role of cultural-traditional variation and selective retention, in either individual or group selection. Elsewhere (Boehm 1981), I have suggested that there are far fewer obstacles to group selection theory at the level of cultural evolution, than at the level of genetic evolution, due to significant mechanical differences between genetic and cultural transmission and selection. It would appear, then, that the present analysis of macaque conflict interference is incomplete in the sense that cultural selection effects have been set aside.

Even without a careful account of cultural selection, this analysis of genetic selection in the area of conflict resolution is suggestive with respect to human pacification behaviors, which are not only similar, but universal. Whether macaques are verging on some kind of protomorality, with their sensitivity to group disruption and with the multifaceted apparent sense of social responsibility exhibited by their leaders, remains in my mind an open question. It is one worthy of further, but necessarily still more speculative sociocultural-biological exploration.

In terms of broader speculations about the natural history of highly social primates, a parasitic selection model may prove useful in hypothesizing about how transitional, protocultural stages of hominid evolution came about. But it is my more immediate hope that the notion of parasitic selection will prove valuable to ethologists who study labile and highly social animals. I believe this model will aid in reassessing the selective basis of helping behaviors, particularly those which still pose altruistic selection paradoxes, but also those which do not.

The term "lability" itself, while obviously very useful, has remained too general as employed by ethologists. Kummer's (1971) notion of adaptive modification has lent it more precision, in spite of the fact that it will be a long time before the operation of behavioral genes will be understood in any detail when behaviors are labile. I believe a parasitic selection model will help further, in relating labile behaviors to less labile ones in terms of genetic selection effects. At the same time, it should facilitate exploration of the mechanics of cultural selection of social behaviors. The result, for all highly social animals, could be a more specific and more integrated approach to the explanation of labile behaviors, be they "altruistic" or "selfish."

Acknowledgments. For comments which I received in time to assist me in rethinking an earlier version of this paper, I am indebted to: Irwin S. Bernstein, Donald T. Campbell, Kevina Vulinek and David S. Wilson. Responsibility, of course, is the author's.

References

Bernstein IS (1965) Role of the dominant male rhesus monkey in response to external challenges to the group. J Comp Physiol Psychol 57:404–406

Bernstein IS (1970) Primate status hierarchies. In: Rosenblum LA (ed) Primate behavior: Developments in field and laboratory research, vol I. Academic Press, London New York, pp 71–109

Bernstein IS, Sharpe LG (1965) Social roles in a rhesus monkey group. Behavior 26:91–104

Boehm C (1978) Rational preselection from Hamadryas to homo sapiens: The place of decisions in adaptive process. Am Anthropol 80:265–296

Boehm C (1979) Some problems with altruism in the search for moral universals. Behav Sci 24:15–24

Boehm C (1981) A fresh view of cultural selection. Am Anthropol, in press (to appear in June 1981)

Dolhinow P (1972) The North Indian langur. In: Dolhinow P (ed) Primate patterns. Holt, Rinehart and Winston, New York, pp 181–238

Eaton GG (1976) The social order of Japanese macaques. Sci Am 235:97–107

Eibl-Eibesfeldt I (1970) Ethology: The biology of behavior. Holt, Rinehart and Winston, New York

Gadgil M (1975) Evolution of social behavior through interpopulation selection. Proc Natl Acad Sci USA 72:1199–1201

Griffin D (1976) A possible window on the minds of animals. Am Sci 64:530–535

Hall KRL (1968) Aggression in monkey and ape societies. In: Jay P (ed) Primates: Studies in adaptation and variability. Holt, Rinehart and Winston, New York, pp 149–171

Hall KRL, DeVore I (1965) Baboon social behavior. In: DeVore I (ed) Primate behavior: Field studies of monkeys and apes. Holt, Rinehart and Winston, New York, pp 53–110

Hoof JARAM Van, deWaal FBM (1975) Aspects of an ethological analysis of polyadic agonistic interactions in a captive group of *Macaca fascicularis.* Proc 5th Int Congr Primatol 24:269–274

Kaplan JR (1976) Patterns of interference and the control of aggression in a group of free-ranging rhesus monkeys. Doctoral Dissertation, Northwestern University, Evanston

Kaplan JR (1977) Patterns of fight interference in free-ranging rhesus monkeys. Am J Phys Anthropol 47:279–287

Kaplan JR (1978) Fight interference and altruism in rhesus monkeys. Am J Phys Anthropol 49:241–249

Kaufmann JH (1967) Social relations of adult males in a free-ranging band of rhesus monkeys. Ecology 46:500–512

Kummer H (1967) Tripartite relations in Hamadryas baboons. In: Altmann S (ed) Social communication among primates. Univ of Chicago Press, Chicago, pp 63–71

Kummer H (1971) Primate societies: Group techniques of ecological adaptation. Aldine, Chicago

Kurland JA (1977) Kin selection in the Japanese monkey. Karger, New York

Lindburg DG (1971) The rhesus monkey in North India: An ecological and behavioral study. In: Rosenblum LA (ed) Primate behavior: Developments in field and laboratory research, vol II. Academic Press, London New York, pp 2–106

Lorenz K (1966) On aggression. Harcourt, Brace Jovanovich, New York

Neville MK (1968) Male leadership changes in a free-ranging troup of Indian rhesus monkeys *(Macaca mulatta).* Primates 9:13–27

Popp JL, DeVore I (1979) Aggressive competition and social dominance theory. In: Hamburg DA, McCown ER (eds) The great apes. Cummings, Menlo Park, pp 316–338

Pulliam R, Dunford C (1980) Programmed to learn: An essay on the evolution of culture. Columbia Univ Press, New York

Reynolds V (1976) The biology of human action. Freeman, San Francisco

Scott JP (1974) Agonistic behavior of primates: A comparative perspective. In: Holloway RL (ed) Primate aggression, territoriality, and xenophobia. Academic Press, London New York, pp 417–434

Southwick CH, Siddiqi MF, Farooqui MY, Pal BC (1974) Xenophobia among free-ranging rhesus group in India. In: Holloway RL (ed) Primate aggression, territoriality, and xenophobia. Academic Press, London New York, pp 185–209

Symons D (1978) Play and aggression: A Study of rhesus monkeys. Columbia Univ Press, New York

Trivers RL (1971) The evolution of reciprocal altruism. Q Rev Biol 46:35–57

Trivers RL (1972) Parental investment and sexual selection. In: Campbell B (ed) Sexual selection and the descent of man. Aldine, Chicago, pp 136–179

Waal FMB de (1978) Join-aggression and protective-aggression among captive *Macaca fascicularis*. In: Chivers DJ, Herbert J (eds) Academic Press, London New York, pp 577–579

Wade MJ (1978) A critical review of the models of group selection. Q Rev Biol 53:101–114

Wilson EO (1975) Sociobiology: The new synthesis. Belknap, Cambridge

Wilson EO (1978) The genetic evolution of altruism. In: Wispé L (ed) Altruism, sympathy and helping: Psychological and sociological principles. Academic Press, London New York, pp 11–37

Wilson DS (1980) The natural selection of populations and communities. Cummings, Menlo Park

Wispé L (1978) Toward an integration. In: Wispé L (ed) Altruism, sympathy and helping: Psychological principles. Academic Press, London New York, pp 303–328

Behavioral Ecology and Sociobiology

ISSN 0340-5443   Title No. 265

Managing Editor: H. Markl, Konstanz

Editors: B. Hölldobler, Cambridge, MA; H. Kummer, Zürich;
J. Maynard Smith, Brighton; E. O. Wilson, Cambridge, MA

Advisory Editors: G. W. Barlow, Berkeley, CA; J. Brown,
Albany, NY; E. L. Charnov, Salt Lake City, UT; J. H. Crook, Bristol;
J. F. Eisenberg, Washington, DC; T. Eisner, Ithaca, NY; S. T. Emlen,
Ithaca, NY; V. Geist, Calgary, Alberta; D. R. Griffin, New York, NY;
W. D. Hamilton, Ann Arbor, MI; D. von Holst, Bayreuth;
K. Immelmann, Bielefeld; W. E. Kerr, Ribeirão Preto, SP; J. R. Krebs,
Oxford; M. Lindauer, Würzburg; P. Marler, New York, NY;
G. H. Orians, Seattle, WA; Y. Sugiyama, Inuyama City, Aichi;
R. L. Trivers, Santa Cruz, CA; C. Vogel, Göttingen; C. Walcott,
Ithaca, NY

The electric eel *(Electrophorus electricus),* often reaching a size of 8
feet and a weight of 200 pounds, electrocutes its prey with a burst
of high-voltage electricity, about 500 Hz. In contrast, the eel locates
prey using an electric organ emitting low-voltage impulses. An important question confronting behavioralists and physiologists alike
is whether these two electrical systems are interrelated in some
fundamental way. An answer will not only reveal important information on the physiology of *E. electricus,* but will also further our
understanding of the basic relationship that exists between the
environment and neuron function.

In response to this and other ecological and sociobiological
questions Springer-Verlag initiated the publication of **Behavioral
Ecology and Sociobiology** in 1976. Since then the journal has become
a major forum, publishing original research on the functions,
mechanics, and evolution of ecological adaptations and emphasizing
social behavior. An international board of editors and advisors, aided
by numerous reviewers, guarantees the very highest standards.
Contributions are welcomed from scientists the world over; publication is almost exclusively in English. Topics treated cover a broad
range, including orientation in space and time, communication and
all other forms of social behavior, behavioral mechanisms of competition and resource partitioning, predatory and antipredatory
behavior, and theoretical analyses of behavioral evolution. Quantitative studies carried out on representatives of nearly all major
groups of the animal kingdom are published, from spiders through
fish, birds, primates, and other mammals. Empirical studies on the
biological basis of human behavioral adaptations are also welcomed.
Behavioral Ecology and Sociobiology has become an important
source of information on the progress in animal behavior research.
Scientists, researchers, and graduate students will regularly find
papers of significance in their particular fields of interest.

For subscription information or sample copy write to:
Springer-Verlag, Journal Promotion Department,
P. O. Box 105280, D-6900 Heidelberg, FRG

Springer-Verlag
Berlin
Heidelberg
New York

V. Geist

Life Strategies, Human Evolution, Environmental Design

Toward a Biological Theory of Health

1978. 9 figures. XXI, 495 pages
ISBN 3-540-90363-1

This book lays the foundation for a universal theory of health applicable to humans and other organisms. Criteria are presented for human life-styles maximizing health.
To this end, the author critically develops an extensive set of major rules organisms must satisfy to maximize reproductive fitness. These are utilized particularly to reconstruct human evolution. The author thereby draws on new insights into the life-strategies of large mammals.

Of necessity a synthesis of many disciplines, this book's conclusions are often at variance with those presently accepted in behavioral and evolutionary biology, and anthropology. A view of human evolution is offered, which sheds new light on previously unexplained features of man and puts forth new theories on the process of evolution in general.
The last part of the book links theory to practice. This study demonstrates how vital it is to understand human evolution and principles of behavior if we are to shape our environment to support life-styles that maximize health.

Primate Evolutionary Biology

Selected Papers (Part A) of the VIIIth Congress of the International Primatological Society, Florence, 7–12 July, 1980

Editors: **A. B. Chiarelli, R. S. Corruccini**
1981. 73 figures. Approx. 140 pages
(Proceedings in Life Sciences)
ISBN 3-540-11023-2

Contents: The Homologies of the Lorisoid Internal Carotid Artery System. – Comparison of Eocene Non Adapids and Tarsius. – Clinal Size Variation in Archaeolemur spp. on Madagascar. – The Anatomy of Growth and Its Relation to Locomotor Capacity in **Macaca.** – Morphological and Ecological Characters in Sympatric Populations of Macaca in the Dawna Range. – Specialization of Primate Foot Reflected in Quantitative Analysis of Arthrodial Joint of Anterior Tarsals. – Morphology of Some of the Lower Limb Muscles in Primates. – Morpho-Functional Analysis of the Articular Surfaces of the Knee-Joint in Primates. – Outlines of the Distal Humerus in Hominoid Primates: Application to Some Plio-Pleistocene Hominids. – Structural-functional Relationships Between Masticatory Biomechanics, Skeletal Biology and Cranio-facial Development in Primates. – Comparison of Morphological Factors in the Cranial Variation of the Great Apes and Man. – Enamel Prism Patterns of European Hominoids – and Their Phylogenetical Aspects. – The Structural Organization of the Cortex of the Motor Speach Areas of the Human Brain and Homologs on the Ape's Brain.

Springer-Verlag
Berlin
Heidelberg
New York